LONE STAR UNIONISM, DISSENT, AND RESISTANCE

For Carolee Simank,

On the occasion of my visit to

Rockdale for Heritage Days,

[signature]

4/21/16

Lone Star Unionism, Dissent, and Resistance

OTHER SIDES OF CIVIL WAR TEXAS

Edited by

Jesús F. de la Teja

UNIVERSITY OF OKLAHOMA PRESS : NORMAN

This book is published with the generous assistance of the Center for the Study of the Southwest, Texas State University, San Marcos.

Library of Congress Cataloging-in-Publication Data
Lone star unionism, dissent, and resistance : other sides of Civil War Texas / edited by Jesús F. de la Teja.
    pages cm
  Includes bibliographical references and index.
  ISBN 978-0-8061-5182-3 (hardcover : alk. paper) — ISBN 978-0-8061-5183-0 (pbk. : alk. paper)
  1. Unionists (United States Civil War)—Texas. 2. Texas—History—Civil War, 1861–1865. I. Teja, Jesús F. de la, 1956– editor.
  E458.7.L66 2016
  976.4'05—dc23
                    2015028027

The paper in this book meets the guidelines for permanence and durability of the Committee on Production Guidelines for Book Longevity of the Council on Library Resources, Inc. ∞

Contents

Illustrations

FIGURES

MAP

TABLES

Lone Star Unionism, Dissent, and Resistance

Introduction

Jesús F. de la Teja

Despite a considerable amount of scholarly study over the years, much of which is referenced in the essays that follow, the subject of Civil War Unionism, dissent, and resistance remains at the margins of Texas history. Historians frequently point to the fact that over 14,000 Texans, almost 24 percent of votes cast—all white males, of course—voted against secession. Scholars have also documented the extreme level of violence that marked secessionists' actions against slaves and abolitionists before the war, Unionists during the struggle, and freedmen and Republicans afterward. Yet the impression persists in the popular imagination of a monolithically pro-Confederate Texas that largely escaped the destruction that occurred in the rest of the South.

The situation is largely the result of the continued emphasis on a military narrative that focuses on the heroic actions of Confederate Texans. Biographies, unit histories, and political narratives on the Confederate side far outnumber works on those topics from the Union side. They do so because studies of the Texas Civil War era, at least as far as what is produced for the general public, have been in the hands of what Walter Buenger calls "updated traditionalists." These writers, many of them outside the academic circles in which the study of Unionists and dissent tend to find more researchers, continue "to mix two strands whose origins date back to before 1960: the impulse to preserve and commemorate the revered past, and the top-down perspective common to many earlier historians but made famous by consensus historians in which elite male political, military, and business leaders stood for the entire community."[1]

It is the experience of those others who have resided on the margins of a Texas history dominated by a Confederate-oriented collective memory that is the focus of this volume. At the start of the war some left, or attempted to leave, Texas to join the Union and found themselves at the working end of a rope or the receiving end of a bullet. Others kept themselves apart and fought off efforts to incorporate them into the Confederacy's struggle. Some Southerners even thought of Texas as a refuge, for themselves and their bondsmen, from the destruction farther east. And, too, there were those future Texans who were the unwilling property of others and for whom the opportunities to participate in the debate over the place of Texas in the Union were irrelevant since they had no place yet as citizens, of either the state or the nation.

This brings me to the man whose tombstone is illustrated here—James Pearson Newcomb. Born in Nova Scotia in 1837, Newcomb and his family came to Texas two years later. By 1854 he was in the newspaper business, publishing what in 1856 became the San Antonio *Herald,* a pro-Union paper. After a brief foray into university education in Vermont he returned to San Antonio, where in 1860 he founded the weekly *Alamo Express,* also a pro-Union paper. In May 1861, Texas Rangers and the Knights of the Golden Circle destroyed his print shop and forced Newcomb to flee to Mexico and eventually to San Francisco, where he performed military service for the Union before taking up journalism again. By 1867 he was back in Texas, however, where he bought an interest in the Republican-leaning San Antonio *Express.* He went on to start and run a number of local and political newspapers, including what eventually became the San Antonio *Light,* and he twice ran for office as a Republican—losing both times.

I bring up Newcomb for two reasons. First, like the vast majority of people who considered themselves "Texans" on the eve of the Civil War, he was an immigrant. Texans then and now tend to be very myopic on this score. As the reader can note in the essays that follow, the white Southern immigrants who came to Texas from the 1820s through the 1850s were quite willing to fashion a unique identity for themselves that excluded or marginalized those who did not look or think like what a Texan should look or think like: white, pro-slavery, anti-Indian, Protestant. The Constitution of the Republic of Texas eliminated the citizenship rights of all people of African descent in the new republic; those

James P. Newcomb gravestone, Alamo Masonic Cemetery, San Antonio, Texas. Photo courtesy of Jesús F. de la Teja.

who had been slaves before coming to Texas returned to that status. Those who had been free or might be freed had no place in the new nation; at best, they could petition the Congress of the Republic of Texas to remain, but with greatly circumscribed rights. Not quite as draconian, Tejanos (Texans of Mexican heritage) faced both racist and nativist attitudes which, as Juan Seguín lamented, made him "a foreigner in my native land."[2] The indigenous population and the immigrant Indians, many of whom had arrived before Anglo-American migration began in the 1820s, were, as Gary Clayton Anderson argues, ethnically cleansed.[3] There was no place at all for tribal peoples in the new Texas. And, not surprisingly, those among the white population who espoused sentiments that did not conform to the norm faced abuse, exile, violence, and even death.

From that first reason springs my second motive for discussing Newcomb, for among his interests was one José Antonio Menchaca. Sometime in the 1870s the newspaperman convinced Menchaca to turn over to him a manuscript containing the old Tejano's recollections of his life through the battle of San Jacinto, and just before he died in 1907 Newcomb wrote an introduction and had the manuscript published in a weekly local-interest magazine, the *Passing Show*. In the process of preparing the memoirs for publication, I needed to know a bit more about Newcomb, who considered Antonio his friend and confidant, but who had held on to the memoirs for over a quarter-century before seeing to their publication. Although I never figured out all of the manuscript's mysteries, I did encounter the interesting life story of a man who never gave up on the Union and also never gave up on Texas. He had the courage to return to the Lone Star State and to remain involved in Republican politics long after it was fashionable. He considered himself a Texan, although he held very "un-Texan" views on things.[4] His tombstone in San Antonio's Alamo Masonic Cemetery tells it all.

My encounter with Newcomb's history cemented for me the idea that the story of Texas Unionism and dissent should be observed in some way in the midst of the nation's and the state's commemoration of the Civil War sesquicentennial. There were plenty of events marking, analyzing, and even celebrating Texas's Confederate experience, but little attention seemed to be going to those other experiences that, though familiar to academics, somehow were not making it into the public consciousness regarding the War between the States. Some people are aware of the massacre of German Unionists at the so-called Battle of the Nueces. Others are familiar with the even more dastardly witch hunt and lynching of Unionists and presumed Unionists at Gainesville. The story of violence against the freedmen during Reconstruction has recently received considerable attention. And there are even a few people who know about East Texas dissenters and Tejano Unionist activities. Still, all of these and other aspects of Civil War–era Texas tend to be studied in isolation, and the emphasis remains on the Confederate side of the story. It occurred to me that bringing all of them together would be a good way of fostering more study and a deeper appreciation for these other Texans.[5]

Moreover, I tend to agree with Kenneth Howell that the Civil War did not end in spring 1865 but continued through Reconstruction. As he explains in *Still the Arena of the Civil War*, "Scholarly celebrations of the Union victory in the Civil War tend to ignore the fact that the United States government ultimately failed to reconstruct southern society in the decades following the war. A more constructive way to study these two periods of American history is to examine the eras as

"Young Texas in Repose." This unflattering representation of
Texas on the eve of annexation serves as a reminder that controversy followed the new state from the beginning. Printed
and published by E. Jones, 128 Fulton St., New York, ca. 1845.
WA Prints+147, Yale Collection of Western Americana, Bei-
necke Rare Book and Manuscript Library.

two distinct phases of a continuous conflict between the northern and
southern states, which lasted from 1861 to 1877."[6] Thus, stories of loyalty
to the Union and dissent and resistance from the racial and political for-
mulas of unreconstructed Southerners deserve consideration on a par
with anti-secession and anti-Confederate activities before and during
the official war.

The result of my deliberations and consultations was the agreement of ten colleagues to participate in a one-day symposium at Texas State University in San Marcos to bring to the public the fruits of their many labors on this other Texas. With funding from the Summerlee Foundation and the support of the Wittliff Collections and the Department of History, the Center for the Study of the Southwest hosted the event in April 2014. The enthusiastic public response to the program provided the green light needed to proceed with the next step, bringing the presentations together in an edited collection of essays. All of the participants responded enthusiastically to carrying out the necessary reassessment and revisions of their works to make this book possible.

This volume starts with the proposition that the collective memory of Confederate Texas is and always has been problematic. Why and how we remember the Confederate experience in Texas—to the degree that there is a collective memory of Texas's role in the Confederacy—Laura McLemore argues, are the outcomes of a people who early on acquired a unique set of characteristics within American society and had little need of adopting Lost Cause attitudes whole cloth. Instead, she tells us in "Gray Ghost: Creating a Collective Memory of a Confederate Texas," Texas politicians sought to move on to making a place for Texas in the new economic order. They left it to women, who increasingly saw themselves as the guardians of the state's heritage, to construct that public memory. Yet, even among these women, who organized themselves under the United Daughters of Confederacy, McLemore claims, the effort was more to foster a sense of culture and appreciation for the state's history and women's place in it than to tie Texas to the Lost Cause bandwagon.

If the collective memory of Texas in the Confederacy never quite fit the Lost Cause paradigm prevalent in the rest of the South, Andrew Torget's essay on "The Problem of Slave Flight in Civil War Texas" leaves little doubt that before the war Texas slaveholders shared their fellow white Southerners' opinion of the happy state of their bondsmen. As Torget explains, white Texans attributed any trouble among their slaves to the influence of outside provocateurs—abolitionists and Republicans—and their efforts to weaken the South. As the war progressed, Texans sobered to the reality that their slaves might have a different opinion of their status than they did. Making creative use of the abundant newspaper advertisements regarding runaways, along with both military and political correspondence, Torget traces both the growing fear whites held of blacks and blacks' increasing opportunities to flee and, thus, put the lie to their masters' belief in their happiness. By the closing days of the war, Torget explains, such were the fears of influential whites that they gave serious consideration to the conscription of able-bodied blacks into the Confederate army, as much to maintain control over the slave population as to provide vital support to the military effort.

Following Torget's survey of slave flight from Texas, Caleb McDaniel examines the phenomenon of wartime southern migration to Texas in "Involuntary Removals: 'Refugeed Slaves' in Confederate Texas." As he notes, many of the Southerners who came to Texas during the Civil War were involuntary migrants—the large number of slaves transported to Texas by their white owners. After an analysis of the motivations of whites in bringing slaves to Texas, McDaniel explores the attitudes of both whites and blacks toward their changed circumstances. Rather than the Lost Cause myth of removal to Texas as a means to protect "dependents" from rapacious Union forces, he finds that slaveholders viewed their bondsmen as a source not only of income but of survival. Slaves, in turn, were crypto-Unionists. Again, challenging the Lost Cause mythology, blacks were not loyal to their white masters but were exercising strategies to regain family, awaiting the right moment to take flight, or hunkering down to outlast the Confederacy. In these ways, refugeed slaves were dissenters who may well have shared with their Texan brethren knowledge of the freedom to come.

Before, during, and after the Civil War there was another type of migration to Texas that has received little serious analysis from the dissent perspective. In "East Texas Unionism: Warren J. Collins, Big Thicket Jayhawker," Victoria Bynum explores the strong resistance to the Confederacy by one group of Southerners in the Piney Woods region of Texas. Her essay makes clear why talking about the Civil War strictly within the 1861–65 timeframe is so problematic. In the absence of records substantiating his motives for rejecting secession and resisting efforts to conscript him, she looks to Warren Collins's battle with gamblers before the war, to his family ties to Mississippi relatives, in particular to Newt Knight, leader of the Free State of Jones, and to his post–Civil War political evolution into socialism. Bynum uses the contrast

between Collins's unsuccessful political career as a socialist and unreconstructed Unionist late in life and his son Vinson's successful career as
an increasingly Lost Cause conservative Democrat to make the case that
the former's opposition to the Confederacy was based on principle, not
expediency. Her conclusion is that for the Texas jayhawkers the Confederate government and the planter class that it represented constituted a
larger threat to their independent backwoods way of life than the federal
government did.

Walter Kamphoefner's "New Americans or New Southerners? Unionist German Texans" explores how that other group of recent arrivals to
the state, the German immigrants of the 1840s and 1850s, confronted
the challenge of simultaneously being Americans and Texans. In part,
Kamphoefner's work refutes recently made arguments that Texas Germans were little different from other Texans in their views or even from
Germans elsewhere in the South. To the contrary, marshalling censuses,
muster rolls, and electoral records, he argues that Texas Germans were,
in fact, different. His evidence indicates that, not only were Germans
not naturally inclined toward slavery, but even among those who did
their duty to the Confederacy there was little sympathy for the cause.
Like Bynum, Kamphoefner in part bases his conclusions on postwar
behaviors, including the quick erection of Comfort's Treue der Union
monument and black-German political alliances during Reconstruction
and beyond.

Just as complex as German Texans' attitudes toward slavery and the
Confederacy were those of Tejanos. Like Walter Kamphoefner, in "'Although We Are the Last Soldiers': Citizenship, Ideology, and Tejano
Unionism" Omar Valerio-Jiménez challenges a historiography that
oversimplifies the behaviors of Mexican Texans. His analysis of South
Texas Tejanos reveals a broad range of behaviors and attitudes that contributed to decisions about whether and how to support one side or
the other in the conflict. Although he mentions the violence, Valerio-
Jiménez is more interested in motivations, something that is harder to
get at given the paucity of writings by Tejanos regarding the reasons for
acting as they did. Nevertheless, their attitude toward African Americans as reflected in their behaviors set a majority of Tejanos apart from
their fellow Texans. Employing examples of intermarriage, accommoda-
tion, and refusal to pursue runaways, Valerio-Jiménez concludes that a

substantial portion of the South Texas Mexican-origin population opposed slavery. This was an opposition that was also driven by the treatment that most Tejanos and Mexicans received at the hands of local and
state authorities. The unique circumstances of the international border
and the ambiguous, or flexible, national identification of its population
also served to distance much of the Mexican-origin population from the
Confederacy.

As Richard McCaslin asserts in "A Texas Reign of Terror: Anti-
Unionist Violence in North Texas," it was white-on-white violence during the war in North Texas that makes clear that the assault on dissenters
was not just based on either race or ethnicity. Although slaves and the few
abolitionists who wandered into the region in the 1850s were the target
of most anti-abolition and anti-Republican hysteria before the war, the
divisions in the region exposed by the process of secession unleashed a
war against suspected Union sympathizers, draft dodgers, and deserters
that undermined some of the very principles the secessionists alleged to
be fighting for. The unbridled ferocity of some secessionists makes the
principled stand of men such as James W. Throckmorton all the more
noteworthy, for, as McCaslin demonstrates, on several occasions those
who dared make their anti-secession sentiments known paid for their
opinions with their lives.

The exceptionally violent nature of Texas society in the Civil War era
had strong repercussions for a black population whose value had before
emancipation been judged in terms of their ability to produce wealth
for their owners. In her essay "In Defense of Their Families: African
American Women, the Freedmen's Bureau, and Racial Violence during
Reconstruction in Texas," Rebecca A. Czuchry examines the repercussions for blacks, particularly for African American women, of whites'
unwillingness to accept the changed status of the former slaves. Using
Howell's long Civil War paradigm, it is obvious that the violence against
blacks (and dissenting whites) was part of the white majority's unwillingness to accept the results of the Confederacy's surrender in 1865. Not
surprisingly, black women fought back against the perpetrators of violence against them as best they could. They refused to accept continued
degradation and abuse but found little support for their efforts in institutions populated by men who either did not care or had little power
to effect change. Nevertheless, the very act of recording the atrocities

committed against them testifies, according to Czuchry, to black women's determination to defend their new status and that of their families.

Defending and promoting freedmen's rights was not just an individual undertaking, it was also a collective endeavor centered in annual celebrations of the date on which the official proclamation of emancipation in Texas took place. By the 1890s the commemoration of that June 19, 1865, announcement by Gen. Gordon Granger had come to be known as Juneteenth, a holiday that has gained traction on a national level. Employing the concept of collective memory as an analytical tool,[7] in "'Three Cheers to Freedom and Equal Rights to All': Juneteenth and the Meaning of Citizenship" Elizabeth Hayes Turner traces the evolution of Emancipation Day celebrations in Texas from Reconstruction through the 1890s, by which time the holiday had evolved into an occasion for political oratory and the assertion of citizenship rights. Turner's essay analyzing the actions of Texas freedmen to celebrate and actively promote their new status stands in marked contrast to Laura McLemore's analysis of the way white Texans thought about and reacted to the defeat of the Confederacy. To the degree that Juneteenth celebrations gained legitimacy and continuity, they marked the real end of the Civil War more than a decade after the Lee's surrender at Appomattox.

Our survey of Texas Civil War Unionism, dissent, and resistance concludes with a case study. What turned one-time Democratic, pro-slavery Southerner Edmund J. Davis into what biographer Carl H. Moneyhon calls "one of the more radical men of Texas history"? As he analyzes the life of Texas's last Republican governor until 1978 in "Edmund J. Davis—Unlikely Radical," Moneyhon reminds readers that, although historians seek patterns and trends, individual motivations and circumstances are an important part of the historical landscape. Holding on to and professing his ideals led Davis to oppose secession politically before the war, then to fight actively against the Confederacy when the possibility of distancing himself from it evaporated with the passage of conscription laws. From there it was a short leap to embracing an ever-expanding sense of what it meant to be an American, which in the end meant support for black political rights in the face of continued former-Confederate resistance.

The story of Davis's struggle to create a new Texas based on Radical Republican principles that included universal adult male suffrage once he became governor is beyond the scope of Moneyhon's essay. But Davis's path to that position lays bare the contradictions, ambiguities, violence, and struggles that have been the subject matter of the essays in this collection. Civil wars are particularly nasty creatures precisely because the essence of civility—an agreement on the rules of public engagement—becomes lost in the struggle to impose ideological order. Rather than a contest over land and resources, civil warfare pits members of the same society against each other. The American Civil War, therefore, was not just a struggle between North and South, it was a struggle between different ideologies, which meant that it made enemies of friends and neighbors.

As the essays in this volume make clear, Texas may have been different from other Confederate states in being on the Mexican border and on the margins of the fighting, but the state and its people faced many of the same challenges in coming to terms with the violence and destruction that the sectional struggle engendered.

NOTES

1. Walter Buenger, "Three Truths in Texas," in *Beyond Texas through Time: Breaking Away from Past Interpretations,* ed. Walter L. Buenger and Arnoldo De León (College Station: Texas A&M University Press, 2011), 1.

2. Jesús F. de la Teja, ed., *A Revolution Remembered: The Memoirs and Selected Correspondence of Juan N. Seguín,* 2nd ed. (Austin: Texas State Historical Society, 2002), 73.

3. Gary Clayton Anderson, *The Conquest of Texas: Ethnic Cleansing in the Promised Land* (Norman: University of Oklahoma Press, 2005).

4. Timothy Matovina and Jesús F. de la Teja, eds., *Recollections of a Tejano Life: Antonio Menchaca in Texas History* (Austin: University of Texas Press, 2013), 21–23; Dale A. Somers, "James P. Newcomb: The Making of a Radical," *Southwestern Historical Quarterly* 72 (April 1969): 449–69; Ernest B. Speck, "Newcomb, James Pearson," *Handbook of Texas Online,* Texas State Historical Association, www.tsha-online.org/handbook/online/articles/fne19.

5. This concern is not to say that there have not been efforts to dig down beyond the superficial characterization of Texas as being in lockstep with the Confederacy during this period of commemoration. For instances, two works that appeared in 2010 attempt to provide rounded coverage of the era. Charles Grear's *Why Texans Fought in the Civil War* (College Station: Texas A&M University Press, 2010) makes an effort to explain the factors that contributed to Texans joining either the Confederate or Union armies. Grear's analysis extends to the German and Mexican Texas populations, which he concludes shared similar motivations. The

majority of his analysis, given that the majority of Texans served the Confederacy, necessarily focuses on the Southern side of the story. Similarly, some of the essays in Kenneth Howell's edited volume, *The Seventh Star of the Confederacy: Texas during the Civil War* (Denton: University of North Texas Press, 2010), consider aspects of dissent and Unionism but, again, the contributions largely analyze the period from a Confederate perspective. Like *Seventh Star of the Confederacy,* an earlier volume edited by Grear that contains essays by Richard McCaslin and Walter Kamphoefner, *The Fate of Texas: The Civil War and the Lone Star State* (Little Rock: University of Arkansas Press, 2008), also touches upon themes of Unionism and dissent but, again, the emphasis is Texas as a Confederate experience.

6. Kenneth W. Howell, ed., *Still the Arena of the Civil War: Violence and Turmoil in Reconstruction Texas, 1865–1874* (Denton: University of North Texas Press, 2012), 23.

7. Collective memory, according to Gregg Cantrell and Elizabeth Hays Turner, in their edited volume *Lone Star Pasts: Memory and History in Texas* (College Station: Texas A&M University Press, 2007), 2, is a group phenomenon that "constitutes shared remembrances; it serves as a coordinator of identity and imbues meaning to past events of historic import"; their chaps. 2, 4, and 6 in particular deal with themes related to the subject matter in this volume.

1

Gray Ghost

CREATING A COLLECTIVE MEMORY OF A

CONFEDERATE TEXAS

Laura Lyons McLemore

I n 1969, the title of a book by Irene Kampen, *Due to Lack of Interest, Tomorrow Has Been Cancelled,* symbolized the ennui resulting from more than a decade of war, social change, and protest in America. In some ways that statement might also apply to post–Civil War reaction to the Confederacy in Texas, if not all over the South. Exhaustion and uncertainty about the meaning of defeat militated against the immediate creation of a collective memory of the Confederacy. Moreover, it would be a mistake to characterize "Confederate memory" in Texas as it has been applied to other states of the former Confederacy. Indeed, few discussions of collective Confederate memory mention Texas. Of course, there are some commonalities—many more, as Walter Buenger has argued, than Texans have been willing to acknowledge—but upon even a brief examination it becomes clear that lumping Texas together with the rest of the Southern states in generalizations about the creation of collective Confederate memory fails.[1] A survey of primary and secondary sources reveals several reasons, the first and foremost of which is that Texans viewed and many continue to view themselves as "Texan" first and foremost. A second is that vast differences of geography and ethnic heritage militated against the formation of a genuinely collective memory of a Confederate Texas. A third is that Texas men were much more interested in getting back to making money than they were in memorializing a lost cause. This left the cultivation of "memory" to the ladies and thus exposed a host of interests that competed with simple memory making.

Memory and collective memory have become popular topics of research, discussion, and debate among sociologists, psychologists, and historians since the early twentieth century, and these experts have not been consistently in agreement. Therefore, some definition of terms may be useful. Most important, what *is* collective memory and what are its implications? Scholars have viewed "social" or "collective" memory as involving particular sets of practices like monument building and general forms like tradition, myth, and identity. The first explicit use of the term "collective memory" is found in the work of Hugo von Hofmannsthal in 1902. Hofmannsthal referred to "the damned up force of our mysterious ancestors within us" and "piled up layers of accumulated collective memory," which suggests that "Confederate memory" may involve pre- and postwar memory as well as memories of the Civil War and Confederate States of America.[2]

Contemporary use of the term "collective memory" began with Maurice Halbwachs in 1925, who established a connection between social groups and collective memory. Halbwachs argued that every memory is carried by a specific social group limited in space and time, that collective memory evokes the presence of the past, and that as a living imagination collective memory is constantly reshaped by the social contexts into which it is received. Commemoration, then, is a calculated strategy for stabilizing collective memories that would otherwise be changeable and temporary; thus, memory and history, in Halbwachs's view, are antithetical—memory distorting the past while history tries to correct memory's inaccuracies.[3]

Halbwachs identified several forms of memory: autobiographical memory, the memory of lived experience; historical memory, that which reaches the present through historical records; and collective memory, the active past that forms identities. In the late twentieth century, French sociologist Pierre Nora conducted perhaps the most influential studies of commemorative narrative and commemoration, *Les Lieux de mémoire* (1984–92). Nora reversed the relationship between memory and history. Instead of being part of a grand narrative, Nora theorized, places of memory are only loosely connected, if at all, and the task of historians is reconstructing a cultural heritage by tying these reference points together.[4]

In the last decade of the twentieth century and first decade of the twenty-first century, a consensus about the meaning of "collective memory" seems no closer than when the term was first used. Some scholars continue to argue that the ideas of individuals are influenced by the groups to which they belong. Others argue that collective memory is not an alternative to history but rather is shaped by it, by commemorative symbolism and ritual, and that commemoration constructs a collective memory where one did not previously exist.[5] All do seem to agree that collective memory involves thoughts shared by a group of people, and that definition will suffice here.

Another term requiring definition is "Confederate," or "Confederacy." In this context, "Confederate" refers to the Confederate States of America, which formed in February 1861 and collapsed in 1865, though both the term "Confederacy" and the concept appear in Texas correspondence as early as 1840.[6] For the purpose of this writing, "Confederate memory" is distinguished from Civil War memory or Reconstruction memory for the simple reason that remembering heroes and heroic adventures is not the same as remembering allegiance to a specific group, the Confederacy, as a nation or as the embodiment of espoused ideals. In that regard, I consider "Confederate" to be distinctly Southern. I would suggest that the conservatism Texas has experienced since the Civil War, and the virulent strain of the past few years, in particular, is not the legacy of the Confederacy so much as it is the legacy of Texan individualism, love of profit, and love of adventure. Texans, with or without slavery, hated the government telling them what to do. Racism, though unquestionably a component, is a value shared much more broadly and is thus not exclusive to the Confederacy. Most of the memoirs of this period were written by men whose memories of themselves and their adventures were a much higher priority than their memories of the Southern Confederacy. There simply is not a lot of evidence that Texas identified itself for any length of time after the Civil War with the other Southern states even though they shared many ideas, behaviors, and prejudices.

Texas's much discussed identity transcends Southern or Confederate identity for a number of reasons. Though many Texas residents had

emigrated from the Old South and shared many characteristics and ideals with people of the Deep South, their experiences once they got to
Texas were not identical. Although highly respected scholars of the Civil
War era argue that Texas is essentially Southern, there is simply no getting around the fact that Texas was on the frontier and therefore had, in
addition to its Southerness, a frontier mentality. Just as Walter Buenger
and Randolph Campbell have pointed to Texans' Southern origins and
characteristics as proof of their Southern mentality, Donald Meinig has
convincingly argued that there are "patterns which yet remain to distinguish Texas from [the rest of] the nation: the serious insistence by the
majority of Texans on thinking of themselves as different . . . the residue
of certain values which sociologists have identified as especially (though
not uniquely) characteristic of the main body of the Texas population;
and the particular regional patterning of peoples, a distinctive mosaic,
related in its parts to, but not duplicated as a whole in, any other parts of
the country."[7] John Bodnar has noted that Davy Crockett represented a
new cultural symbol that competed with George Washington, a symbol
of a frontier rather than a national community.[8] Col. John S. "Rip" Ford,
a states' righter who helped write the Texas secession ordinance, served
on and off as a Texas Ranger and as a colonel in the Confederate cavalry.
Yet he was described as "an adventurer at heart." His memoirs are full of
anecdotes. It seems, though, that he found his greatest adventures in the
Texas Revolution, the Mexican War, and Indian wars.[9]

The great adventures of Texans' creation narrative caused them to
identify themselves as Texans more than as Southerners as well. They
wrested Texas from Mexicans and from Indians, and for a decade they
governed themselves as an independent republic. Whatever memories
or ideals some Texans shared with the old South they left behind, being
on the frontier was an experience shared by *all* Texans regardless of
their origins. As Campbell explained, memory of the cattle kingdom
was built upon "heroically individualistic ranchers and cowboys successfully braving nature, defeating Indians, and civilizing the plains and
prairies west of the one-hundredth meridian." This was exactly what
Texans who participated in the Civil War remembered: heroically individualistic Texans and Rangers successfully braving nature, defeating Indians, and dominating, if not civilizing, the plains and prairies.

Campbell continued, "This memory emphasizes all things western and allows Texans to escape from their essentially southern heritage. Being western may create problems for those who worry about such things as destroying the buffalo and dispossessing the Indians, but this western past is still far more appealing than a southern past that involves slavery, secession, Civil War, and defeat."[10]

It is not too difficult to see how Texans may have developed a strong sense of identity separate from the older states of the Deep South. The Civil War was sandwiched between the Texas Revolution and the cattle kingdom, both of which dominated collective memory of Texans. The war they won won out. They identified with Texas heroes (many of whom like Rip Ford fought in both the Texas Revolution and the Civil War) and with the cattle range. The Confederacy simply could not compete. This is perhaps nowhere better illustrated than in the response of Adina de Zavala to the question whether the Daughters of the Republic of Texas should allow, without public protest, the Daughters of the Confederacy to erect a fountain to their cause in Alamo Plaza in front of the post office. "I think a fountain is all right and a great convenience—we had spoken of the matter ourselves," de Zavala wrote to Adele Looscan in June 1902. "However," she continued,

It is on ground sacred alone to the Heroes of the Alamo. On the square of the old Mission San Antonio de Valero where our men were hemmed up so many days and every inch is watered with their blood. It seems to me that every delicacy of sentiment and feeling would have kept them from this sacred spot. Some of our Daughters are furious and beg me to prevent "the sacrilege" if I can. I hate any unpleasant feeling though I do think they should not have trespassed. I am for peace—letting them alone—and letting the stigma of at least, "bad taste" rest upon them. Of course, most of us are D[aughters of the] Confederacy too—but we did not like the Chapter's actions during last Convention and feel that Societies as well as individuals should have some delicacy of sentiment, and that there are certain spots in S[an] A[ntonio], the Alamo in particular, that should be left sacred alone to the [memory of the] old Republic.[11]

In the 1880s and 1890s, when the myth of the Lost Cause was burgeoning across the South, the ladies in Texas were putting pictures of Texas heroes on schoolroom walls and campaigning to have public schools named after the heroes of San Jacinto.

Texans also identified themselves with the frontier for geographic and cultural reasons. Terry Jordan has hypothesized that there were actually two clearly defined areas in Texas, one typically lower Southern and the other unmistakably characteristic of the upper South. By 1861, Jordan notes, these two "Souths," always socioeconomically different, had drifted far apart politically.[12] Jordan shows that frontier conditions, culture, and even dialect separated the experience of these Texans. Moreover, except for El Paso, most of Texas west of the ninety-ninth parallel was unorganized politically when Texas seceded in 1861. Ty Cashion in his essay "What's the Matter with Texas" reinforces this notion of the frontier or "West" as experiential as much as spatial.[13]

Another reason collective memory of a Confederate Texas is so elusive is that there were so many competing memories within Texas itself. In addition to the "two Souths" dichotomy described by Jordan, there was also a black memory of Confederate Texas which, much like the Mexican memory of the Texas Revolution, has been all but excluded from any "collective" memory of Confederate Texas. As Buck Barry's account revealed, another memory of the Civil War era in Texas was that of Indian fighter. Still another was the memory of women left at home. Halbwachs theorized that individual memory can be recalled only in the social framework within which it is constructed. Individuals, he surmised, belong to many social groups, and a collective memory inheres in each. Halbwachs discussed the frameworks of family, religion, and nation, showing how each conditions the ways in which memory is activated.[14]

In Texas, secessionists, Unionists, slaves, women, Mexicans, Germans, and other groups all perceived the Confederacy differently, if they considered it at all. Certainly there existed a powerful contingent who identified with the Confederacy and its precepts, but it could not claim uniformity of experience with these other competing groups. Perhaps the most obvious example would be black countermemory. Campbell has noted that white Texans tend to remember slavery as a relatively unimportant institution in Texas, or, to the extent that slavery did exist, they recall it as a largely paternalistic, benevolent institution. This is not what African Americans who were enslaved remember.[15] Historian Robert Cook, in an article on Civil War centennial celebrations, noted that a black countermemory existed, stressing the evils of slavery, the attainment of emancipation, black military support for the Union, and the benefits Reconstruction offered freedpeople.[16] Elizabeth Hayes Turner has written that "white recollections denied the importance or the wisdom of emancipation," but Juneteenth celebrations, observed continually since 1866, always held meaning and historical memory for blacks. That these annual observances did not cease, even in the days of the civil rights movement when they were less public, provided "trenchant testimony to the strength of an emancipationist memory."[17]

Further evidence of the elusiveness of a collective memory of Confederate Texas lies in the fact that Texas's experience of the Civil War was not the same as that of other states in the Confederacy. Most of the war was fought elsewhere. As Charles Ramsdell observed, Texas suffered less than her sister states throughout the war and during the first two or three years was fairly prosperous. No hostile armies laid waste her towns and fields or withdrew slaves from the plantations. Good crops were raised every year. During most of the war Texas ports were open, and steamers and blockade runners made their way to and from Vera Cruz, Havana, and the ports of Europe. Moreover, the Mexican border offered peculiar advantages for a safe overland trade, and through that channel the staples of Texas were exported and exchanged for necessary supplies or specie.[18] Houstonian T. W. House served the Confederacy loyally and well but never had much hope that the Confederate armies could defeat the far larger, better-equipped forces of the Union. He therefore avoided accumulating Confederate currency and added to his gold reserves whenever possible. At war's end, he had $300,000 in gold laid away in England.[19]

Even before the outbreak of the Civil War, Houston was poised for industrial growth. The year 1860 was the richest year commercially that Houston had ever had. In early January 1860, the Texas Telegraph Company began service to Galveston. The San Jacinto Yacht Club held its first regatta on April 12, 1860. The Houston Base Ball Club was organized. In 1860, Irishman Dick Dowling chartered a bank at the corner of Main Street and Congress Avenue for the purpose of dealing in the exchange of liquors for gold, silver, and bank notes. In every direction new houses appeared. Out on the prairie to the south and west the city spread street by street, until it was impossible to find the landmarks as they had been even three or four years before, while stately brick stores arose on every block.

When the war ended, Houston continued its expansion. In 1867, Hugh Rice, an Irish immigrant, became engineer-in-chief of a survey of Buffalo Bayou, the San Jacinto River, and Galveston Bay. His report urged "widening the channel at the city of Houston for the purpose of affording seagoing and other ships ample room to turn around without delay or inconvenience." Houston remained characteristically intent on the future. By 1867 the city was connected to every telegraph line in the United States. Though still under the cloud of the Civil War, the city petitioned Congress to designate it a port of entry. On March 30, 1870, when Texas was readmitted to the Union, Houston, though still under state-appointed government, was flourishing. It rode through the 1870s on a surge of enterprise and prosperity. The city invested in the Buffalo Bayou Ship Channel Company. In July 1870, after three years of consideration, Congress designated Houston a port of delivery and called for a surveyor of customs to be posted in the city.[20]

Texas's other major cities, San Antonio, Austin, and Galveston, all experienced rapid growth in the decade after war's end. Buenger has noted Texas's divergence from the economic patterns that plagued the South heading into the twentieth century. In Texas, more prosperous tenants and small-scale, landowning farmers were able to find political or geographic solutions to the South's biggest problem at the beginning of the Depression, the imbalance of land and people. Even the unskilled were able to find work in Texas's rapidly growing cities.[21]

The importance of this urban growth to Texas's postwar collective memory has been studied in depth by Kenneth W. Wheeler, who pointed out that not all immigrants to antebellum Texas were Southern farmers by any means, and many of those from the North and from overseas were merchants and skilled craftsmen. Commercial activities developed quickly in the new republic, despite its financial destitution, and resulted in urbanization. Houston, Galveston, and Austin were deliberately planned to become great cities, with foresight and imagination, and San Antonio set its own special pattern for growth. Wheeler explained that each of the four cities had some unique feature, and that these were already markedly evident by the time of the Civil War. "The pattern for early urban development in Texas," he wrote, "was formed by the end of the Civil War. Cities would rise on the upper Texas plains (Dallas, Fort Worth, Lubbock, Amarillo), but in the older section of the state none would seriously rival those already established. Galveston, Houston, San Antonio, and Austin had each developed its own particular characteristics and had shaped the design of its future growth. Moreover, by 1865 the permanent relationship between the four was cemented."[22]

By 1900, Texas was home to three of the largest cities of the former Confederate South. Luxuries such as gas lighting, electricity, telephones, and servants eventually relieved genteel women in urban areas of the constant drudgery of housework, freeing them for cultural pursuits. In towns along shipping routes and railroads, increasing population brought a measure of prosperity and provided the first setting for the women's club movement in Texas.[23]

The growth of cities emphasized the many competing agendas that discouraged the formation of a monolithic collective memory of Confederate Texas. These included the motives of women, professional historians, and commercial interests. By the 1880s, women, who had been organizing social groups outside their homes since the early 1870s, were beginning to look beyond church mission and benevolent societies, which were the earliest women's organizations in cities like Houston and Galveston. The Ladies Reading Club, organized in Houston in 1885, allowed women to branch out from benevolence and charity to intellectual matters, handling abstractions, dealing with contradictory ideas and written assignments, delivering papers in front of other women, speaking in mixed groups, arranging conventions, traveling to conventions unaccompanied by male escorts, doing committee work, and leading others into the public forum.[24]

By 1880, the memory of Reconstruction was fading, and the myth of the Lost Cause was spreading. Everything connected with the Lost Cause seemed to interest Americans of the 1890s—so long as it was presented in a romantic, sentimental framework.[25] The creation of the myth of the Lost Cause fitted perfectly a pattern of an invented collective memory. The tradition evolved out of the defeat, poverty, and dislocation that followed the Civil War.[26] However, although Texas's pride may have been wounded, its experience after the defeat of the Confederacy differed significantly from that of the other Southern states. To the extent that Texas women embraced the myth of the Lost Cause, it was most certainly an invented, collective memory of convenience for them.

Women were considered at the end of the nineteenth century as the "custodians" of culture, especially of "preservation of links with the past." "Thank God the woman of Texas can always be trusted to lead in all great reforms and patriotic movements," a Texas legislator wrote to Mrs. Mary Jane Briscoe in 1897. "God bless them and aid them in all their efforts to elevate our race."[27] Lawyer Charles B. Emanuel summarized men's attitudes in a speech he delivered at the Rusk, Texas, Confederate reunion in 1901. Emanuel argued that men's work ended with the war, and the next task, that of "preserving the memories of the gallant heroes who fell in defense of our native land," was left to the women.[28] The first organization to form for this purpose was the Daughters of the Republic of Texas (DRT) in 1891. Miss Betty Ballinger of Galveston laid out the purpose of the organization in terms of the traditional role of Southern women: "The future of Texas is in the hands of her sons [who], dazzled by the splendor of the present have forgotten the heroic deeds and sacrifices of the past. But it is not so with woman. Surrounded by the history of the family life, it is her duty to keep alive the sacred fire of tradition. Let us leave the future of Texas to our brothers, and claim as our province the guarding of her holy past." Her choice of words echoed the sentiments of many clubwomen across the country, particularly in the South, as they tried to balance traditional roles with their desire to enlarge the scope of womanhood.[29]

The first project undertaken by the DRT was urging the State to purchase the San Jacinto battleground and erect a monument to its heroes—their husbands and fathers. If memory creation through monument building represents cultural power, this was an opportunity for women to exercise that power.[30] In 1896 and 1897, two chapters of the region-wide United Daughters of the Confederacy (UDC) organized in Texas. Through these groups, women supported—and sometimes competed with—the goals of aging veterans and their sons about how best to justify the South's stubborn stand and stinging loss. Their activism was an important and distinctive element of virtually all Confederate memorialization.

In the years immediately after the war, Southern commemorative efforts centered around respectful burial of the dead and creation of mourning rituals. The cemetery was the focus of memorialization. Confederate Decoration Day was celebrated each spring, during which women and children spread flowers on graves and townspeople gathered to hear speeches praising the dead.[31] Many of the women who joined the UDC were already members of the DRT and had gained some experience with memorializing Texas heroes and lobbying the legislature. Monument building was an activity in which they could exercise power on the public stage. Women seized this opportunity for power in Texas, erecting more than fifty of the sixty-five large, public monuments to the Confederate generation in the state.

It seems clear that they were motivated by much more than nostalgia for the Confederacy. Women were motivated by many interests other than memory, such as expanding their public influence, social climbing, artistic movements such as City Beautiful, and elevating the status of their state. Women's historian Kelly McMichael, in her study of Confederate memorials in Texas, noted that, though they always claimed monuments were an "object lesson in history," UDC members engaged in monument building for a host of reasons in addition to memorializing Southern soldiers. They understood the potential power in memory construction and used it to project the morals they valued, morals such as honor, sacrifice, and patriotism. Soldiers represented these values, which were worthy of honor and deserved to be memorialized in stone. But they were the mothers, daughters, or wives of these soldiers. They had worked in complementary roles with their fathers and husbands, and they wanted women's efforts remembered. Much of the UDC's monument work in Texas attempted to guarantee that women were recognized and remembered for their efforts through word, art, and symbol. In the ideal, the monuments represented an acceptable public and culturally powerful position for women.[32] "I am an enthusiast in Texas history and think I see where Texas women can do much with equal grace and ease to enrich our state literature by saving from irrevocable loss the memory of our pioneer women," wrote Dora Fowler Arthur, editor of the women's section of the *Texas Magazine* in Austin.[33] That the erection of Civil War monuments in Texas was as much a memorial to Texas heroes as to the Confederacy was demonstrated when the Sherman Chapter of the UDC unveiled its monument on April 21, 1897, the day set aside to commemorate the Battle of San Jacinto.

Engagement in the UDC and other clubs also gave many Texas women a vehicle for social climbing. "The whole thing will forever remain in the hands of a clique," De Zavala complained to Looscan in 1907. Though specifically referring to the DRT, she continued, "Have you noticed that it is the same clique that has grabbed all the patriotic societies? It is a well-organized clique—they stand well together. They first took possession of the smaller clubs and societies then widened their influence. Of course Mrs. [Cornelia Branch] Stone did not get the place on her merits or personal influence but on the representation that Texas should have it and she was Texas on the spot.[34]

De Zavala's estimate of Cornelia Stone was echoed by Betty Ballinger. "Long ago I became persuaded from things happening in our own chapter, that Mrs. Stone cared only for her own personal advancement and would stoop to actions which I could not countenance," Miss Betty confided to Looscan.[35] McMichael noted that, though the Daughters argued that they erected Confederate monuments purely to venerate the old soldiers and instruct Southerners, the UDC and individual women consistently made sure that the public knew who raised the funds and organized the campaigns. Katie Cabell Currie Muse, the individual most responsible for Dallas's monument, basked in the recognition she received at the grand ball held at the Oriental Hotel in Dallas the night before the unveiling of the Confederate monument in that city. She claimed that she was totally surprised when she was led onto the dance floor, proclaimed "the daughter of monuments," and presented with a diamond, ruby, and sapphire brooch on behalf of the local United Confederate Veterans camp.[36]

All this is not to say that some women were not sincerely devoted to the memory of the Confederacy. Adelia Dunovant, founder of the Oran Roberts Chapter of the UDC, grew up in South Carolina and came to Texas only after the Civil War. She sought to rehabilitate the memory of her father, a plantation and slave owner. Justification for the plantation culture of her youth motivated her. And though, like Dunovant, many Southern women involved in the patriotic hereditary clubs connected to the Confederacy sought a sense of ennobled Southern womanhood

"O great Confederate Mothers, we would paint your names on monuments, that men may read them as the years go by and tribute pay to you, who bore and nurtured hero-sons and gave them solace on that darkest day, when they came home, with broken swords and guns!" Confederate monument, Texarkana. Courtesy of Laura Lyons McLemore.

based on Old South values or extolled the virtues of a past "Southern life," many other Texas women tended to see the UDC as another vehicle for improving Texas society and culture and reminding Texans of their obligations and duties as citizens.[37]

For example, note the difference between Looscan's reasons for studying history, which she presented in her address to the Ladies Reading Club of Houston in 1890, and Dunovant's address, "The Study of History," delivered to the Lamar Fontaine Chapter of the UDC in Alvin, Texas, in 1899. Looscan spoke in broad terms of studying history for personal edification, to bring the individual into "sympathetic relations with the great individual minds that have shaped the form and determined the character of what we call history," to give those who inhabit the present a sense of their place in the great continuum, and to appreciate their position as American women as well as the benefits they derive from that position. Dunovant's message, on the other hand, differed in both tone and emphasis. History was, she declared, "a tribute at the feet of our beloved South." By "diving into historic recesses," she assured her listeners, they could rescue the principles of the South "from the grave of oblivion" and glorify them. Her reasons for studying history were its indestructibility, the "regal robe" it draws around the UDC, and its utility for inculcating younger generations with Southern principles.[38] Those Daughters most dedicated to glorifying the principles of the South tended to be latecomers to Texas from other states in the Deep South, like Dunovant, or to be the product of a plantation upbringing, like Stone, whose father was a planter and slave owner in Liberty County, Texas, before the outbreak of the Civil War.[39]

Texas women also saw their activities as participating in the future of their burgeoning communities. As an extension of their traditional domestic roles, women assumed responsibility for promoting appreciation for art, drama, and music as well as literature, because culture and the arts were, by the late nineteenth century, widely considered female terrain. Memorials were a way of introducing art into public space and creating a sense of cultured sophistication in Texas cities. Women of the Texas Federation of Women's Clubs seemed to see their mission as looking to the prosperous American future more than the past. The future was Union, not the defeated Confederacy.

The women's movement, closely related in some of its phases to urban aesthetics, was well represented at the Chicago World's Fair in 1893. The growing role of women in the spreading village improvement movement, in municipal reform, and in the cultural life of the nation was reflected in the exposition's Women's Department and in the Women's Building, designed by a woman. In the minds of the cultural elite and in the mass mind, the fair was linked with American progress in the urban arts and sciences. The fair was also an expression of the best features of the United States. It was in the highest sense a patriotic exercise.[40] Katie Currie (later Katie Muse), the Texas UDC division's first president, traveled to the World Columbian Exposition and Fair in Chicago and returned home to Dallas motivated to create a woman's club dedicated to the "beautification and moral uplifting" of Texas.[41] Stone, also a Texas UDC president, declared, "The history of a people and their monuments measure their consequence as a nation, and the character of their intelligence, their morals, religion and civilization." Confederate memorial monuments thus served multiple purposes. Although they may ostensibly have been intended to preserve the memory of the Confederacy and those who fought for it, they also served to remind Texans of their own accomplishments. Finally, the Daughters set themselves to the task of creating memory, drawing strength potentially from the power of culture building in the interest of crafting a memory of women.[42]

The monument building of Texas women coincided with the development of a faculty of professional historians at the University of Texas. Though some were Southerners by birth, their interest in cultivating scholarship produced resistance to the myth of the Lost Cause or the perpetuation of a collective memory of Confederate Texas. George P. Garrison, first head of the history department at the University of Texas and organizer of the Texas State Historical Association, saw Texas as a key part of that greater national experience with conflict and expansion. He "proved to be more American than Texan, and more nationalistic than provincial," and was influential in weakening the perception of a collective memory of Confederate Texas.[43] Eugene Bolton, who came to the University of Texas in 1901 by way of Wisconsin and Pennsylvania, developed an interest in the history of Spanish expansion into North America within a year of his arrival. Bolton, like Garrison, was a

Progressive historian who regarded Texas history as part of the national settlement process and emphasized the influence of Spain advancing into the Southwest rather than its roots in the American South. Bolton became coeditor of the *Quarterly of the Texas Historical Association*. It was in large part through his influence that the title changed to *Southwestern Historical Quarterly* and the scope expanded to include all the Spanish borderlands. Eugene C. Barker, who succeeded Garrison as department chair in 1910, also succeeded him at the helm of the Association and as general editor of the *Quarterly*.

Barker's selection of articles on Texas history after 1860 reflected an emerging bias among his contributors for the era of the Republic and clearly indicated the future of Confederate memory in Texas. As Richard McCaslin, author of the centennial history of Texas State Historical Association, observed, there were far fewer good contributions on the Civil War period than on the post-Reconstruction era, and many who wrote about the war avoided military topics. Barker's major research project was the life of Stephen F. Austin and the editing of Austin's papers. Charles Ramsdell joined the history department at the University of Texas in 1906. Most Texas historians during the first two decades of the twentieth century, both professional and amateur, tended to focus on the Western frontier heritage of the state. Ramsdell, as a student of William A. Dunning, did tend to view Texas history from the Southern perspective, and he was known for his scholarship on the old South, but he never fully embraced all of the strongly pro-Southern biases of Dunning.[44]

Among the most potentially influential forces for a collective memory of Confederate Texas was George W. Littlefield, a former Confederate officer, university regent, and one of the wealthiest men in Texas. Littlefield was a Mississippi native who moved to Texas in 1850. He complained about the Northern bias he saw in American history textbooks, in particular a book by Henry W. Elson, *History of the United States*. Barker deflected Littlefield's complaint by pointing out that the university needed resources to support research and scholarship in Southern history. "Until this collection is made," he warned Littlefield, "the resolutions and protests of patriotic societies against the misrepresentations of the South are as sounding brass and tinkling symbols." As a result, Littlefield eventually endowed a fund for the purchase of materials for the study of Southern history.[45] Ironically, the Littlefield Fund and Southern History Collection represented Confederate memory employed in the service of Texas.

Commercial interests and the pursuit of profit also inhibited the development of a robust collective memory of Confederate Texas. John E. Bodnar, in his book on public memory, commemoration, and patriotism, *Remaking America,* noted that public memory emerges from the intersection of official and vernacular cultural expressions. "The former originates in the concerns of cultural leaders or authorities at all levels of society. Whether in positions of prominence in small town, ethnic communities, or in educational, government, or military bureaucracies, these leaders share a common interest in social unity, the continuity of existing institutions, and loyalty to the status quo. They attempt to advance these concerns by promoting interpretations of past and present reality that reduce the power of competing interests that threaten the attainment of their goals." Bodnar observed that, whereas official culture seeks to mediate assorted interests so as to assure "ascendancy," vernacular culture is fickle and changeable and can be "reformulated from time to time by the creation of new social units such as soldiers and their friends who share an experience in war or immigrants who settle a particular place."[46]

Raw political and economic conflict dominated the final quarter of the nineteenth century. A growing business class in the North and the South sought to nationalize the economy and expand corporate power. Workers, farmers, immigrants, and other ordinary people struggled to regulate that effort in ways that would temper the breathtaking pace of change and allow for their participation in the formation of public and economic policy. The resulting clash of interests produced not only class and political conflict but sharp cultural exchanges over the issue of public memory. The Lost Cause, according to Bodnar, was a way of meeting the psychological needs of defeated Southerners but also the powerful interests of a rising class of Southern industrialists who were anxious to resume activity with the North and who were assuming roles once played by the region's aristocracy. In their attempt to absolve the region of guilt and resume commerce with a growing national economy, these interests deemphasized commemorative activities centered on grief and sorrow for the dead and defeat itself and fostered a memory designed to speed the process of reunification while preserving something of a sense of regional pride. Cast in these terms, "collective memory" of the Confederacy was a trick played on ordinary people for the convenience of the elite.[47]

Similarly, Kenneth M. Hamilton, in his study of Harrison County, Texas, found the myth of the Lost Cause as the collective memory of Confederate Texas insufficient to explain the extreme white repression of blacks there between 1865 and 1868. His research demonstrated that the pursuit and protection of wealth was at the root of the repression, much as some actions of the Ku Klux Klan attributed to a collective memory of the South were actually nothing more than a mask for unadulterated hatred and racism (not necessarily exclusively toward former slaves).[48]

In the 1890s railroad companies were able to exploit national battlefields to stimulate tourist traffic and veterans from the North and the South.[49] Centennial celebrations of the Civil War, which coincided with the civil rights movement of the 1960s, revealed similar profit motives. Certain memories of the Confederate struggle did help to sustain actions to preserve segregation, which were no match for the powerful processes of change at work in the region. Government officials and agencies in several Southern states welcomed the prospect of tourists flocking to the region. A resurgence of Confederate memory among members of the Texas UDC and Sons of Confederate Veterans did prompt those two groups to hold up plans for a centennial celebration in the state because the organizers used the term "Civil War" instead of acknowledging the South as a distinctly Southern nation. But these misgivings were overcome. State legislatures voted substantial funding for new agencies in anticipation of the financial rewards likely to accrue from the "heritage" bonanza.[50]

∎   ∎   ∎

Collective memory of Confederate Texas is as elusive as a ghost. Sometimes it emerges plainly in Texas politics and culture, but like an apparition it tends to dissolve when one reaches out to capture and examine it. Whether memory is displaced by history or takes over when history no longer survives, a truly collective memory of Confederate Texas would be difficult if not impossible to conceive because there are so many constituencies with competing experiences and memories. Even if the term "collective memory" were applied only to the dominant Anglo-American population of Texas, there were, in fact, two (white) memories of a "Confederate Texas." The first was that remembered by contemporaries, those who were involved; the second was constructed by some contemporaries and by subsequent generations for specific purposes. The first consisted of personal accounts—often inconsistent and sometimes contradictory—military strategies, and memorial biographies that helped people grieve and come to grips with loss. The second, including memorializing, monument building, and sentimentalizing, was brought to serve a host of agendas for various constituencies not always closely tied to Confederate identity. Further, what might be considered the hallmarks of a collective memory of Confederate Texas would be the same ones that inhabitants of Texas would recognize as Texan: a conservative approach to government, an eye for the main chance, a lust for adventure, fierce individualism, and a strain of racism that extended to the Other, whether Mexican, black, or something else. It is a collective memory that existed before the Confederacy came into being and endured long after it collapsed. At the end of the day, collective memory has to do with collective identity. One may safely conclude that Texans identify themselves first and foremost as Texan, which evokes the frontier, wide-open spaces (even in Texas's largest cities), cowboys, and the Alamo, the iconic symbol of freedom.

NOTES

1. Walter L. Buenger, "Flight from Modernity: The Economic History of Texas since 1845," in *Texas through Time,* ed. Walter L. Buenger and Robert A. Calvert (College Station: Texas A&M University Press, 1991), 310–41.

2. Jeffrey K. Olick and Joyce Robbins, "Social Memory Studies: From 'Collective Memory' to the Historical Sociology of Mnemonic Practices, *Annual Review of Sociology* 24 (1998): 105–106.

3. Alon Confino, "Collective Memory and Cultural History: Problems of Method," *American Historical Review* 102 (December 1997): 1392, 1399; Patrick Hutton, "Recent Scholarship on Memory and History," *History Teacher* 33 (August 2000): 537–38.

4. Hutton, "Recent Scholarship," 538.

5. Olick and Robbins, "Social Memory Studies," 112.

6. Elizabeth Howard West, "Southern Opposition to the Annexation of Texas," *Southwestern Historical Quarterly* 18 (July 1918), 76.

7. Donald William Meinig, *Imperial Texas: An Interpretive Essay in Cultural Geography* (1969), quoted in John H. Jenkins, *Best Texas Books* (Austin: TSHA Press, 1988), 381.

8. John E. Bodnar, *Remaking America: Public Memory, Commemoration, and Patriotism in the Twentieth Century* (Princeton, N.J.: Princeton University Press, 1992), 26.

9. Jenkins, *Basic Texas Books,* 167–68.

10. Randolph B. Campbell, "History and Collective Memory in Texas: The Entangled Stories of the Lone Star State," in *Lone Star Pasts,* ed. Gregg Cantrell and Elizabeth Hayes Turner (College Station: Texas A&M Press, 2007), 278.

11. Adina de Zavala to Adele B. Looscan, June 3, 1902, Adele Briscoe Looscan Papers MC041, San Jacinto Museum of History, LaPorte, Tex. [hereafter Looscan Papers].

12. Terry G. Jordan, "The Imprint of the Upper and Lower South on Mid-Nineteenth-Century Texas," *Annals of the Association of American Geographers* 57 (December 1967), 686.

13. Ty Cashion, "What's the Matter with Texas," *Magazine of Western History* 55 (Winter 2005), 4.

14. Susan A. Crane, "Writing the Individual Back into Collective Memory," *American Historical Review* 102 (December 1997), 1376.

15. Campbell, "History and Collective Memory," 277.

16. Robert Cook, "(Un)furl That Banner: The Response of White Southerners to the Civil War Centennial of 1961–1965," *Journal of Southern History* 68 (November 2002), 882.

17. Elizabeth Hayes Turner, "Juneteenth: Emancipation and Memory," in Cantrell and Turner, *Lone Star Pasts,* 144.

18. Charles W. Ramsdell, "Texas from the Fall of the Confederacy to the Beginning of Reconstruction," *Quarterly of the Texas State Historical Association* 11 (January 1908), 199.

19. Marguerite Johnston, *Houston the Unknown City, 1836–1946* (College Station: Texas A&M University Press, 1991), 67.

20. Ibid., 59, 60, 67, 79, 82.

21. Walter L. Buenger, "Texas and the South," *Southwestern Historical Quarterly* 103 (January 2000), 311–12.

22. Kenneth W. Wheeler, *To Wear a City's Crown: The Beginnings of Urban Growth in Texas, 1836–1865,* quoted in Jenkins, *Basic Texas Books,* 573.

23. Elizabeth Hayes Turner, *Women, Culture, and Community* (New York: Oxford University Press, 1997), 153.

24. Audrey Crawford, "A Women's Tour of Early Houston," Summer Seminar for Public School History Teachers at the University of Houston, June 10, 2002;

Johnston, *Houston the Unknown City,* 91, 95; Joan Marie Johnson, *Southern Ladies, New Women: Race, Region, and Clubwomen in South Carolina, 1890–1930* (Gainesville: University Press of Florida, 2004), 1; Turner, *Women, Culture, and Community,* 152.

25. Rollin G. Osterweiss, *The Myth of the Lost Cause, 1865–1900* (Hamden, Conn.: Archon Books, 1973), 63.

26. Kelly McMichael, "Memories Are Short but Monuments Lengthen Remembrances: The United Daughters of the Confederacy and the Power of Civil War Memory," in Cantrell and Turner, *Lone Star Pasts,* 97.

27. Dr. L. D. Hill to Mrs. Briscoe, May 10, 1897, Mary Jane Briscoe Papers, San Jacinto Museum of History, LaPorte, Tex.

28. McMichael, "Memories Are Short," 100.

29. Betty Ballinger quoted in Elizabeth Hayes Turner, "Ballinger, Betty Eve," *Handbook of Texas Online,* Texas State Historical Association, www.tshaonline.org /handbook/online/articles/fba51.

30. McMichael, "Memories Are Short," 96.

31. Cynthia Mills and Pamela H. Simpson, eds., *Monuments to the Lost Cause: Women, Art, and the Landscapes of Southern Memory* (Knoxville: University of Tennessee Press, 2003), xvi.

32. McMichael, "Memories Are Short," 96–97.

33. Dora Fowler Arthur to Adele B. Looscan, October 27, 1896, Looscan Papers.

34. Adina de Zavala to Adele B. Looscan, November 27, 1907, Looscan Papers.

35. Bettie Ballinger to Adele Looscan, January 28, 1908, Looscan Papers.

36. McMichael, "Memories Are Short," 100.

37. Turner, *Women, Culture, and Community,* 167; Kelly McMichael, *Sacred Memories: The Civil War Monument Movement in Texas* (Denton: Texas State Historical Association, 2009), 8.

38. Andrea Kökény, "The Construction of Anglo-American Identity in the Republic of Texas, as Reflected in the 'Telegraph and Texas Register,'" *Journal of the Southwest* 46 (Summer 2004): 283–308; Mrs. M. Looscan, "President's Address," *Annual Reports of the Ladies' Reading Club of Houston, Texas* (Houston: Gray's Printing Office, 1890), 13–14, Box 117, Looscan Papers; Adelia A. Dunovant, "Study of History," Proceedings of the Fourth Annual Convention (United Daughters of the Confederacy, Texas Division, 1900), 1–5, Box 118, Looscan Papers. Francesca Morgan comments on the differences among Southern clubwomen in *Women and Patriotism in Jim Crow America* (Chapel Hill: University of North Carolina Press, 2005), 30–31. See also Karen L. Cox, *Dixie's Daughters* (Gainesville: University of Florida Press, 2003), 65.

39. "Adelia Dunovant," Oran M. Roberts Chapter 440 United Daughters of the Confederacy Houston, Harris County, Texas, www.lksfriday.com/UDC/UDC-030. htm; Elizabeth Brooks, "Mrs. H. C. Stone," in *Prominent Texas Women* (Akron, Ohio: Werner, 1896), 179–81.

40. William H. Wilson, *The City Beautiful Movement* (Baltimore, Md.: Johns Hopkins University Press, 1989), 57–58, 64.

41. McMichael, *Sacred Memories*, 15. See also Gregg Cantrell, "The Bones of Stephen F. Austin: History and Memory in Progressive-Era Texas," in Cantrell and Turner, *Lone Star Pasts*, 42.

42. McMichael, "Memories Are Short," 95 (quote), 105.

43. Richard B. McCaslin, *At the Heart of Texas: 100 Years of the Texas State Historical Association, 1897–1997* (Austin: TSHA Press, 2007), 24.

44. Ibid., 43, 56–57, 60, 43.

45. Gaines M. Foster, *Ghosts of the Confederacy: Defeat, the Lost Cause, and the Emergence of the New South, 1865 to 1913* (New York: Oxford University Press, 1987), 190.

46. John E. Bodnar, *Remaking America: Public Memory, Commemoration, and Patriotism in the Twentieth Century* (Princeton, N.J.: Princeton University Press, 1992), 13–14, 28–29.

47. Ibid., 31.

48. Walter. L. Buenger, "Memory and the 1920s Ku Klux Klan in Texas," in Cantrell and Turner, *Lone Star Pasts*, 120; Kenneth M. Hamilton, "White Wealth and Black Repression in Harrison County, Texas: 1865–1868," *Journal of Negro History* 84 (Autumn 1999), 340–59.

49. Bodnar, *Remaking America*, 28.

50. Cook, "(Un)furl That Banner," 884–85.

2

The Problem of Slave Flight in Civil War Texas

Andrew J. Torget

From the first moment Anglo-Americans began migrating into Texas with their slaves, those enslaved people had been running away. This, of course, had always been a problem for slaveholders across the southern United States—slaves tended to run away, undermining the system that surrounded them and resisting their masters whenever the opportunity arose. In most cases, those slaves escaped for only a few days at a time. Some fugitives left to visit family and loved ones on nearby plantations; others ran in protest, hoping to force their masters into concessions of various sorts; still others escaped for any number of reasons, taking to the surrounding woods for whatever temporary freedoms the countryside could provide. Nearly all of them returned within days or weeks to their farms and plantations, where life resumed usual rhythms. There were, however, a smaller number of slaves toiling in the American South who undertook the far riskier challenge of making a permanent escape to freedom, and for those bold souls Texas offered unique opportunities.[1] Unlike Mississippi or Alabama, Texas shared a porous border with Mexico and a sparsely settled western frontier where Anglo-Texan authority remained tenuous at best. Beginning in the 1820s, and continuing through the eve of the Civil War, enslaved men and women in Texas confounded their masters by running away in a bid for permanent freedom.

Such escapes made Texas slaveholders uneasy. Although hard numbers remain elusive, it does not appear that Texas slaves ran away—whether to Mexico or in any other direction—with greater frequency

than their counterparts in other Southern states. Yet, as several historians have noted, Texas slaveholders by the 1850s had nonetheless developed a pervasive fear that the trickle of fugitive slaves making their way
toward Mexico could become a flood, which they believed would have
painful consequences for the state. Beyond destabilizing Texas farms—
and thereby disrupting the region's cotton economy—any significant
increase in slave flight to Mexico or the western territories would make
Texas appear to be a particularly risky location to set up a new farm and
thereby swiftly disrupt the steady stream of Southern migrants making
their way during the 1850s into Texas from nearby slaveholding states.
Any decrease in that stream of migration would, in turn, threaten land
values and economic stability in the state, and thereby the well-being
of every white Texan. Anglo-Texans, in response, did whatever they
could to discourage such escapes—establishing county slave patrols,
organizing slave-capture raids into northern Mexico, and passing state
laws offering rewards to anyone who recaptured a fugitive slave—as they
worked to contain the problem of slave flight.[2]

The outbreak of the Civil War, therefore, presented a particularly
daunting challenge to Texas slaveholders by offering their slaves new opportunities and encouragement for both rebellion and escape. Yet many
Anglo-Texans did not see it that way, at least not at the start of the war.
Indeed, many white Texans proudly boasted in 1860 and 1861 that their
reliance on slaves would prove to be a source of great strength and stability for the new Confederate nation, not a critical weakness or liability.
They earnestly proclaimed what they called the "natural loyalty" of their
enslaved men and women, insisting that black people's "happiest position is *Chattel Slavery*," which was clearly the "*natural* condition of the
negro."[3] Some Texas farmers even argued that secession would instead
mark the end of slave flight as a significant problem in the state. By walling themselves off from the pernicious influence of abolitionists in the
northern United States (whose misguided propaganda, they believed,
was the primary cause of their slaves running away), white Texans instead believed that the creation of the Confederacy would allow them to
control and contain their slaves far more effectively. Their slaves, they
insisted, would prove to be loyal Confederates in the coming war, not
secret Unionists among them.

Such illusions, however, would be dashed during the course of the Civil War. As it turned out, Texas slaves did rebel and run as the circumstances of the war provided them new opportunities for escape. Because U.S. forces never managed a sustained invasion of Texas before 1865, Texas slaves never ran in numbers comparable to the rest of the Confederacy. Yet the steady stream of reports appearing in Texas newspapers detailing massive defections of slaves in nearly every other Confederate state put white Texans on edge, as it became increasingly clear that enslaved people would run to Union lines for freedom whenever the opportunity presented itself. As the needs of the Confederate armies, in turn, demanded ever more able-bodied men, fears in the state also began to rise of slave rebellions that could follow when fewer white men remained in each county to enforce order. By the end of the Civil War, defections of Texas slaves to Mexico and surrounding territories had forced Confederate authorities to react and thereby forced many Anglo-Texans to abandon their earlier faith in the natural loyalty of their slaves. Indeed, if anything marked the Texas home front during the years between 1861 and 1865, it was how the increasing problem of slave flight—both inside and outside the state—pushed white Texans to confront the uncomfortable realization that their slaves were not natural Confederates.

At the outset of the Civil War, most white Texans insisted—at least publicly—that the 182,000 enslaved men and women in the state would never rise up against them. Even before Texas seceded, Austin's *State Gazette* dismissed fears of Texas slaves turning against Confederates in a long article detailing British attempts to entice slaves to abandon their masters during the American Revolution and the War of 1812. Such attempts at destroying the revolutionaries from within had invariably failed, the paper insisted, because the vast majority of slaves refused to rebel against their masters, demonstrating that "under proper regulations we need not apprehend much trouble from that quarter."[4] That the newspaper's editor felt the need to reassure his readers on the matter of slave loyalty revealed that not everyone shared his deep confidence. Yet many other white Texans in 1860 and 1861 made similar claims in public venues about the certain loyalty of their slaves, and they clearly believed their own rhetoric. One man in Washington County, for example, predicted that Texas slaves would gladly join their masters in opposing

Abraham Lincoln's attempts to secure "the abolition of slavery in the Southern States." Should the U.S. Army dare to make their way into Texas, he explained, "not only will they have to counter men fighting for their homes, and their dearest rights, but they will find negroes themselves in the Southern ranks, fighting with their masters, to drive back the invaders."[5] Rather than a vulnerability of the Confederacy, many white Texans pointed toward their slaves as a source of great strength for their new nation's defense.

Some Texans went to remarkable lengths to demonstrate not only that their servants were fiercely loyal but that the slaves themselves regarded Lincoln and Northerners as troublesome threats. One planter in Wharton County penned a public letter detailing "a novel scene" he claimed to have witnessed during the 1860–61 Christmas holidays, when "several hundred" slaves from nearby plantations gathered for their annual celebration. "As the festivities drew to a close," the planter reported, "we discovered two buck negroes carrying something in the shape of a human being." It was an effigy of Abraham Lincoln, whom the slaves had dubbed "the king of the abolitionists," and it soon became clear they intended to put him on trial. What followed was a public excoriation of Lincoln, John Brown, and their anti-slavery allies, as the slaves— according to the planter—loudly denounced outsiders for "putting de fool in de black people's heads." One of the slaves played the part of Lincoln, protesting that he only wanted "to give you poor niggers your freedom." The crowd, in response, shouted down the offer as the "liberty to starve and freeze" and then lynched the dummy before burning it and scattering the ashes. Although it is doubtful that any such scene played out the way the Wharton slaveholder described, he nonetheless held it up as evidence for his fellow planters that their slaves rejected Lincoln and his Republicans just as fully as they did.[6]

Although they put on a brave face in public—and certainly believed what they said—such rhetoric among white Texans poorly masked grave fears about possible slave revolts and rebellions. Indeed, ever since the massive 1791–1804 slave rebellion of Saint-Domingue destroyed the French colonies on what became modern-day Haiti, slaveholders across the American South lived with an ever-present fear of their slaves rising against them in violent insurrection. Yet, remarkably, most Texas slaveholders on the eve of the Civil War did not appear to believe that such revolts would begin with discontent among the slaves themselves. Because most white Texans believed that their slaves were naturally loyal and contented—one planter called enslaved blacks "the only happy race on God's earth"—they instead blamed any rebelliousness among the enslaved on pernicious outside influences.[7] It was, they insisted, the abolitionists, Republicans, and their free black allies who fostered disloyalty by purposefully duping Texas slaves into revolts with false promises of freedom and liberty. And by 1860–61 it seemed that those forces of anti-slavery were prepared to go to any lengths necessary to convince Texas slaves to slit the throats of their masters. John Brown's infamous 1859 raid on the federal arsenal at Harper's Ferry, where he intended to spark a massive slave rebellion by arming the local slave population, provided a chilling example to white Southerners everywhere of the ongoing campaign among abolitionists to disrupt and destroy the supposedly loyal bond that linked together master and slave.

An even more terrifying example came to Texas in July 1860, when a series of fires—sparked by faulty phosphorous matches that spontaneously ignited in extreme summer heat—burned several North Texas towns. As the downtown sections of Dallas and Denton smoldered in ashes, local newspapers blamed the fires on abolitionists who had supposedly infiltrated the region and recruited allies among the local slave population in order to spark a violent insurrection. Waves of panic soon swept the state, and vigilante mobs murdered dozens of slaves and any whites suspected of anti-slavery sentiments in an effort to root out anyone disloyal to the slave regime in Texas.[8] What was so remarkable about these events—which became known collectively as the "Texas Troubles"—was how they revealed both the deep-seated fears that white Texans harbored about slave insurrections as well as their deep-set convictions that such rebellions came primarily from the evil influences of their enemies in the northern United States. "An Abolitionist, it should be recollected," warned the *Navarro Express* more than a year after the fires, "can steal negroes, entice them away, or incite servile insurrections," and the newspaper urged the Texas legislature to make an exception to its prohibitions against blacks testifying against whites in court. If the defendants were abolitionists suspected of meddling with the slaves, argued the newspaper, then it was imperative to allow the testimony of enslaved people in order to root out "such offenders."[9]

The secession of Texas therefore appeared to offer local slaveholders increased protection from the possibilities of slave rebellion and flight. By walling themselves off entirely from the pernicious influence of abolitionists, free blacks, and Lincoln's Republicans, they could help ensure the unbroken allegiance of their slaves by protecting them from false promises of freedom. To be sure, the decision of Texas to leave the Union in February 1861 was foremost an effort to shield the legal status of slavery within the state from the anti-slavery designs of the Lincoln administration. But for many white Texans, secession also represented an opportunity to shore up the long-term loyalty of the local slave population by shielding them from outsiders determined to lead those slaves toward rebellion. On the eve of the Civil War, then, Anglo-Texans hoped that the creation of the Confederacy would strengthen the bonds between masters and slaves.

As fighting began during the spring and summer of 1861, Confederate Texans nonetheless remained nervous about how their slaves would behave. The Texas legislature passed a new runaway slave law in April 1861, clarifying the responsibilities of country sheriffs for capturing and returning fugitives.[10] In response to local demands, county governments, particularly in North Texas, expanded the work of slave patrols in order to guard against possible insurrections, and the Texas legislature passed a law in January 1862 requiring that such patrols be made weekly rather than monthly.[11] "Too much liberty is allowed to negroes," grumbled Corsicana's *Navarro Express* in an editorial demanding more slave patrols.[12] Perhaps one reason white Texans remained nervous was how rapidly the slave population had expanded during the previous decade—rising from 58,000 in 1850 to more than 182,000 by 1860, a remarkable 213 percent increase. The vast majority of enslaved people in Texas, therefore, had only arrived within the past few years, and fears remained that these recent arrivals could be particularly susceptible to abolitionists seeking to infiltrate their ranks. During the summer of 1861, almost exactly one year after the Texas Troubles, nervous citizens in Nacogdoches discovered "a plot to burn that town," which they blamed on two white men who had supposedly attempted to incite local slaves into "a general insurrection in the county."[13]

To the collective relief of Texas Confederates, there were no outright revolts among the enslaved in Texas during the first few years of the war, nor any meaningful increases in the number of slaves who ran from Texas plantations. As a rough gauge, surveying Houston's *Telegraph* reveals that the frequency of advertisements seeking the return of runaway slaves did not vary in almost any way from the late 1850s through the early 1860s. There was nothing in the content of these early wartime advertisements, moreover, suggesting that the war itself had changed either the circumstances or motivations for the enslaved to escape.[14] Indeed, motivations of any kind were rarely cited in ads, although planters—as always—tended to blame outside influences for the escapes. In his offer of $50 for the return of his escaped slave Bill, A. B. McAlpin speculated that the fugitive "has probably been decoyed off by some white person."[15] During the first few years of the war, local plantations and farms largely operated as they always had, and perhaps white Texans interpreted the lack of overt rebelliousness as a sign that their slaves were, indeed, as loyal as they had hoped.

Yet slaves throughout the rest of the Confederacy abandoned plantations and ran to Union lines whenever U.S. forces came near, forcing white Texans to read alarming newspaper accounts of slaves attempting to liberate themselves from the earliest days of the war. As Union troops made their way through Virginia and the Mississippi River Valley during 1861 and 1862, reports streamed into Texas newspapers of enslaved African Americans escaping their masters. During the space of ten days during the summer of 1862, for example, Texans read about 3,000 slaves who had fled to the Union army along the Mississippi River (including reports that tallied losses by individual slaveholders), and another seven hundred who ran to Federal lines in Arkansas.[16] Some of these escaped slaves ran to Union camps and simply refused to leave; others boarded trains they thought bound for Union lines; still others climbed aboard ships, stole horses, or otherwise made their way to wherever U.S. soldiers marched. In July 1862, a San Antonio newspaper reprinted a letter from Natchez, Mississippi, that summed up what quickly became obvious to all Confederates: "The appearance of the Yankees has a bad effect on the negroes. The jail on this side of the river is full of negroes. We have just heard that 300 arose on the other side and killed two overseers, and then took possession of the two plantations."[17]

Stories of African Americans willingly abandoning their masters to join the enemy, of course, directly contradicted what white Texans believed about the natural loyalty of their slaves. Most Texas newspapers responded by reassuring their readers that in nearly all cases the slaves had been "stolen" by the invading Union troops rather than running away of their own volition. Reporting on the movement of the U.S. Army in Arkansas in July 1862, the Clarksville *Standard* printed reports that the hundreds of slaves moving with the Federals had been "kidnapped, the most of whom were tied hands and feet to prevent them from escaping to their masters."[18] Other newspapers reported that Union troops not only stole slaves whenever they could but also abused them by forcing these captives to labor against their will "day and night" in constructing Federal defenses.[19] Some papers even reported that slaves captured by Yankees would escape whenever they could in order to return to their former masters and plantations. In September 1862, for example, Houston's *Telegraph* reported that "some thirty negroes that had been stolen from Louisiana planters near Milliken's Bend, have returned."[20] Although masters were losing slaves across the Confederacy, white Texans refused to believe that their slaves could be either disloyal or sympathetic to the Union. The rise of runaways, they insisted, was instead the fault of U.S. forces, which, in the words of the Houston *Telegraph*, "insulted the women, laid waste the country, and stole hundreds of negroes" everywhere it went.[21]

Although they assured themselves that slaves were not running of their own accord, white Texans nonetheless saw clearly why similar destruction and loss of slaves had not devastated their own farms and plantations: Union forces had not yet invaded Texas. In every part of the Confederacy invaded by Federal troops, enslaved people ran away in droves because they believed that following the Union armies would protect them from pursuit and recapture by their former masters. In sections of the Confederacy that rarely saw Federal troops, however, far fewer enslaved people attempted to escape their masters simply because they lacked the unique opportunities offered by the presence of such troops. White Texans recognized this pattern, even if they concluded— incorrectly—that it proved their slaves rebelled only when anti-slavery Northerners forced them. Texas's position along the extreme western edge of the Confederacy made the state far less appealing for invasion by

Federal forces than the Mississippi River, and so white Texans escaped the disruptions that came to Mississippi, Alabama, and Louisiana during the 1862 Union onslaughts in the west, and thus large-scale rebellions among their slaves.[22]

Because Confederates across the South also recognized the security that Texas offered, the state became a magnet for white Southerners nervous about maintaining control over their slaves. Refugees began making their way into Texas as early as 1861, although displaced Confederates began flooding into the state in earnest after the Union invasion of the Mississippi River Valley in early 1862.[23] Along with the arrival of U.S. forces in Louisiana and Mississippi came mass escapes by local slaves—"generally when told to run away from the soldiers, they go right to them," grumbled Louisianan Kate Stone—and soon the roads to Texas became clogged with slaveholders desperate to hide their slaves from the Federals.[24] Arthur Fremantle, an Englishman traveling through the Confederate states to see the war for himself, marveled at the number of planters he saw in Louisiana "driving their families, their slaves, and furniture towards Texas." "One of them had as many as sixty slaves with him of all ages and sizes."[25] The traffic increased dramatically after the fall of Vicksburg and Port Hudson in July 1863, which gave the U.S. military unchallenged control over the entire Mississippi River, and continued in earnest through 1865. During the course of the war, refugee Confederates transported as many as 50,000 slaves into Texas for safekeeping—swelling the state's overall enslaved population to around 230,000—as farmers across the western Confederacy imagined Texas as a place where their slaves could be kept safe from the pernicious influence of Union troops.[26]

Yet Confederates in Texas remained nervous, and a short-lived U.S. invasion of Galveston during the fall of 1862 revealed the deep-set fears that white Texans harbored about the stability of the local slave populations. Union gunboats sailed into Galveston Bay in October 1862, forcing the island's Confederate defenders to retreat to the mainland. Maj. Gen. John Bankhead Magruder, commander of the Confederate District of Texas, ordered emergency preparations for the defense of the state and issued public warnings of the destruction he predicted would accompany a Union assault on Texas. "Should the enemy make successful raids from the coast into the country," he warned, "nothing can be expected from his forbearance." The general pointed to Louisiana as an example of how the U.S. Army planned to use Texans' slaves against them. "In all cases, the negroes would be taken off, made to work on the fortifications of the enemy, and then armed against us. The people of Texas ought to be fully warned by the fate of planters in other States." It was not losing their investments in slaves that proved most terrifying—it was, instead, the prospect of those slaves being forcibly turned against their former masters. "The slaves are not only armed, drilled, and used as a military police, and as soldiers against us," cautioned Magruder, "but those who are not suited to the service are hired to citizens who profess loyalty to Lincoln, at ten dollars a month, to work on their own plantations, and these negroes maltreat their former masters, and insult, in their presence, their wives and daughters, without punishment or rebuke."[27] Although Confederate troops managed to retake Galveston in January 1863, preventing a Union assault of the state's mainland, white Texans nonetheless found themselves increasingly on edge about the threat of Union soldiers using their slaves against them.

The endless stream of reports filtering into the state, detailing how slaves continued to abandon plantations throughout the Confederacy, left white Texans particularly alarmed about runaway slaves becoming an asset for the Union armies. Men in the state began debating whether it was time to give their slaves formal roles in the Confederate armies as a means of countering the problems caused by slave flight. As early as August 1862, for example, the editor of Houston's *Telegraph* came out publicly in favor of "enrolling 50,000 able bodied negro men" for service in the Confederate armies, arguing that every slave put to work in the army camps would free a white man to concentrate on fighting the Yankees. "These negro conscripts would only be employed to perform the heavy labor and drudgery incident to camp and army life," thereby greatly increasing the fighting strength of the Rebel armies. The editor of the *Telegraph* was clearly disturbed by the never-ending reports of runaway slaves making their way to Union lines, concerned that rebellious slaves could become a source of great strength to marauding enemy. He therefore urged his fellow white Texans to begin formally committing their own slaves toward supporting the Confederate armies as the only reasonable means for countering the advantages runaway slaves could offer the Union's military. Some of these slaves positioned along the Confederate front lines might run away, of course, but the editor insisted that the benefits would surely outweigh the risks. "Whatever objections may be urged against the expediency or policy of the plan, those are silenced by the consideration that if we do not, our enemies will."[28]

Such concerns grew into outright alarm with Abraham Lincoln's announcement of the preliminary Emancipation Proclamation in September 1862. Hoping to convince white Southerners to abandon the fight, and knowing that the measure would greatly weaken the Confederacy, Lincoln promised to declare free all enslaved people living within rebellious territory on January 1, 1863. Yet if Lincoln believed that threats to free their slaves would convince Texans to return to the United States before the deadline, he soon realized his mistake. White men and women throughout Texas, as well as the other seceded states, saw the proclamation as validation of all the fears they had long held about the abolitionist intents of their Republican enemies, and so they denounced Lincoln and his anti-slavery allies for making slave rebellion their explicit war policy. "The programme of the enemy," seethed the Houston *Telegraph*, "is to destroy our labor as the best way of destroying us." In their newspapers, white Texans had already followed in terrifying detail how Union armies had forcibly freed slaves wherever they went in other Confederate states—and now Lincoln's proclamation took away any hope they might have harbored that they could escape the same fate if the U.S. military ever mounted a successful invasion of the state. "The enemy has taught us—not alone by his raids in Louisiana, South Carolina, Florida, Virginia and Arkansas, but by the proclamation of his President," warned the *Telegraph* editor, "that he is determined to steal the slaves and set them free." Fostering slave flight and rebellion was now an explicit war aim of the Union, just as white Texans had always feared.[29]

At that same moment, the simultaneous expansion of the Confederate draft exacerbated concerns among white Texans about their ability to control their slaves. The C.S.A. government first instituted a draft during the spring of 1862, when it declared all able-bodied white men between the ages of eighteen and thirty-five years eligible to be conscripted into military service. By September 1862, concerns about fielding enough soldiers prompted the Confederate Congress to raise the upper age limit to forty-five years. The measures proved immensely unpopular throughout the Confederacy, where so many men and women had championed the creation of their nation as a means of preventing the national government from infringing on the rights of the people and the states. Even more galling to some was a provision that allowed any plantation with twenty or more slaves to exempt one white man from the draft.[30] The intent of the exemption was to keep enough white men on the home front to ensure the obedience of the millions of slaves serving as the foundation of the Confederate economy and, therefore, the continued production of food and clothing necessary for the Confederate war effort. Yet many white Texans who did not qualify for the exemption—which was the overwhelming majority of the population—complained loudly about a measure that seemed crafted primarily to serve the interests of the wealthy. "Again it is asked," observed the *Telegraph*, "why were slave owners exempted? Here you give privileges to a class of rich men, while the poor man is required to risk his life in the army!"[31]

Yet the "Twenty-Negro Law," as it became known, also had many supporters within Texas, precisely because of growing fears within the state about the need to control the slave population. By the end of 1862, Texans had already sent tens of thousands of white men into the Confederate armies, and the rapid expansion of the draft promised to take many more.[32] Fears abounded that the exodus of so many able-bodied Anglo men from Texas farms and plantations would mean there was little to stop local slaves from rebelling or running away. Indeed, by late 1862 many white Texans had largely abandoned their earlier rhetoric about the "natural" loyalty of their slaves, as the course of the war made them feel increasingly vulnerable to internal rebellion. In the town of Marshall, Col. Malcolm Graham made a public speech wherein he defended the "Twenty-Negro" exemption as the first of many measures he believed would be needed to control Texas slaves and "prevent servile insurrections" as U.S. forces bore down on the Confederacy.[33]

The editor of the *Telegraph* felt much the same and urged his readers to support such measures as necessary for ensuring that both Confederate armies and plantations had enough men for "the certain defense of our country, our rights, property and liberty." "Our negro slaves, who constitute a large part of the laborers in the fields in our social system, and when properly controlled, a useful and beneficial class, when left to themselves or insufficiently governed, become drones, non-producers, and dangerous nuisances, imperiling the safety of our homes and people," the editor warned. "The provision is a matter of *police* only," he insisted, "that suitable men may have charge of the slaves—keep them in order and see that they perform their proper work." Proponents of the law, in fact, argued that any attempt to abolish the measure would surely have disastrous consequences for both the state and the Confederacy because it would prevent white Texans from enlisting. "What man rich or poor," the *Telegraph* demanded to know, "would be willing to go into the army without a guarantee that the slaves at home or his neighborhood had some one in charge of them to protect his family?"[34]

Such appeals tapped into deep fears among white Texans, as the increasing number of white men leaving for the armies heightened local paranoia about slave rebellion. In September 1862, nervous authorities in Bastrop County discovered what they described as "a horrible, and deeply plotted scheme of a servile insurrection" among more than sixty slaves in western Texas. "The plan was," according to the *Bellville Countryman*, "that the negroes should secure all the fire-arms, knives, &c., that they could get their hands on" and then "kill their masters, and all others who might be in the way, take their horses and go over to the Yankees, or make for Mexico." The signal for the supposed insurrection would be the departure of a new regiment of local Bastrop men on their way to join Confederate forces, when area slaves apparently hoped to take advantage of the reduced number of white men to watch over them.[35] No such rebellion ever took place, but the episode nonetheless revealed how conscriptions of local white men into Confederate forces, when combined with regular newspaper reports of slaves rebelling in other parts of the Confederacy, heightened fears among white Texans about the problems of slave flight and rebellion.

By 1862–63, citizens in Washington County had become particularly nervous about the expansion of the draft undermining their ability to control their slaves. A letter signed by twenty-four of Washington's leading residents petitioned Governor Lubbock to provide "one of our citizens R F Harris" a special exemption from being "forced into the service." Harris, they explained, "has a pack of negro dogs which is of great service in keeping the negroes in subjection and without which the community would be subject to frequent disturbances and outbreaks among them." Located in the heart of the Brazos River valley,

Washington County boasted the second-largest slave population in the state, and the increasing number of local white men leaving to serve in the Confederate armies had people on edge. Clearly no one in Washington was counting on the supposed natural loyalty of their slaves to keep them safe. Local white Texans instead put their stock into more practical, proven, and violent methods—such as Harris's dogs—for preventing slave flight and rebellion. And so they requested that "Harris be released from military duty and that his name be erased from the muster roll" in order to ensure continued security of the county.[36]

Although Texas slaves never did resort to violent rebellion, white Texans nonetheless became increasingly paranoid about the possibility. Just as their counterparts in Nacogdoches and Bastrop had in 1861 and 1862, authorities in Denton "discovered" in 1863 yet another plot among the slaves to overthrow their white masters. "Originating with disaffected white men and extending to negroes," the plan was reportedly "to murder indiscriminately all the whites, except known Abolitionists, reserving only young women for wives of the blacks." It is not clear how the plot was discovered, but "the citizens of Denton County" acted swiftly, arresting "some 17 or 18 negroes and 5 or 6 white men" whom they placed under armed guard and reporting the situation to Confederate military authorities in Houston. Nothing, again, ever came of the supposed conspiracy, but the frequency with which white Texans uncovered such would-be rebellions offers perhaps the best window into the growing fears that Confederates in the state harbored about the loyalty and dependability of their slaves.[37]

Such paranoia may have been driven, in part, by growing restlessness among enslaved Texans. There is some evidence that Texas slaves ran from plantations with growing frequency during the later years of the war. Because U.S. troops never marched through Texas, the state never witnessed a mass exodus of enslaved people to match what happened in Louisiana or Mississippi. Yet surveying the Houston *Telegraph* reveals a significant increase in the number of advertisements listed for the recapture of runaway slaves during the later years of the war. The frequency of these ads, for example, increased by a remarkable 144 percent between 1862 and 1863.[38] Although we cannot know for certain how closely the increase in runaway slave ads correlated to fluctuations in the number of actual fugitives, it seems reasonable to assume that such a large increase in ads reflected some level of increase in the number of slaves fleeing Texas plantations. The timing of this upward shift in runaways, more-over, correlates to Lincoln's Emancipation Proclamation, although again it is impossible to recover whether that had any influence. What does become clear from the ads, however, is that many of the masters who placed ads believed their slaves ran toward Louisiana, the closest loca-tion of U.S. forces.[39] And at least some of those slaves were running away in groups. In July 1863, John Ewing offered a $50 reward for the capture of "my negro boy Abe," who was "trying to make his escape to Galveston with my other negroes."[40] Two months later, F. G. Banks advertised for the return of Frank, Issac, and Charles, who "are trying to make their way to Louisiana."[41]

Slaves across Texas, indeed, continued to run away throughout the war years. As early as 1861, Texans reported to Confederate authorities about slaves and free blacks fleeing toward Indian country. In November 1861, Col. William Young of the Texas Volunteer Cavalry sent a letter to the Confederate secretary of war warning "that there were at one place in the Cherokee Nation, on the Canadian River, 200 runaway and free negroes in regular drill, whose object is supposed to be hostile to the Confederates."[42] The authorities in Richmond, Virginia, took such mat-ters seriously, and by early 1863 Confederate troops had been dispatched "to scout for runaway negroes and other depredators" lurking just north of the Red River in Indian Territory.[43] One Texan became so incensed by the prospect of runaway slaves aiding the North that he raised his own private cavalry unit specifically dedicated to "guerrilla warfare," re-cruiting men with promises that they would spend their time killing Unionists and "capturing negroes who have deserted to the enemy and sending them further South. We will, also, find good masters for all the free negroes who have given aid and comfort to the enemy."[44] By the time of Lincoln's Emancipation Proclamation, the problem of runaway slaves had become a consuming interest for white Texans.

The war itself provided new opportunities for Texas slaves to escape. The lifeblood of the Texas and Southern economy had long been cot-ton, and with the onset of the Union blockade of the Confederate coast in 1861 there was a great deal of money to be made for any Confeder-ate who could smuggle cotton bales to European buyers. Because their state shared a porous border with Mexico, Texans began as early as 1861

> RANAWAY from my plantation in Wharton coun-
> ty, about the 1st of September, the following de-
> scribed negroes:
>   FRANK, aged 50 years, 5 feet 8 or 9 inches high,
> heavy set, should weigh about 150 lbs., dark copper
> color, grey headed, pleasant countenance, quick spo-
> ken and intelligent.
>   ISAAC, aged 30 years, 5 feet 8 or 9 inches high,
> should weigh 140 lbs., black, bow legged, very promi-
> nent eyes and red, very low forehead.
>   CHARLES, aged 1 years, 5 feet 10 or 11 inches high,
> color brown, would weigh 170 or 180 lbs.
>   Said negroes are trying to make their way to Loui-
> siana. The boy Charles was separated from the other
> two before crossing the Brazos river. Frank and
> Isaac were seen near Montgomery. Any one taking
> up the above negroes will be liberally rewarded.
>   Address   F. G. BANKS,
>   oct 7tw 3t   Chappell Hill, Texas.

An increasing number of enslaved Texans ran from their masters by 1863, such as these three men who attempted to make their way from Wharton County, Texas, to Louisiana. *Houston Tri-Weekly Telegraph*, October 7, 1863.

to smuggle their bales to eager markets in Matamoros and Monterrey. Long wagon trains soon began making their way from East Texas down toward the Rio Grande, and by 1863–64 the commerce had grown to enormous proportions. One man would later recall how, as a fourteen-year-old living along the border, he had marveled at the procession of "ox trains, mule trains, and trains of Mexican carts, all laden with cotton coming from almost every town in Texas" that created "a never ending stream of cotton pouring into Brownsville."[45] By the end of the war Confederates had managed to smuggle 320,000 bales—144 million pounds of cotton—through Mexican ports and past the Union blockade and received all manner of military supplies and goods in return. Transporting that much cotton, however, required manpower, and by the summer of 1863 both planters and the Confederate government were using slaves to drive heavily loaded wagons toward the Mexican border.[46]

Just as slaves in the Mississippi River Valley ran to Union lines whenever the opportunity presented itself, Texas slaves ran to Mexico during the war for the same reasons. In July 1863, several Texas newspapers carried a story about "three darkeys" who reportedly "stole a bale of cotton" near the border in order to "cast it into the river and floated across the Rio Grande on it." The lesson to be learned, noted one newspaper, was that "parties are taking great risks when they bring niggers to this frontier."[47] Other runaways floated bales across the river, and still others apparently commandeered boats along the shores of the Rio Grande and paddled across. Although hard numbers remain elusive, it is clear that the stream of Texas slaves making their way into Mexico was significant. Angry slaveholders often followed these fugitives into Mexico, and raiding parties of Anglo-Texans periodically made their way through Mexican border towns in search of escaped slaves. Hoping to keep the lucrative cotton trade moving, authorities in northern Mexico moved to facilitate the recapture of slaves. In November 1864, a newspaper correspondent stationed in Brownsville reported that "negroes that run off from this side of the river are immediately returned, and we have the privilege of searching for them on the Mexican side."[48] Yet the frequency of runaways had become disturbing enough that the Houston *Telegraph* warned its readers in December 1864 against taking "their trusty negroes" to the border on cotton trade trips, since border towns like Matamoros were now "overrunning with these trusty, now insolent, negroes."[49] In early 1865, just months before the war's end, Confederate officials forged a formal agreement with their Mexican counterparts for the return of any Texas slaves captured south of the border, as well as permission for "armed parties" to "cross the river in pursuit of fugitives" in order to deal with the problem.[50]

Enslaved people did not need to travel to the Mexican border to take advantage of unusual circumstances brought on by the war. From the earliest days of the conflict, the United States maintained a constant blockade of the port of Galveston as part of its effort to isolate the Confederacy and undermine its extensive cotton economy. Union ships docked within sight of the town of Galveston, providing enslaved men and women living along the Texas coast with a tantalizing image of freedom. Bands of slaves near Galveston would, whenever the opportunity presented itself, steal an unguarded boat or skiff and then attempt to navigate their way to the Union fleet. During the brief Federal occupation of Galveston in October 1862, at least three Texas slaves successfully made their way by boat to freedom across Union lines. In reporting the incident, the *Galveston Weekly News* implored its readers to "be careful to have all boats carefully secured, or occurrences of this kind may happen every night."[51] In July 1863 the same newspaper reported that "five

negroes attempted to escape from Galveston to the Federal blockaders" in a stolen boat, but the unlucky slaves were quickly run down and
captured by a Confederate steamship—which pursued and recaptured
the escapees despite being fired on by U.S. ships—before they could
make it.[52] Less than a year later, another group of African Americans
attempted a similar escape, although they were also caught "while in the
act of going over to the blockaders."[53]

Regular threats of invasion by Union forces provided still other opportunities for Texas slaves to escape. Threats of such invasions in 1863
and 1864, for example, prompted Confederate authorities to order the
impressment of enslaved Texans to build defenses both along the state's
coastline and around major towns. In the aftermath of a Union assault
along the Texas border in September 1863, Confederate general John
Magruder dispatched Confederate troops and impressed slaves to the
Texas coast to construct defenses in anticipation of a full-out Federal
invasion. He also dispatched "about 500 negroes to San Antonio and
about 1,000 to Austin for that purpose," as he sought to prepare Texas
towns for the certain assault. Such matters were absolutely necessary,
he explained, because the Federals intended "to liberate the negroes, to
lay waste the country, destroying not only crops, but farming implements, to slay or imprison men, and to subject our women to every spe-
cies of insult and brutality." Yet what became so deeply frustrating to
Magruder, and other Confederate authorities, was the overt resistance
they received from Texas slaveholders unwilling to send their slaves to
work on these frontline defenses. Some of that resistance came from
concerns of Texas masters that their slaves could be abused and mis-
used by Confederate officers, but a significant portion were motivated
by fears that their slaves might have new opportunities for escape. Indeed, the frequency of slaves escaping from Confederate work details
was enough to alarm even General Magruder.[54] "The frequent escapes
of Negroes from the different Departments to which they have been assigned to labor," grumbled the general in December 1863, "renders it
imperatively necessary for some course to be adopted to prevent so serious and growing an evil."[55]

By the last years of the war, the persistent problem of slave flight across
the Confederacy forced many white Texans to consider conscripting

slaves into the C.S.A army as a means of preventing their escape to Union lines. By the fall of 1863, for example, the Houston *Telegraph* had begun calling for "the enrollment of negroes as soldiers in all respects like white men." Such a measure, insisted the editor, was necessary to bolster the fighting capacity of the Confederacy. But it was also just as necessary to ensure that their slaves did not run away to the Federals and thereby bolster the enemy. If Union forces ever managed an invasion of Texas—and by late 1863 most white Texans believed such an assault was all but inevitable—then it seemed certain that mass escapes by Texas slaves would follow. Yet by enrolling those slaves in Confederate fighting units (as cooks, teamsters, camps workers, or even soldiers if necessary), white Texans could effectively preempt any such escapes and thereby prevent the Union armies from arming their slaves against them. If Texas Confederates believed at the start of the war that their slaves were natural allies, the brutal realities of the war convinced them by 1863 to adopt a more practical outlook.

Such appeals resonated widely among Texas Confederates. One white Texan wrote an open letter to the *Telegraph* in support of conscripting African Americans into the C.S.A. army, arguing that the continued flow of runaway slaves in the rest of the Confederacy to Union forces left white Texans little choice in the matter. "It is but necessary to show what the enemy is doing with the negro, and, *unfortunately, our negro*, to demonstrate the importance of adopting a similar course," he insisted. Given a choice between enlisting their own slaves or watching the Federals arm them, "I deem it plain that the policy of not using the negro in our army is suicidal in the extreme." "Leave upon the plantations," he urged his fellow Confederates, "only the class of negroes the Yankees will not have, and the balance put in the army. I will not waste time in trying to show that the negro will be much more secure in camp than on the plantation."[56] The only certain way to prevent mass defections of their slaves, in other words, was to encircle them with the Confederate forces.

Desperate rebels across the Confederacy debated conscripting their slaves throughout the last year of the war, although nothing came of it. Indeed, by early 1865 the last remnants of the Confederate armies had become so battered that little could be done to save either the cause or slavery as an institution. When the war finally ended in April 1865, moreover, there had been no great slave revolt or rebellion within Texas. The lack of any sustained Union invasion of Texas had spared the region's plantations and farms from a mass exodus of enslaved people. What had changed so drastically by the war's end, however, were the expectations of white Texans about the loyalties of black Texans. Despite the absence of any overt rebellion, most white Texans no longer believed—or at least now had grave doubts—that their enslaved servants were natural Confederates and stalwart allies in their fight against the Union. Years of sustained slave flight by black Texans—whether to Indian Territory, across the Rio Grande, or away from Confederate defense projects— had provided their masters ample evidence of the desires for freedom among Texas slaves. The never-ending reports of large-scale slave flight in every other part of the Confederacy convinced every sober-minded white Texan that the same would have been true in the Lone Star State if U.S. forces ever arrived. Indeed, by the end of the war that was precisely what every white Texan had come to expect: a Federal invasion followed by rampant slave flight. Texas Confederates, as a result, had come to embrace a position in 1865 that would have been unthinkable in 1861: bring their slaves into the army, even arm them as soldiers, in order to prevent them from joining the Union side. The very certainty of slave rebellion, they had come to believe, meant that the end of slavery in Texas was likely to be a violent and bloody affair.

Yet no Union invasion ever took place, and change came instead in the form of Union general Gordon Granger, who arrived in Galveston and proclaimed the end of slavery in Texas on June 19, 1865. The 230,000 enslaved men, women, and children toiling in Texas, he announced, were now free, although what that would mean in practice remained anything but certain. One immediate outcome was that all the runway slaves who had been jailed in Texas during the war were now to be freed. In July 1865, the sheriff in San Antonio released "eight runaway negroes confined in the jail" who had been captured on their way toward Mexico. After news of Granger's announcement, the sheriff had unshackled the prisoners "with the statement that they were free" and sent them "'home' again, with proper passes, to Eastern Texas, Louisiana and Arkansas."[57] They were no longer fugitives but free men and women returning to their homes and families.

NOTES

1. The standard work on runaway slaves in the U.S. South remains John Hope Franklin and Loren Schweniger, *Runaway Slaves: Rebels on the Plantation* (Oxford: Oxford University Press, 1999), although the work does not address Texas directly. I would like to thank Katherine Bynum for her terrific research assistance on this essay, as well as Vicki Betts, Mike Campbell, Rick McCaslin, and Richard Lowe for their sage advice and recommendations.

2. Among the works on slave flight in pre-1860 Texas, the most comprehensive remains Rosalie Schwartz, *Across the Rio to Freedom: U.S. Negroes in Mexico* (El Paso: University of Texas at El Paso Press, 1974). See also Ron Tyler, "Fugitive Slaves in Mexico," *Journal of Negro History* 57 (January 1972): 1–12; William Carrigan, "Slavery on the Frontier: The Peculiar Institution in Central Texas," *Slavery and Abolition* 20 (August 1999): 63–86; Sean Kelley, "'Mexico in His Head': Slavery and the Texas-Mexico Border, 1810–1860," *Journal of Social History* 37 (Spring 2004): 709–23; and James David Nichols, "The Line of Liberty: Runaway Slaves and Fugitive Peons in the Texas-Mexico Borderlands," *Western Historical Quarterly* 44 (Winter 2013): 413–33.

3. Gideon Lincecum to R. M. Hannay, July 7, 1864, in *Gideon Luncecum's Sword: Civil War Letters from the Texas Home Front*, ed. Jerry Lincecum, Edward Phillips, and Peggy Redshaw (Denton: University of North Texas Press, 2001), 280.

4. Austin *State Gazette*, January 5, 1861.

5. J.L.F. to the Editor of the Telegraph, May 8, 1861, printed in *Houston Weekly Telegraph*, May 22, 1861.

6. Whartonian to "The Editor of the Democrat," printed in *Houston Weekly Telegraph*, January 29, 1861.

7. Ibid.

8. For the 1860 fires in North Texas and the panic that followed, see Donald Reynolds, *Texas Terror: The Slave Insurrection Panic of 1860 and the Secession of the Lower South* (Baton Rouge: Louisiana State University Press, 2007).

9. Corsicana *Navarro Express*, November 7, 1861. For similar screeds against abolitionists within Texas, see *Dallas Herald*, January 9, 1861, and *Colorado Citizen*, May 18, 1861.

10. "An Act providing for the disposition of runaway slaves," April 8, 1861, reprinted in Clarksville *Standard*, June 1, 1861.

11. "An Act . . . to Provide for the Appointment of Patrols," January 13, 1862, reprinted in H. P. H. Gammel, *The Laws of Texas, 1822–1897* (Austin: Gammel Book, 1898), 5:498.

12. Corsicana *Navarro Express*, May 22, 1861.

13. *Dallas Herald*, August 7, 1861; *Houston Weekly Telegraph*, August 7, 1861.

14. Using runaway slave advertisements as a gauge of the frequency of runaway slaves is an imperfect measure at best. Most runaways, for example, were never advertised in the newspapers, and masters often advertised for their runaways in newspapers printed in areas they expected their fugitive slaves to be found. Yet these ads represent one of our only sources available for attempting to quantify

the frequencies of escape and can therefore offer a window onto this phenomenon not available anywhere else. Surveying the *Telegraph* (counting only original ads, not including reprints) reveals nine runaway slave ads placed in 1857, eight in 1858, seven in 1859, and twelve in 1860. By comparison, there were nine original ads placed in the *Telegraph* during 1862, the first full year of the war.

15. *Houston Tri-Weekly Telegraph*, August 1, 1862.

16. *Houston Tri-Weekly Telegraph*, August 4, 1862; Clarksville *Standard*, July 26, 1862. For other examples, see Clarksville *Standard*, June 22, 1861, April 3, 1862; San Antonio *Semi-Weekly News*, July 14, 1862; *Houston Tri-Weekly Telegraph*, April 6, May 21, June 6, 1862, June 27, July 25, August 15, September 8, 1862.

17. San Antonio *Semi-Weekly News*, July 14, 1862.

18. Clarksville *Standard*, July 26, 1862.

19. *Houston Tri-Weekly Telegraph*, July 25, 1862.

20. *Houston Tri-Weekly Telegraph*, September 8, 1862.

21. *Houston Tri-Weekly Telegraph*, June 27, 1862.

22. Randolph B. Campbell, *An Empire for Slavery: The Peculiar Institution in Texas, 1821–1865* (Baton Rouge: Louisiana State University Press, 1989), 231.

23. Austin *State Gazette*, July 6, 1861; *Houston Weekly Telegraph*, July 17, 1861.

24. Entry for July 5, 1862, in John Anderson, ed., *Brokenburn: The Journal of Kate Stone, 1861–1868* (Baton Rouge: Louisiana State University Press, 1956), 128.

25. Arthur Fremantle, *Three Months in the Southern States: April–June 1863* (New York, 1864), 81, 86.

26. On slaves "refugeed" to Texas, see Campbell, *Empire for Slavery*, 243–46, and Dale Baum, "Slaves Taken to Texas for Safekeeping during the Civil War," in *The Fate of Texas: The Civil War and the Lone Star State*, ed. Charles Grear (Fayetteville: University of Arkansas Press, 2008), 83–103.

27. John Bankhead Magruder to "The Citizens of Texas," printed in *Houston Tri-Weekly Telegraph*, December 24, 1862.

28. *Houston Weekly Telegraph*, August 27, 1862.

29. *Houston Weekly Telegraph*, November 12, 1862; see also November 19, 1862.

30. James, McPherson, *Battle Cry of Freedom: The Civil War Era* (Oxford: Oxford University Press, 1988), 427–31, 611–12.

31. *Houston Tri-Weekly Telegraph*, December 8, 1862.

32. The records make it difficult to estimate exactly how many white Texans served in the Confederate armies at any given point. Most estimate that 25,000 Texans signed up within the first year of the war, and Stephen Oates, "Texas under the Secessionists," *Southwestern Historical Quarterly* 67 (October 1963), 187, estimated that 88,000 Texans served during the course of the war.

33. *Houston Tri-Weekly Telegraph*, December 19, 1862.

34. *Houston Tri-Weekly Telegraph*, December 8, 1862.

35. *Bellville Countryman*, September 13, 1862.

36. Petition from Washington County to F. R. Lubbock [1862 or 1863], in *The Indian Papers of Texas and the Southwest, 1825–1916*, ed. Dorman Winfrey and James Day, 4:71–72 (reprint; Texas State Historical Association, 1995).

37. Samuel Roberts to Edmund Turner, August 29, 1863, in *The War of the Rebellion: A Compilation of the Official Records of the Union and Confederate Armies* [hereafter *OR*], Series 1, Vol. 26 (pt. 2), 187–88.

38. Surveying the *Houston Tri-Weekly Telegraph* (counting only original ads, not including reprints) reveals twenty-two runaway slave ads placed in 1863, compared to nine in 1862.

39. See, for example, *Houston Tri-Weekly Telegraph,* February 16, May 13, July 13, July 15, October 30, 1863.

40. *Houston Tri-Weekly Telegraph,* July 15, 1863.

41. *Houston Tri-Weekly Telegraph,* October 7, 1863.

42. W. M. C. Young to J. P. Benjamin, November 3, 1861, *OR,* Series 1, Vol. 4 (pt. 1), 144–45.

43. "A Soldier of the 29th" to the Clarksville *Standard,* March 30, 1863, and reprinted April 25, 1863.

44. *Houston Weekly Telegraph,* March 12, 1862.

45. John Warren Hunter, "The Fall of Brownsville on the Rio Grande, November, 1863," quoted in Ron Tyler, "Cotton on the Border, 1861–1865," in *Lone Star Blue and Gray: Essays on Texas in the Civil War,* ed. Ralph Wooster (Austin: Texas State Historical Association, 1995), 212.

46. J. B. Magruder to Kirby Smith, July 3, 1863, *OR,* Series 1, Vol. 26 (pt. 2), 102; F. W. Rhine to Simeon Hart, July 20, 1863, *OR,* Series 1, Vol. 26 (pt. 2), 154; H. P. Bee to Edmund Turner, November 15, 1863, *OR,* Series 1, Vol. 26 (pt. 2), 414–15.

47. *Flag,* July 17, 1863, reprinted in *Houston Tri-Weekly Telegraph,* July 31, 1863.

48. Austin *Weekly State Gazette,* November 16, 1864.

49. *Houston Tri-Weekly Telegraph,* December 29, 1864, quoted in James Marten, "Slaves and Rebels: The Peculiar Institution in Texas, 1861–1865," in Wooster, *Lone Star Blue and Gray,* 252.

50. James Slaughter to S. D. Yancey, January 2, 1865, *OR,* Series 1, Vol. 48 (pt. 2), 1311–12.

51. *Galveston Weekly News,* October 22, 1862.

52. *Galveston Weekly News,* July 29, 1863.

53. *Galveston Weekly News,* April 20, 1864.

54. For discussions of such impressments, see V. Sulakowski to Edmund Turner, April 30, 1863, *OR,* Series 1, Vol. 15 (pt. 1), 1063–64; J. B. Magruder to Francis Lubbock, June 4, 1863, *OR,* Series 1, Vol. 26 (pt. 2), 33–36 (second quote); P. N. Luckett to Edmund Turner, September 27, 1863, *OR,* Series 1, Vol. 26 (pt. 2), 263–64; Edmund Turner to A. G. Dickinson, November 23, 1863, *OR,* Series 1, Vol. 26 (pt. 2), 440–41; J. B. Magruder to Pendleton Murrah, November 23, 1863, *OR,* Series 1, Vol. 26 (pt. 2), 441 (first quote); J. B. Magruder to Major-General Price, December 3, 1864, *OR,* Series 1, Vol. 41 (pt. 4), 1096–97.

55. J. B. Magruder to T. C. Armstrong, December 7, 1863, printed in *Houston Tri-Weekly Telegraph,* December 11, 1863.

56. *Houston Tri-Weekly Telegraph,* October 28, 1863.

57. *Houston Tri-Weekly Telegraph,* July 14, 1865.

3

Involuntary Removals

"REFUGEED SLAVES" IN CONFEDERATE TEXAS

W. Caleb McDaniel

In 1910, historian Charles Ramsdell claimed that "slaves were in fact more plentiful than ever before" in Confederate Texas, "for great numbers of them had been run in . . . for safe-keeping" by white refugees fleeing from Union armies. Ramsdell exaggerated, but not by much. According to various estimates, Confederate refugees in Texas brought with them between 50,000 and 150,000 enslaved people during the war, swelling a population of slaves that numbered around 200,000 in 1861.[1]

Historians have typically examined these so-called refugeed slaves in the aggregate, however, rather than as individual actors in their own right. Since Ramsdell, various attempts have been made to estimate their numbers and understand the experiences of the white refugees who brought enslaved people into the state. Yet recent scholarship on the politics of the enslaved and the "war within" Southern households now makes it possible—and necessary—to consider what Ramsdell did not: the experiences of refugeed slaves themselves.[2]

Scholars now know that no group of Southerners prayed for Union victory, or helped it along, more fervently than the enslaved; no consideration of Southern "Unionists" can be complete without them. Indeed, the determined resistance of enslaved people, whether overt or covert, required the constant threat or use of white violence to suppress. By refusing to work, running to Union lines, and sometimes laboring or fighting for the Union army and navy, enslaved people helped to undermine the Confederacy from within.[3]

Enslaved people in Texas at first appear to be only exceptions to this rule. Distant from the war's main battlefields, and supposedly ignorant of emancipation until after the war ended, enslaved Texans had fewer opportunities to escape slavery's clutches. According to most studies of the subject, slaves in Texas continued to labor in the fields and helped to enrich the state even during war. In fact, more attention has been paid to questions about the political loyalty of white refugees than to the politics of the enslaved people they brought with them. Ramsdell's view, that refugeed slaves only boosted the state's prosperity by increasing its labor force, remains prevalent today.[4]

Yet the lack of serious disruptions to slavery in Confederate Texas does not prove an absence of dissent among enslaved people who were brought there. True, slavery as a system remained mostly impervious to challenges from enslaved people in Texas, just as white Unionists in Texas proved unable to challenge the Confederate government seriously. Nonetheless, in this chapter I argue that enslaved people need to be considered together with white Unionists as potential and actual dissenters. And this is particularly true of slaves who hailed from regions of the Confederacy that were much closer to the front lines of the fight for emancipation. The white Confederate exodus to Texas should be understood not just as a movement of bedraggled white refugees or as a boon to the wartime economy but as a massive, forced relocation of black Southerners that likely swelled the state's population of Unionists and dissenters.

Seeing refugeed slaves as Unionists and dissenters requires first seeing past stereotypical images of white refugees as helpless sojourners and exiles—images that Lost Cause apologists for the Confederacy helped to propagate after the war. A state historical marker erected as late as 1965 in Hopkins County emphasized the "poverty, loneliness, and sorrow" of Confederate refugees, highlighting the story of Louisiana planter Amanda Stone and her "heartbroken" family after they fled from their Mississippi River plantation to Texas. Refugees at the time emphasized the same themes, complaining in their letters home of what one called the "miserable life of a refugee."[5]

The idea of white refugees as impoverished and miserable went hand in hand with a distorted image of refugeed slaves, whom white

Southerners usually depicted, paradoxically, as both faithful servants and helpless dependents. For example, in its sole mention of the enslaved people brought to Texas by the Stones, the Hopkins County marker claimed the Stones "had to lease farm land, to support the family and 90 slaves dependent upon them," implying that slaves placed additional burdens on their white providers. In reality, the Stones and other white refugees were often dependent for *their* survival on the continued labor and commercial value of the people they enslaved. Amanda Stone's daughter Kate admitted as much to her diary in early 1865: "If the Negroes are freed, we will have no income whatever, and what will we do?"[6]

Stone knew that, by removing to Texas, refugee slaveholders secured significant, if small, streams of income and seized new, if tenuous, economic and social opportunities. These advantages explain why slaveholders exerted considerable effort—and frequently, violent force—to relocate so many people beyond the reach of Union armies. Lost in the marker's lament for the Stones' plight are the means that they and other refugees used to keep "the Negroes" enslaved, as well as their motivations for doing so.

The arrival of refugeed slaves in Texas began almost as soon as the first shots of the Civil War had been fired. Slaveholders from Missouri began arriving in Texas even before the First Battle of Bull Run. The fall of New Orleans to Union forces in 1862 generated another stream of refugees from the sugar-rich districts of lower Louisiana in the Lafourche district. But the exodus of slaveholders from Louisiana and Arkansas peaked in 1863, when Union forces under the command of Gen. Nathaniel P. Banks moved up Louisiana's major bayous as far as Alexandria. Writing near Monroe, Louisiana, on May 10, 1863, British traveler Arthur J. Fremantle noted that "the road to-day was alive with negroes, who are being 'run' into Texas out of Banks's way."[7]

Fremantle was not the only observer to note the throngs on Texas roads; the Marshall *Texas Republican* reported in 1864 that "there are more Negroes in the State now than were ever here before" and proposed that the state take advantage of that fact by employing newly arrived slaves to improve public roads. Two years later, the same paper speculated that "there are, perhaps, to-day, double the number of negroes that

View of Brownsville during the Civil War. From *Frank Leslie's Illustrated Newspaper.*
Texas State Library and Archives Commission, Prints and Photographs Collection,
1980/10-4.

were in the State in 1861" because of those who "came with the refugees
that flocked into Texas from Missouri, Arkansas, and Louisiana."[8]

Using county tax records, historian Dale Baum has estimated that
many of these slaveholding refugees settled with their slaves in the
cotton-growing counties that lined the Sabine, Trinity, and Brazos Rivers. But refugees also gravitated toward two urban centers. First, many
entered Texas by traveling through Shreveport to Marshall, which by
1864 was the headquarters of numerous military bureaus and a magnet for Confederate refugees. By January 1864, one local reported to the
governor that Marshall was "filled with Govt. functionaries, Govt. details, and men, and families, whose misfortunes, have driven them temporarily among us, for safety, and protection." A second refugee center
was in Houston, whose proximity to Galveston and the Mexican border
made it a crossroads of the cotton trade.[9]

Wherever they went, refugee slaveholders looked quickly for opportunities to make money, just as they always had. Avid in their pursuit of
profits before the war, refugees now had to secure sources of income just
to make ends meet. Their primary methods were to "hire out" enslaved
people to contractors who paid the slave owner for a slave's labor while
meeting some of the owner's expenses, or to rent land on which refugeed
slaves could be put to work. Near Houston and in the fertile counties
along the Brazos, cotton beckoned to those who could rent plantations,
hire out field laborers, or use their wagons to transport bales to market
along the Mexico border. Railroad companies also hired slaves to lay

track or chop lumber. But counties in northeastern and northern Texas also appealed to refugees. There, they could rent farms to produce grain or hire out enslaved laborers to work in nascent iron, manufacturing, and salt industries.[10]

Around Marshall, Tyler, and Shreveport, for example, companies that had contracted to manufacture supplies for the military frequently sought to hire slave laborers. The Sulphur Forks Iron Works near Texarkana hired at least sixty slaves to chop wood for its furnace, and one man who was refugeed from Louisiana recalled in a twentieth-century interview that his master had put fifty young slaves to work making bullets in Tyler. Meanwhile, near urban areas refugees could often find locals willing to pay for slaves trained in particular skilled trades or in domestic work. As Kate Stone reported to her diary not long after arriving in Texas, her new neighbors were "all eager to hire Negroes. There is a furor for them."[11]

Refugees who made it to Texas with significant numbers of slaves usually pursued several such opportunities at once, even if it meant dispersing families and slaves. One former slave who was taken from Tennessee to Webberville, Texas, during the war recalled that the men would "plow, plant, gather crops, split rails, cut wood, and do a little of everything; de wimmen was hired out fo' cooks, nusses, and sich." The adult children of David and Mary Weeks, whose family presided over an extensive network of sugar plantations in southern Louisiana, followed a similarly eclectic pattern with the slaves they brought to Texas.[12]

The Weeks children—led by the eldest sons Alfred C. Weeks and William F. Weeks—were among those who fled to Texas in the summer of 1863 as Banks's forces moved up the bayou. After investigating the "hiring" rates for slaves in Texas, William and Alfred took several dozen enslaved men from their New Iberia plantations to the Houston area, where they hired out some slaves to a local railroad company at favorable rates of $40 a month. William Weeks hired out another enslaved man to make barrels and several other slaves as domestic servants in Houston. And he placed others on area farms to cultivate cotton with the help of letters of introduction from Houston merchant Robert Mills.[13]

Members of Weeks's extended family settled in Freestone County (where his sister Harriet and a family friend took more than one hundred enslaved people to grow wheat), in Wharton County (where his step-sister and her husband hired out 114 slaves), in Mansfield, Louisiana (where the Weeks's stepfather John C. Moore hired out another hundred), and near Natchitoches (where Moore's grandson had found "profitable business" by putting refugeed slaves to work on an abandoned plantation). A younger Weeks brother, Charlie, traveled back and forth between Texas and Louisiana, hiring out slaves to a fellow refugee named Skaggs, hauling supplies for the military in Texas, and working as an overseer in the railroad camp where William Weeks hired out some of his slaves. By the end of the war, William had managed to help several Weeks families, including those of his siblings Harriet and Charlie, to resettle on rented cotton farms in Walker County.[14]

As the movements of the Weeks family show, refugeed slaves who came to Texas often endured multiple relocations as slaveholders reacted to local conditions. In August 1863, Robert Campbell Martin, Sr., another refugee Louisiana sugar planter, settled first in Cherokee County, Texas, having brought at least twenty-seven people on a five-week journey from his Albermarle plantation. Several other refugees from Louisiana had already settled in the area, too, but all were "dissatisfied" with the low demand for slave labor and looked to "invest elsewhere" if they could. Martin spent the rest of his Texas exile growing provision crops, making short trips to the Houston area, and looking for information about where to "hire out" slaves. Toward the end of 1864, for instance, Martin learned from his son Robert C. Martin, Jr., of a distillery in Jefferson willing to hire almost all of his "Negroes" at $50 per month per hire (with food provided by the employer). Another son had located a Louisiana refugee willing to hire four of his father's men at $350 per year to chop wood, and Martin's later relocation to Nacogdoches appears to have been guided partly by such information.[15]

Before that final relocation, Martin also put at least some of his "Negroes" to work producing salt, which proved to be a common job for refugeed slaves in the region. Before the war, manufacturing salt had been a seasonal task in Louisiana, where planters periodically took small groups of slaves to the state's known salt domes to dig wells, chop lumber, and boil salt water in large cauldrons. Typically, a few trips a year extracted enough salt for the plantation's immediate needs. But the war intensified demand for salt throughout the Trans-Mississippi

Department, especially once the Union blockade of the Gulf Coast cut off imports of this essential preservative.[16]

Numerous entrepreneurs in both Louisiana and Texas raced to capitalize on the salt shortages, creating a ready market for slave-hiring contracts at the very moment when many planters were trying to move enslaved people away from Federal lines. The Stones, for example, sent "the best and strongest of the Negroes" with an overseer to work at a salt works in Winnfield, Louisiana, several months before they fled for Texas themselves. Other slaveholders took laborers to Rayburn's Saline near Lake Bistineau, where more than one hundred furnaces were in operation during the war, or to the rock salt deposit discovered in 1862 at Avery Island. There, more than five hundred slaves helped excavate millions of pounds of rock salt before the mine fell to Union forces in 1863, forcing the Avery family to flee to Houston with many of their slaves.[17]

Texas salines, most of which boiled salinated water pumped from underground, also expanded their operations during the war. J. S. O. Brooks, a salt maker in Smith County, sold salt for as much as $40 or $50 per 200-pound sack in "new issue" Confederate currency, and more than $100 in "old issue." Using similar methods, salt makers at Steen Saline in northern Smith County and Jordan's Saline (or Grand Saline) in Van Zandt County produced hundreds of sacks of salt a day at the height of wartime production. The state government, too, sought to exploit the opportunity for profits in salt. The legislature appropriated to the Texas Military Board up to $50,000—almost the same amount spent by the board on the manufacture of rifles—to fund salt production at Jordan's Saline, where the Board hoped to turn salt into a "source of revenue to the state."[18]

All this new production required labor—to chop lumber for fuel, transport the lumber to furnaces, pump and boil water, and haul the finished product. The agent for the state salt works told the Military Board that approximately ten to fifteen slave "hands" were needed per furnace, along with white overseers to supervise each group. As late as December 1864, Brooks was advertising in the Marshall *Texas Republican* about his willingness to hire up to "100 Negroes" for the next year "or during the war" to produce salt at his saline; later reports suggest that as many as two hundred to three hundred slaves may have worked there. Another saline operator confirmed that by 1863 slaves were already being hired "at enormous prices."[19]

These Texas salt makers benefited from the presence of so many refugee slaveholders looking for employment for their slaves and for themselves—especially since by making salt white men could sometimes secure exemptions from the draft. Upon his arrival in Cherokee County, for instance, Martin Sr. discovered that his neighbor John Williams and his son-in-law Richard Pugh (also a relative of Martin's) had between them brought more than one hundred enslaved people to Texas and had already hired many of them to Brooks. Another Louisianan was working a salt spring himself about 75 miles away near Tyler. And still another Martin relative, William Littlejohn, obtained a contract to haul salt to Shreveport using his teams and enslaved drivers. Martin later learned from Williams that "a *high price* could be obtained" in Confederate notes or in salt for hired out "Negroes" near Larissa, where Williams and Pugh later found work for themselves as employees at a local saline.[20]

Other refugee slaveholders attempted to cut out the hiring middle man and pursue commercial salt production for themselves. One such group found an unexpected windfall in Van Zandt County, where one of Texas's largest salt domes happened to rest beneath the land of a Confederate deserter and eventual Unionist named Samuel Q. Richardson. Richardson had purchased a Grand Saline salt works valued at $50,000 in 1859, but after the war began his property was soon overrun by squatters who dug their own wells, set up their own furnaces, cut down Richardson's trees, and began producing salt, often boasting they had the right to do so for the public good.[21]

Richardson later claimed that the squatters' threats to his personal safety had forced him to enter the Confederate army, but he quickly deserted in October 1863 and sought "protection under the Federal authorities" in Missouri, where he remained with a relative until June 20, 1865. Upon returning home, Richardson found thirty-five people still working thirty-seven furnaces and claiming his land as their own. "Most of them," Richardson complained in a letter to the governor about his plight, "are refugees from Arkansas, Louisiana, Mississippi and Missouri," who, by bringing their own slaves to the salt works, helped to quadruple Van Zandt County's once minuscule slave population during the war.[22]

Whether they were squatters, renters, hirers, or employees, few refugee planters looked on their new situations as ideal. Many arrived in
Texas having lost all or most of their once considerable property to confiscation and the abrasions of war. Martin Sr., for example, made it to
Cherokee County with only about thirty people—about a quarter of the
number he once enslaved. The other three-quarters escaped from Martin's plantation before he left for Texas, and on a brief attempt to return
home in 1864 to recapture his slaves Martin failed to get farther than
Alexandria before learning that the Union military had occupied his
plantation and placed hundreds of newly freed people to work there. By
the fall of 1864, Martin, now back in Texas, lamented that he had been
"permanently ruined by the war—the small number of Negroes which I
have in this state not even supporting themselves." Most refugee planters voiced similar complaints. In response to a question about his Texas
luck, William F. Weeks replied to his wife, "I have had none, have made
nothing here but a little Confederate money, and not enough of that to
buy me a suit of clothes."[23]

Yet such pessimism belied the advantages won by refugee planters,
like Weeks and Martin, who were able to reach Texas with at least some
of their slaves. By "hiring out," refugees secured needed income while
shifting the cost of provisions for enslaved people to third parties. Moreover, since slaves could still be sold in Texas until the last days of the
war at reasonably high prices, refugeed slaves offered planters valuable
access to financial and commercial opportunities and could be sold as a
last resort. Indeed, in the same letter of complaint he wrote to his wife,
Weeks reported that he had managed, even in his dire straits, to purchase
forty bales of cotton that he intended to transport to Matamoros to sell.
Writing to his stepfather at around the same time, Weeks took a more
sanguine view of his prospects, declaring, "I am doing very well so far."
Weeks noted that the railroad supplied him with beef and owed him between $15,000 and $20,000 for services rendered and laborers hired, and
his brother likewise believed he had "done well . . . in coming to Texas."[24]

Indeed, complaints aside, refugees "ran off" slaves precisely because
they could do well—or at least do better—in Texas than they could do
by staying at home. Dependent on their human property for everything
they had, but reluctant to admit it was so, refugees like Martin and Weeks
went to great lengths to salvage even a small portion of their holdings.

As historian Willie Lee Rose once wrote, in their determination "to retrieve the most portable part of [their] evaporating fortunes," planters on the run had "borne witness by action to [their] private conception of chattel slavery." In that conception, enslaved people represented *wealth* above all. They entered into the calculations of slaveholders primarily insofar as they helped white families to do "well" or not. Martin Sr. testified to the same conception when he explained why, on his five-week journey to Texas, he decided to stop in Mansfield to acquire carts "to haul" some of the enslaved youths he brought to Texas: "Expenses of marching are excessively high," he told his son, "and the value of negroes may be consumed in this way."[25]

Both at the time and later, some white Southerners attempted to swaddle these naked calculations of value and expense, opportunity and cost, with a more paternalistic conception of slavery as an organic bond between loving master and faithful servant. After the war, Lost Cause apologists depicted enslaved people as simultaneously helpful and helpless dependents who would have remained loyal to their white providers had Northern meddlers not intervened. In late nineteenth- and early twentieth-century memoirs, refugeed slaves in particular often appeared in family and regional lore as exemplary servants who, as one twentieth-century romanticization of a refugee diary put it, "faithfully followed" their masters and "never failed" to meet the smallest need of their careworn caretakers. In the mid-1880s, Sarah Avery Leed, a descendant of the refugee Avery family, recorded and praised the names of "family servants" like Sabra, who served as a valet for his young master in the Confederate army, or Jane, a "faithful & devoted nurse" who attended her mistress as she fled first to Texas and then to Cuba.[26]

Even such nostalgic accounts failed to blot out all evidence to the contrary, however. Leed's account noted, for example, that Sabra's brother Joe "went with [the Avery] family to Texas [in] 1863 & remained there" instead of returning to serve the family. And interviews with former slaves by the Federal Writers Project in the 1930s confirmed that seeming devotion to Confederate masters often masked far different feelings. One interviewee named William M. Adams recalled a white minister asking a group of slaves for a show of hands from those who hoped for Confederate victory. "We all raised our hands because we was scared not to," he admitted, "but we sure didn't want the South to win."[27]

Even when enslaved people seemed, at first glance, to go willingly to Texas, closer inspection of sources makes it possible to discern their true and complex loyalties. As historian Thavolia Glymph notes, "The decision of a slave to stand side by side with an owner during the war," or to move with an owner to Texas, "had little to do with the concept of loyalty as it is typically understood in our everyday usage. Its complexities and ambiguities of meaning to those who fought or lived through the Civil War must be teased out" of archives kept by their enslavers, who usually imagined slaves either as faithful servants or ungrateful dependents. In reality, Confederate refugees never could take for granted that "run off" slaves would cooperate in their relocation, and even apparent cooperation often masked sharply divergent aims.[28]

Slaveholders at the time were far more acutely aware of those divergent aims than their later apologists allowed. Indeed, that is why so many decided to remove enslaved people to Texas in the first place. By 1863, as James Oakes writes, "everyone knew that runaway slaves and Union armies formed a nearly irresistible magnetic attraction," and white refugees to Texas often came from combat zones where hundreds of enslaved people had already fled to Union lines. After the fall of New Orleans in 1862, Kate Stone—who still resided at her Brokenburn plantation in northeastern Louisiana—noted in her diary that "the Yankees have taken the Negroes off all the places below Omega, the Negroes generally going most willingly."[29]

For the rest of the year, Stone's mother resolved to "have the Negro men taken to the back country" whenever Union gunboats seemed to be approaching on the river, "if she can get them to go. Generally when told to run away from the soldiers, they go right to them," wrote Kate, "and I cannot say I blame them." By early 1863, Stone reported that "a great number of Negroes have gone to the Yankees from this section," and she began to carry a pistol as protection against enslaved people who were beginning to show "a very surly, aggressive temper." In March, just before her family fled to Texas, a fatalistic Stone recorded that "all the Negroes are running away now."[30]

By that time, overseers hired by the Stones had already managed to take most of their "Negro men" to a distant salt works. But given the widespread dissent that Stone observed at Brokenburn, it is telling that she referred to these enslaved men being "carried" off, "brought," or "taken to" places "of greater safety." Few went willingly, and when the Stones did finally flee, they were forced to leave "the most valuable [house servants] we own" behind.[31]

Problems with runaway slaves did not stop once refugees got on the road. As other historians have noted, refugeeing often created new opportunities for enslaved people to run away. Richard L. Pugh's wife reported that many enslaved men ran away from her father, John Williams, while he was en route to Texas, even though, as already noted, Williams and Pugh finally arrived at a Texas salt works with nearly one hundred people still under their control. Yet refugeed slaves continued to run away in Texas. Martin Sr. had barely arrived in Cherokee County before one enslaved man, James, "ran off"—"causelessly," in Martin's view.[32]

Other enslaved people found opportunities to escape after being hired out in Texas. An advertisement in the July 4, 1863, issue of the Clarksville *Standard* reported that five enslaved men had run away from Jordan's Saline, most likely a reference to the salt works there. One runaway "was brought from Missouri to Texas," with the other four "belonging to John Anderson late from Mississippi." On the same day, a Marshall ad reported on another runaway who "was brought two weeks since from Carroll Parish, La., by way of Shreveport and Marshall." In February 1864, William F. Weeks likewise learned from his agent Robert Mills that two slaves hired out "in the service of the government have escaped," only to be recaptured on a local plantation. Later that year, William's brother Charles C. Weeks groused to his wife about the enslaved people he had brought to Texas, noting the regularity with which "the vile animals runaway."[33]

Such comments again betrayed refugees' private conceptions of enslavement and belied nostalgic myths about faithful slaves who followed their masters to Texas. In reality, the process of refugeeing people depended at every turn on violence and the vulnerability of human bodies. For example, many refugees took advantage of poor health among the enslaved people they sought to remove. One of the few enslaved people whom the Stones managed to remove from Brokenburn on their initial flight "was sick, groaning most of the way." The men whom they earlier removed to a salt works were also "very sick," including three who died after their arrival there, and Stone's brother reported from Titus County, Texas, that another man taken there was "almost dead."[34]

Martin Sr. likewise reported, "Many of my Negroes were sick on the way up" to Texas, and once he arrived among other Louisiana refugees in Cherokee County he found that "all have much sickness among Negroes." One enslaved woman in Cherokee County who was later interviewed by the WPA remembered burying a child on the road from Mississippi. And John Leigh, a refugee relative of the Weeks family, reported that so many of the slaves he brought to Texas were sick that his three-week caravan from Louisiana was "nothing more nor less than a travelling infirmary."[35]

Refugee planters sometimes suspected their relocated laborers of feigning sickness; in one letter, after noting that "our blacks continue very sick," Robert Campbell Martin, Jr., reported that his father-in-law, William Littlejohn, had threatened to whip one enslaved woman "if she did not get better." But though some sickness may well have been a cloak for dissent, more likely is that refugee planters were reaping the results of an antebellum regime that worked to keep enslaved people only as well fed and healthy as required to keep their value from being "consumed," as Martin Sr. had put it. With food scarce and normal patterns of healing disrupted, enslaved people in poor health had fewer opportunities to resist their removal to Texas.[36]

On the other hand, planters understood that removing healthy people to Texas and holding them there against their will required coercion, especially since so many had seen firsthand the opportunities for freedom created by the war. White refugees resorted to familiar means of terror and abuse to combat resistance from those well enough to offer it. After Aleck, a man owned by the Martin family, began to "put on some *airs*" before he got to Texas, his overseer "took a bridle rein to his *bottom*." And after recapturing two enslaved men who ran away from him in Texas, Charles C. Weeks "had them pickled"—a brutal process that involved whipping slaves and rubbing salt or lime into the open wounds.[37]

Other planters used violence before departing for Texas to impress on enslaved people the risks of resisting; one man interviewed by the WPA recalled sitting with other enslaved people in a wagon, about to depart for Texas, and watching as his owner turned a pack of dogs on a man who had resisted orders. He then whipped the man with a "cat-o-nine-tails" before driving off, leaving his victim lying "bloody" and "fainted" on the ground as a warning to those who might think of leaving the wagons.[38]

Lost Cause mythology concealed the violence inherent in refugeeing as much by popularizing images of gentle plantation mistresses as by perpetuating the image of faithful slaves. For many postwar writers, the archetypical refugee was a poor widow or mother ill prepared to manage large groups of refugeed slaves. Later Hollywood depictions of fleeing plantation belles like Scarlet O'Hara only reinforced that idea. Yet, as Glymph has shown, slaveholding women were well practiced in the application of violence, even within the supposedly more congenial domestic sphere. For example, Maggie Martin, wife of Robert Campbell Martin, Jr., reported a female relative dealing with an allegedly lazy servant, Alice, by entering her bedroom wielding a *"shovel . . .* [and] looking very much like a young *lioness."*[39]

Litt Young, a WPA interviewee who remembered being refugeed from Vicksburg to Marshall, likewise recalled his "mistress," Martha Gibbs, as a "big, rich Irishwoman" who "warn't scared of no man" and who "buckled on two guns" before visiting the slave quarters on her plantation each morning. After the fall of Vicksburg, Union soldiers temporarily arrested Gibbs, but after her release, Young said, she "seized a bunch of us Niggers and started to Texas," employing a gang of "Irishmen guards, with rifles, to keep us from running away." Amanda Stone pursued a similar course; after the Stones left Brokenburn, she accompanied her son back to the plantation with a group of armed men, surrounded the cabins where her enslaved people were living with some of her own furniture, and then returned west "in triumph with all the Negroes" who had remained, except for four elderly people and one man who had joined the Union army.[40]

In short, refugee planters had to work hard to relocate enslaved people who had already made clear—through flight, fight, or everyday resistance—their dissent from the Confederate regime. Force would be required. Sometimes, however, that realization dawned slowly on planters. Some still believed laborers might willingly follow them away from the front lines. And, occasionally, enslaved people did seem to indicate a preference for going to Texas rather than staying.

Sarah Wadley, a young woman whose family temporarily hosted the Stones at their western Louisiana plantation after their flight from

Brokenburn, recorded one such story in her Civil War diary. Sarah's father, William Wadley, not only managed a large plantation but also oversaw a group of nearly seventy slaves owned by the Vicksburg, Shreveport and Texas Railroad. In August 1863, Wadley began making plans to remove both groups either to Texas or back to the family's original home in Georgia. According to Sarah, "Father gave all the negroes choice yesterday evening," telling them they could either go with her brother Willie to "a place of safety" or that they might "bundle up their things and go to the Yankees." All eagerly agreed "to go with Willie," including "one of the railroad negroes" whom Sarah overheard telling her father that "I come from Georgia and you did too and I calculate to die by you." A few days before, another enslaved man named Prince, who was married to one of the Wadleys' slaves, had come to request that William Wadley purchase him, emphatically declaring that he had "no notion of going" to the Yankees.[41]

Statements like these may have reflected uncertainty on the part of enslaved people about what advantages and protection the Union army could realistically afford in 1863. According to Sarah's diary, for instance, Prince had heard from black acquaintances in Monroe that "the Yankees takes all the young looking fellows and puts them in the army." In 1863, the Union army had also employed black laborers in dangerous and often fatal jobs like digging canals around Vicksburg—information that may have given men like Prince pause when considering their next steps.[42]

Even more likely, however, is that Prince desired to go with the Wadleys to remain with his wife, Emmeline. As historian Calvin Schermerhorn and others have shown, enslaved people often prioritized the preservation of family groups even over individual freedom. Wash Ingram, a formerly enslaved man from Virginia, remembered the great lengths to which his father went to reunite with him even after securing freedom for himself. Sometime before the war, Ingram's father had escaped their shared master and managed to find work in a mine close to his family; but when Wash and others were taken to Mississippi and sold to a man who "bought a big gang of slaves and refugeed part of 'em to Louisiana and part to Texas," the elder man made a dramatic relocation of his own. Wash recalled that while he and others were traveling to Texas in "ox-wagons" and were camped at Keachie, Louisiana, "a man come ridin' into camp and someone say to me, 'Wash, dar's your Pappy.'" Someone had told Wash's father "dat his chil'ren is dar in camp, and he come and fin' me and my brothers. Den he jine Master Ingram slaves so he can be with his chil'ren."[43]

Pappy's extraordinary efforts to find his sons may have been exceptional, but his fidelity to family was not. Prince likely made a similar decision to join the Wadleys so that he could be with his wife, and even the railroad laborer who declared that he would die by Wadley may well have been calculating on getting back to his Georgia home. Indeed, whites who understood the strong pull of family on the people they enslaved could apply a different kind of pressure on those they refugeed, even without resorting to the whip. Some refugee families appear to have moved enslaved people in stages, separating family groups as they did so. Kate Stone revealed, for example, that three men who had been sent to the Winnfield salt works ran away to reunite with their wives, who remained on the river, "but were caught." Another Mississippi River refugee hired out his enslaved men at the Lake Bistineau salt works while keeping their wives with him on a rented farm, and the Wadleys eventually moved some of the "railroad negroes" to an iron works in Texas while keeping the spouse of at least one hired out man in Louisiana. The Martin family, too, appear to have dispersed enslaved family members among various members of their own family living on both sides of the state border.[44]

Some refugeed slaves may well have chosen to remain with a white family either to prevent such separations or to remain informed of the whereabouts of kin. What is clear is that after the war ended people who had been refugeed often prioritized reunion with family members as they planned their next moves. The editors of the most recent volume of the Freedom and Southern Society Project note that many refugeed slaves in Texas desired to return to the places they had been relocated from and "set out to remedy separations inflicted by former owners." According to one report, "toward the end of 1865, some 300 per day traversed the Texas-Louisiana border along a single road."[45]

Not all returned at their own behest, or under conditions totally under their control. One refugee planter agreed to transport his now legally emancipated slaves back to their home in Louisiana but then, while en route, forced them to either sign a labor contract or be abandoned

on the road. Martin Sr. flogged one man he had refugeed while carrying him back to Louisiana in the fall of 1865. Another in his party was
confined to the wagon with diarrhea, just as many sickly slaves had been
on the way to Texas.[46]

Meanwhile, some refugeed freedpeople who were healthy enough to
resist appear to have gone along with former masters' wishes only so
that they would be transported back to kin; before leaving Texas, Martin
reported that his "Free Negroes" and those of another refugee "generally
. . . desire to return to La. and are obedient in all respects." Farther north,
in September 1865, Kate Stone wrote that the people who had been hired
out on a Lamar County farm were all in a "state of insubordination, insolent and refusing to work," but they were "all crazy to return to Louisiana." After her brother made clear that he did not intend to take them
back, Stone claimed that the family's former slaves—who still numbered
eighty or ninety—were suddenly "on their best behavior."[47]

To Stone, this turnabout indicated "what a treacherous race they are."
Yet, in retrospect, such scenes suggest that the behavior of refugeed
slaves had been strategic all along. Some enslaved people, like those who
had told William Wadley they preferred to go to Texas, had been on
what white planters considered their best behavior even during the war.
But given the violence inflicted on those whose behavior was deemed
bad, the poor conditions under which many people were moved, and
the incentives to comply with orders to maintain family networks, it
would be a mistake to conclude that slaves' seeming cooperation indicated anything like what we understand as loyalty.[48]

Indeed, even those refugee planters once convinced that their servants were faithful learned to think differently while in Texas. In October
1864, after Sarah Wadley's father left for Texas with a "guard of soldiers"
and the "railroad negroes" who had declared that they preferred to stay
with him, eight of the men ran away as soon as Wadley dismissed the
guards, including "one in whom Father placed great confidence."[49] And
despite Martin's claims that his "Free Negroes" were behaving well so
that they could return to Louisiana, an August 1865 letter written in Nacogdoches told a different story: "Several of the Negroes I am rid of. Old
Wilson I told he could work his way in the world & down to La. if he
could. He has set off. Alex ran off, and Ralph was told that he was seen
near Logansport. He will turn up at Mansfield I reckon. Jo has also run

off I presume. I ordered him to go back to my negro quarters and work in furrow filling. This he did not do."[50]

The possibility of such defections had already shaken Martin's confidence a few months earlier. Before it was clear that the war had ended, Martin had resolved to sell the "Negroes" he had left in both Texas and Louisiana, "for I am tired of owning them—if I do so even." In such moments of candor, refugee planters revealed the truth about their situation: first, that their ownership of slaves was crucial to their own economic prospects, and second, that their hold on enslaved people in Texas always remained tenuous. Enslavement on the run depended on intentional violence or accidents of health and kinship that kept slaves from acting at once on their true aspirations for freedom.[51]

It is difficult to know what refugeed slaves did when they ran away from their refugee owners, but they may well have spread local knowledge about Union activities long before June 19, 1865, traditionally held to be the date when enslaved Texans learned of freedom for the first time. Refugeed people generally came to Texas from areas where the magnetic attraction between Union soldiers and runaway slaves was already widely known. As historian Randolph Campbell notes, "the influx of refugees" and the people they brought with them probably attracted the attention of local slaves and "brought additional information about the meaning of the war."[52]

Still, if many enslaved newcomers to Texas ran away, many more did not. Nor did the activities of refugeed slaves ever directly aid Union armies, which remained far away from places like Hopkins County and Jordan's Saline. This does not mean, however, that the influx of refugeed slaves did not bring serious dissent into the state. Enough evidence exists to undo the myth, cherished by some white Southerners, that most were faithful slaves who followed their masters to Texas instead of running to Union lines. In Campbell's apt words, what Confederates and their sympathizers interpreted as loyalty was, "as always with the majority, largely a matter of their circumstances."[53]

■ ■ ■

Enslaved people brought to Texas had relatively few ways to support Union efforts directly, in view of their circumstances: surrounded on all sides by armed Confederates willing to use force to keep them enslaved;

dispersed across the state and often weakened by sickness; uncertain about what sorts of protection the Union could provide; and committed to keeping families together when possible. Some expressed dissent explicitly by running away, but it is difficult to imagine how refugeed slaves could have fundamentally altered these general circumstances, any more than white Texas Unionists could have overturned secession. Samuel Q. Richardson, the white salt maker suspected of anti-secession sentiments and chased off of his land by Confederate squatters, could not even save his saline.

Yet if refugeed slaves, who surely understood the forces arrayed against them, sometimes complied with orders, that did not mean they accepted these circumstances. Just as Richardson initially joined the Confederate army but then showed his true loyalties by deserting to Missouri, some refugeed slaves initially went to Texas and worked without appearing to be forced. Always, however, they watched and waited for opportunities to advance their own interests, even as their owners pursued opportunities of very different kinds.

On the whole, the range of strategies employed by refugeed slaves probably resembled the decisions made by white Texas Unionists who have received far more study from historians of the state. As historian James Marten notes, some white dissenters in Texas "reluctantly joined the Confederate cause, others defied the rebels and actively worked for a Union victory, while many simply kept their heads down," cloaking their dissent until it seemed possible to act on it most effectively and safely.[54] The evidence surveyed here suggests that refugeed slaves probably acted with similar savvy—but in the face of dangers and obstacles far greater than those that white Unionists faced. Though often caricatured by white Southerners as perfectly passive dependents or as perfectly faithful servants, enslaved people brought to Texas should be considered seriously as part of the mosaic of dissenters who challenge a monolithic view of the state as solidly Confederate.

NOTES

1. Charles William Ramsdell, *Reconstruction in Texas* (New York: Columbia University Press, 1910), 23. Contemporary estimates placing the number of refugeed slaves at 150,000 have appeared in many subsequent studies. See Yael A. Sternhell, *Routes of War: The World of Movement in the Confederate South* (Cambridge, Mass.:

Harvard University Press, 2012), 99; Ira Berlin et al., eds., *The Destruction of Slavery* (Cambridge: Cambridge University Press, 1985), 676; Leon F. Litwack, *Been in the Storm So Long: The Aftermath of Slavery* (New York: Alfred A. Knopf, 1979), 32. See also W. Caleb McDaniel, "How Many Slaves Were Refugeed to Confederate Texas?" June 25, 2013, http://wcm1.web.rice.edu/how-many-refugeed-slaves-in-texas.html.

2. Throughout this article, I have used the term "refugeed slaves" to refer to enslaved people brought to Texas by white Confederates. This term has been used extensively in previous historiography and thus serves as familiar shorthand for the group of people under consideration here. For attempts to estimate the number of slaves brought to Texas, see Dale Baum, "Slaves Taken to Texas for Safekeeping during the Civil War," in *The Fate of Texas: The Civil War and the Lone Star State*, ed. Charles D. Grear (Fayetteville: University of Arkansas Press, 2008), 83–103; Randolph B. Campbell, *An Empire for Slavery: The Peculiar Institution in Texas* (Baton Rouge: Louisiana State University Press, 1989), 245. On white refugees, see Sternhell, *Routes of War;* Mary Elizabeth Massey, *Refugee Life in the Confederacy* (Baton Rouge: Louisiana State University Press, 1964).

3. For recent statements of these points, see Stephanie McCurry, *Confederate Reckoning: Power and Politics in the Civil War South* (Cambridge, Mass.: Harvard University Press, 2010); Thavolia Glymph, *Out of the House of Bondage: The Transformation of the Plantation Household* (New York: Cambridge University Press, 2008), 97–136.

4. See Ramsdell, *Reconstruction in Texas,* 23; Campbell, *Empire for Slavery,* 245.

5. William F. Weeks to [John C. Moore], January 12, 1864, *Records of Ante-Bellum Southern Plantations,* ed. Kenneth M. Stampp (Frederick, Md.: University Publications of America, 1985–2000) [hereafter RASP], Series I, Part 6, Reel 17, Frames 810–11. For the text from the marker, see www.9key.com/markers/marker_detail.asp?atlas_number=5223007305.

6. John Q. Anderson, ed., *Brokenburn: The Journal of Kate Stone, 1861–1868* (Baton Rouge: Louisiana State University Press, 1995), 335.

7. Arthur J. Fremantle, *Three Months in the Southern States* (Edinburgh: William Blackwood and Sons, 1863), 85. On the timing of refugee streams, see Baum, "Slaves Taken to Texas," 86–87, 91; Massey, *Refugee Life in the Confederacy,* 91–93; Barnes F. Lathrop, "The Pugh Plantations, 1860–1865: A Study of Life in Lower Louisiana" (Ph.D. thesis, University of Texas, 1945), 195–98; Robert L. Kerby, *Kirby Smith's Confederacy: The Trans-Mississippi South, 1863–1865* (New York: Columbia University Press, 1972), 107–109; Barnes F. Lathrop, "The Lafourche District in 1861–1862: A Problem in Local Defense," *Louisiana History* 1, no. 2 (Spring 1960): 99–129; Barnes F. Lathrop, "The Lafourche District in 1862: Invasion," *Louisiana History* 2, no. 2 (Spring 1961): 175–201.

8. Marshall *Texas Republican,* October 7, 1864, April 17, 1866.

9. Baum, "Slaves Taken to Texas"; R. R. Haynes to Pendleton Murrah, January 5, 1864, Records of Texas Governor Pendleton Murrah, Texas State Library and Archives Commission [hereafter TSLAC]. See also Massey, *Refugee Life in the Confederacy,* 90–94.

10. On these various opportunities, see Kerby, *Kirby Smith's Confederacy,* chap. 2.

11. Anderson, *Brokenburn*, 242. For the bullet making, see interview with Lyttleton Dandridge, in *Slave Narratives: A Folk History of Slavery in the United States from Interviews with Former Slaves*, Vol. 2: *Arkansas Narratives*, Part 2, Project Gutenberg, www.gutenberg.org/ebooks/13700. On the Sulphur Forks Iron Works, see Thomas G. Clemson to E. Kirby Smith, December 12, 1864, Compiled Service Records of Confederate Soldiers, M258, Roll 0111, National Archives and Records Administration, Washington, D.C. [hereafter NARA].

12. Interview with Mattie Williams, in *The American Slave: A Composite Autobiography*, Supplement, Series 2, ed. George P. Rawick (Westport, Conn.: Greenwood Press, 1979), 10:4104. For more information about the Weeks family's movements, see http://wiki.wcaleb.rice.edu/Weeks%20Family. On William F. Weeks before the war, see Richard Follett, *The Sugar Masters: Planters and Slaves in Louisiana's Cane World, 1820–1860* (Baton Rouge: Louisiana State University Press, 2005), 15.

13. See, for example, John Moore to J. A. Johnson, July 7, 1863, RASP, Series I, Part 6, Reel 18, Frame 116f; C. E. Gregory to William F. Weeks, March 25, 1864, RASP, Series I, Part 6, Reel 18, Frames 376–77; Certificate for Slaves Hired, RASP, Series I, Part 6, Reel 18, Frame 429; C. E. Gregory to William F. Weeks, June 30, 1864, RASP, Series I, Part 6, Reel 18, Frame 489; Letters of Introduction for William F. Weeks, October 9, 1863, RASP, Series I, Part 6, Reel 18. Later, in 1864, Weeks used personal connections to Louisiana governor Henry W. Allen to investigate the possibility of running wagon trains to Mexico to trade cotton for manufactured goods and gold. See "Weeks, W. F.," Confederate Citizens File, Confederate Papers Relating to Citizens or Business Firms, 1861–65, Record Group 109, M346, NARA; William F. Weeks to John C. Moore, December 22, 1864, RASP, Series I, Part 6, Reel 18, Frames 713–14; Letters of Introduction for William F. Weeks, RASP, Series I, Part 6, Reel 18.

14. See the numerous wartime letters pertaining to Harriet Weeks Weightman (or H. C. Meade), John F. Leigh, Charles C. Weeks, and John C. Moore in RASP, Series I, Part 6. Quote taken from "Maggie" to "Bud," May 25, [1864], RASP, Series I, Part 6, Reel 18, Frames 85–88.

15. Robert Campbell Martin, Jr., to Robert Campbell Martin, Sr. [December 1864], transcription in Martin-Pugh Collection, Item 633, and Thomas Pugh Martin to Robert Campbell Martin, Sr., January 7, 1865, transcription in Martin-Pugh Collection [hereafter MPC], Item 638, Nicholls State University. See also Thomas Pugh Martin to Robert Campbell Martin, Sr., January 31, 1865, MPC, Item 645, and Thomas Pugh Martin to Robert Campbell Martin, Jr., February 19, 1865, MPC, Item 652; Lathrop, "Pugh Plantations," 447.

16. Kerby, *Kirby Smith's Confederacy*, 68–70; Ella Lonn, *Salt as a Factor in the Confederacy* (University: University of Alabama Press, 1965).

17. Anderson, *Brokenburn*, 170; W. Magruder Drake, "Two Letters of H. Winbourne Drake, Civil War Refugee in Northwest Louisiana," *Louisiana History* 7, no. 1 (Winter 1966): 71–76; Kerby, *Kirby Smith's Confederacy*, 70.

18. John Williams to Robert Campbell Martin, Sr., October 16, 1864, MPC, Item 612; Letter from Texas Military Board to A. H. Abney at Salt Works, January 17,

1865, Records of the Texas Military Board, 2–10/304, TSLAC. On the Texas salt works generally, see "Salt Industry," *Handbook of Texas Online,* Texas State Historical Association, www.tshaonline.org/handbook/online/articles/dks01; Kerby, *Kirby Smith's Confederacy,* 68–70. On Brooks Saline, see Loy J. Gilbert, "Salt of the Earth: Making Salt at the Neches Saline," *Chronicles of Smith County, Texas* 11, no. 2 (Fall 1972): 1–12. On the appropriation for salt, see also "Report of the Special Examination of the Records of the Military Board of Texas," Records of the Texas Military Board, 2–10/298, TSLAC, and Letters from State Military Board to A. H. Abney, April 1864 and August 16, 1864, both 2–10/304, TSLAC.

19. A. H. Abney to Texas State Military Board, November 1, 1864, Records of the Texas Military Board, 2–10/304, TSLAC; Marshall *Texas Republican,* December 2, 1864; J. L. McMeans to Francis R. Lubbock, June 22, 1863, Records of Governor Francis R. Lubbock, TSLAC.

20. Robert Campbell Martin, Sr., to W. W. Pugh, September 2, 1863, MPC, Item 373; Maggie Martin to Robert C. Martin, Sr., January 18, 1863, MPC, Item 319; John Williams to Robert Campbell Martin, Sr., October 16, 1864, MPC, Item 612. On the connection of Williams and Pugh to salt works, see Pugh-Williams-Mayes Family Papers, *Records of Southern Plantations from Emancipation to the Great Migration,* ed. Ira Berlin (Bethesda, Md.: University Publications of America, 2000–), Series B, Part 3, Reel 7.

21. Samuel Q. Richardson to Andrew Jackson Hamilton, September 30, 1865, Records of the Governor Andrew Jackson Hamilton, TSLAC.

22. Ibid. On Van Zandt's surge in slave population, see Baum, "Slaves Taken to Texas," 90.

23. Robert Campbell Martin, Sr., to W. W. Pugh, September 2, 1863, MPC, Item 373; Robert Campbell Martin, Sr., to Albert C. Martin, October 24, 1864, MPC, Item 614; William F. Weeks to Mary Palfrey Weeks, October 31, 1864, RASP, Series I, Part 6, Reel 18, Frames 656–58. See also Lathrop, "Pugh Plantations," 292.

24. William F. Weeks to John Moore, October 31, 1864, from Gentry, RASP, Series I, Part 6, Reel 18, Frames 654–56; C. C. Weeks to John C. Moore, February 14, 1864, RASP, Series I, Part 6, Reel 18, Frames 335–36.

25. Willie Lee Rose, *Rehearsal for Reconstruction: The Port Royal Experiment* (New York: Oxford University Press, 1964), 108; Lathrop, "Pugh Plantations," 291.

26. Francis Fearn, *Diary of a Refugee* (New York: Moffat, Yard, 1910), 30–31; List of Avery Family Servants, RASP, Series J, Part 5, Reel 11, Frames 988–91.

27. List of Avery Family Servants; WPA interview quoted in Campbell, *An Empire for Slavery,* 247.

28. Glymph, *Out of the House of Bondage,* 104.

29. James Oakes, *Freedom National: The Destruction of Slavery in the United States, 1861–1865* (New York: W. W. Norton, 2013), 318; Anderson, *Brokenburn,* 127.

30. Anderson, *Brokenburn,* 127, 171, 173.

31. Ibid., 165, 192.

32. Robert Campbell Martin, Sr., to W. W. Pugh, September 2, 1863, MPC, Item 373. On opportunities for flight caused by refugeeing, see Berlin et al., *Destruction*

of Slavery, 35, 676; Steven Hahn et al., eds., *Land and Labor, 1865* (Chapel Hill: University of North Carolina Press, 2008), 72–77. On the flight of Williams's slaves, see Moon-Ho Jung, *Coolies and Cane: Race, Labor, and Sugar in the Age of Emancipation* (Baltimore, Md.: Johns Hopkins University Press, 2006), 51.

33. Clarksville *Standard,* July 4, 1863; Marshall *Texas Republican,* July 4, 1863; R. D. G. Mills to William F. Weeks, February 28, 1864, RASP, Series I, Part 6, Reel 18, Frame 355; C. C. Weeks to Mary Palfrey Weeks, July 4, 1864, RASP, Series I, Part 6, Reel 18, Frames 499–501.

34. Anderson, *Brokenburn,* 191, 204, 220.

35. Martin, Sr., to W. W. Pugh, September 2, 1863, MPC, Item 373; Elvira Boles quoted in Litwack, *Been in the Storm So Long,* 33; John F. Leigh to John Moore, November 7, 1862, RASP, Series I, Part 6, Reel 17, Frames 769–71.

36. Robert Campbell Martin, Jr., to Maggie Martin [February 7, 1864], MPC, Item 418. On slaveholders' efforts to keep slaves just well and fed enough to work, see Walter Johnson, *River of Dark Dreams: Slavery and Empire in the Cotton Kingdom* (Cambridge, Mass.: Harvard University Press, 2013), 179.

37. William G. Thomas to [R .C. Martin, Jr.], May 27, 1863, MPC, Item 355; Charles C. Weeks to Mary Palfrey Weeks, July 4, 1864, RASP, Series I, Part 6, Reel 18, Frames 499–501.

38. Allen Manning interview in Rawick, *American Slave,* 7:215–22A.

39. Maggie Martin to R. C. Martin, Jr., December 7, 1863, MPC, Item 403. See Glymph, *Out of the House of Bondage.*

40. Litt Young interview in Rawick, *American Slave,* 10:4300–304; Anderson, *Brokenburn,* 208–209.

41. Diary of Sarah Lois Wadley, August 8, 1859–May 15, 1865, Manuscripts Department, Southern Historical Collection, University of North Carolina at Chapel Hill [hereafter Wadley Diary], http://docsouth.unc.edu/imls/wadley.

42. Wadley Diary. On the dangerous military labor being performed by "contraband" slaves in Louisiana around this time, see John D. Winters, *The Civil War in Louisiana* (Baton Rouge: Louisiana State University Press, 1963), 106–107.

43. Interview with Wash Ingram in Rawick, *American Slave,* 5:1854–55. On devotion to family, see Calvin Schermerhorn, *Money over Mastery, Family over Freedom: Slavery in the Antebellum Upper South* (Baltimore, Md.: Johns Hopkins University Press, 2011).

44. Anderson, *Brokenburn,* 204; Drake, "Two Letters of H. Winbourne Drake," 75; Wadley Diary. See references to "Ralph" and "Alice" in MPC.

45. Hahn et al., *Land and Labor,* 60–61, 82–83.

46. Ibid., 322; Robert Campbell Martin, Jr., to Maggie Martin, October 29, 1865, MPC, A-17-B, Item 719.

47. Robert Campbell Martin, Sr., to Robert Campbell Martin, Jr., August 14, 1865, MPC, Item 680; Anderson, *Brokenburn,* 362–63.

48. Anderson, *Brokenburn,* 363.

49. Wadley Diary.

50. Robert Campbell Martin, Sr., to Robert Campbell Martin, Jr., August 14, 1865, MPC, Item 680.

51. Robert Campbell Martin, Sr., to Robert Campbell Martin, Jr., May 25, 1865, MPC, Item 674.

52. Campbell, *Empire for Slavery,* 246.

53. Ibid., 248.

54. James Marten, *Texas Divided: Loyalty and Dissent in the Lone Star State, 1856–1874* (Lexington: University Press of Kentucky, 1990), 32.

4

East Texas Unionism

WARREN J. COLLINS, BIG THICKET JAYHAWKER

Victoria E. Bynum

During the Civil War the Big Thicket of East Texas, a tangle of forest that spans portions of five counties, provided an effective refuge for upwards of one hundred deserters from the Confederacy. At the northwestern end of Hardin County, near Honey Island, Warren Jacob Collins led a remnant band of deserters that included his brothers, Stacy Collins, Jr., and Newton Carroll Collins, and fifteen to twenty other men. Like most Big Thicket deserters, the men rejected the derogatory term "bushwhackers" in favor of "jayhawkers," which linked them ideologically to the more famous Unionist Kansas jayhawkers. And no one made a stronger claim to principled Unionism than Warren Collins—whose Southern frontier roots reached all the way back to the colonial South Carolina backcountry.

A study of Warren Collins's political views—and the context in which he developed those views—provides a window on one segment of the white Southern yeomanry that *did not* rush forward at the behest of Confederate state leaders. Although plenty has been written about Warren and the jayhawkers, a lack of Confederate military reports and letters concerning this remote outpost of the Civil War home front has forced historians to rely mostly on folklore to piece together the story.

Thanks to the rich lore emanating from the ecologically fascinating Big Thicket, we know quite a bit about *how* jayhawkers lived during the war, but little about their political views. Over time, Warren Collins has become the quintessential backwoodsman who just wanted to be "left alone." Ever the trickster and backwoods brawler, he is presented as clever and forever ready to fight rather than take orders from *any-one*. But shorn of his Unionist beliefs, he appears simply suspicious of all government, reacting against authority (usually with fists) without clear thought. And yet later in life this same man embraced socialism and even ran for political office on a socialist ticket in early twentieth-century Texas.[1]

Neither folklore nor published family histories explain how "Old Warren," the "Daniel Boone" of East Texas, evolved from Southern Unionist during the Civil War to Southern socialist in 1909. We get a hint after his death in 1926, when his obituary reported that he "took a keen interest in politics up until the last days of his life and always took a fearless stand on any issue regardless of its public favor." The obituary failed to identify, however, what those fearless stands were. It is not surprising, then, that Warren Collins is rarely mentioned in histories of Civil War or New South Texas.[2]

For those devoted to the Confederate cause, ignoring Warren Collins's political views and affiliations, while anchoring him within the trope of the backwoodsman, implies that he was simply too isolated in his Big Thicket world—perhaps too primitive—to realize that the Confederacy represented his true interests. Political and economic conflicts between slaveholders and nonslaveholders of the Piney Woods of Texas and Mississippi are thus overshadowed by images of provincial backwoods hotheads who reflexively opposed all authority, whether imposed by the Union or the Confederacy. All too easily, Warren Collins slides into a caricature of the headstrong Southern man of honor, fighting for the same principles that led to creation of the Confederate government in the first place.[3]

This is not to diminish the importance of folklore and local history. Both offer richly detailed narratives about Big Thicket life that provide an all-important context for understanding the politics of the region's Civil War dissenters. Because of local lore, we have detailed knowledge of how well armed jayhawkers were, and how well supplied by woods and creeks that offered wild oats, game, and fish. We know that Big Thicket outliers (conscript deserters and resisters) knew the densely forested, vine-covered terrain of the Big Thicket like no one else, as did their families, who provided them with staples such as coffee, corn, tobacco, and salt. In this remote corner of the state, neither deserters nor

The Big Thicket of southeast Texas remains prime hunting and fishing land 150 years after Warren Collins and family made the isolated area their home. Photo courtesy of the History Center, Diboll, Texas.

the civilians who aided them were easily captured, executed, or tortured by Confederate militia and home guard soldiers.[4]

In fact, jayhawkers lived rather well during the Civil War. Surrounded by beehives, the men cut down trees, gathered honey from the hives, and set up a thriving system of barter. According to local memory, Warren Collins's men took a large plank and placed it between two pear trees to fashion a table. There, they laid out honey, deer meat, and whatever else the woods had to offer. Wives and friends then retrieved the goods and sold them in Beaumont, where they bought tobacco and coffee to return to the deserters' makeshift table. To assure a fresh supply of water, the men even dug and camouflaged three wells (appropriately named "Union Wells") near the Polk County line.[5]

In late November 1864, an anonymous report appeared in the *Houston Tri-Weekly Telegraph* that described the living arrangements of some twenty-eight jayhawkers living on the western edge of the Big Thicket. Deserters there had "built comfortable shanties, cleared land, planted corn, [and] erected a tan yard for making leather of the hides of stolen cattle." The informant went on happily to report that some twenty-four of the men had been tracked down with "negro dogs." In what may have been a reference to Warren Collins's remnant band, he also admitted that some twenty other deserters remained at large in "another place in the Thicket."[6]

The most enduring and popular folktale about Warren Collins's war years is that of the "Kaiser Burnout."[7] The story goes that Capt. Charles Bullock of the Twenty-Fourth Texas Cavalry was determined to capture the notorious deserters of the Big Thicket. Allegedly, Bullock *did* capture them, only to have them escape right under his nose. And it was the wily and clever Warren Collins who pulled it off. Warren, folks said, took to playing his fiddle and dancing a little jig for guards in the front part of the jail while his fellow jayhawkers slipped out the back. Somehow, legend has it, Warren then slipped away, too!

In fall 1864 (or spring 1865, depending on the version), Capt. Bullock turned his mission over to one Capt. James Kaiser. Unable to penetrate the jayhawkers' hideout, Kaiser decided simply to burn the men out. He commanded his men to set the woods on fire, and so they did, allegedly burning 2,000–3,000 acres of Big Thicket land. Two outliers reportedly died in the flames, but not a single one was captured. Warren Collins, whose military records reveal no trace of him after November 1864, remained an outlaw in a Confederate nation that soon was breathing its last breaths.

Verifying the Burnout has not been easy. There is no doubt about the existence of Capt. Charles W. Bullock, and environmental experts agree that *someone* burned the 100-acre portion of the Big Thicket known as Kaiser's Burnout, but no Capt. James Kaiser appears in Texas military records. Historians point out, however, that one Capt. H. W. Kyser (the only officer in Texas with that surname) of Company G, Twelfth Texas Cavalry, was at one point commanded to hunt jayhawkers and deserters in Hardin County. Historians, then, may well be close to verifying the Kaiser Burnout, although the image of Warren Collins fiddling and jigging his way out of jail remains in the realm of folklore.[8]

As in the case of folktales, local history provides distinct clues to understanding the politics of Warren Collins's behavior. Take, for example, news journalist Dean Tevis's article from the 1930s about Warren's efforts to clear the town of Beaumont of gamblers back in 1854.[9] Lumber mills barely had a presence in East Texas before the Civil War, but, Tevis told readers, the early timber industry had already attracted commercial development and men on the make, with the inevitable influx of gamblers and prostitutes. Eager to line their pockets in burgeoning frontier boom towns, gamblers from New Orleans and places east of the Mississippi entered Texas via Beaumont. "In a good many pockets silver jingled merrily," noted Tevis.

The ordinary farmers and herders of Jefferson County, unhappy about this turn of events, moved to rid Beaumont of these purveyors of graft and greed. A war in the courts ensued, with several families organizing themselves and filing numerous "true bills" against the gambling houses. Serving on the grand jury that heard these bills was none other than Warren Collins, who voted in favor of each and every one of the bills.

Undaunted, gamblers turned back the challenge. Flush with cash, they hired lawyers and procured land surveyors who craftily determined that Collins did not even live in Jefferson County. One surveyor testified that the Collins homestead in fact was located just over the county line—in Liberty County! The court judge then quashed the indictments against the gamblers. Predictably, a few years later, surveyors found that Collins did indeed live in Jefferson County—in the portion soon to be designated Hardin County.

The story of Warren Collins and the gamblers is told with humor and the usual references to Warren's penchant for fist fights. But what might this story tell us about Warren's view of social order and good government? Tevis, who wrote to entertain rather than to analyze, was silent on that score. Yet, when viewed in the larger context of Collins family history, Warren and his neighbors' efforts to clean up their neck of the woods tell us plenty. To begin, they tell us that these were not stereotypical frontier rabble rousers, "poor whites," or debtors on the lam from Eastern bill collectors; rather, according even to Tevis, they were the "better element" of East Texas's pine barrens culture—folks wedded to a way of life with a distinct ethos of long duration.

Warren Collins and his associates were of the frontier yeomanry that opened and settled the southwestern frontier. Warren's own father, Stacy Collins, Sr., pioneered in settling Mississippi Territory during his long migration west from Spartanburg, South Carolina. Sometime around 1809, Stacy migrated to Georgia, where he met and married Sarah Anderson. The couple remained in Georgia (where their first four children were born) for several years before moving on to Mississippi. By 1816, they had bought land in Wayne County; by 1820, in Covington County, out of which Jones County, Mississippi, was carved in 1826. All along the way, relatives traveled alongside them, each family carving out its own homestead. Much later, Stacy and Sarah would take another caravan of family members on to East Texas.[10]

As they moved, Stacy Collins and his comigrants worked to establish stable, orderly communities. Between 1814 and 1815, Stacy's name appeared regularly on frontier petitions urging the federal government to protect yeoman land titles and replace corrupt local officials with federally appointed magistrates and judges. (On one petition, the men likened corrupt militia to marauding Indians, with the militia defined as the greater problem.) Paraphrasing the Declaration of Independence in 1815 with a preamble that included the words "when in the course of human events," the men urged the federal government to make Mississippi a "Sister State" in the "American Union." As much as Warren's generation hated gamblers, his father Stacy's generation deplored the anarchic, rootless wanderers who brought vice and violence to the rapidly developing southwestern territories.[11]

After settling in Jones County, Stacy raised livestock and grew mostly corn and sweet potatoes without the benefit of slaves. In 1826, he served as county tax assessor. By 1850, ten of his and Sarah's fourteen children were married, had families of their own, and were among the most prosperous and civic-minded of the county's plain farmers. Their eldest son, Vinson, regularly held public office. Although two of their daughters married slaveholders, none of their eight sons ever owned slaves, although their economic statuses indicated that they could have had they so chosen.[12]

Around 1852, Stacy, Sarah, and four of their sons migrated from Mississippi to Jefferson County, Texas. For the parents, this migration represented the culmination of a lifetime of exodus from societies in which commercial agriculture and slavery were on the rise. Stacy died soon after his arrival in Texas, but the union-building, anti-slavery ideals that he instilled in his sons would soon nurture their opposition to the cause of secession.[13]

The Texas Collinses carried on the yeoman-herder traditions of their father and were typical of East Texas's backwoods people in their continued reliance on a hunting and gathering lifestyle subsidized by minimal

farming. Warren Collins built his home of notched pine saplings, reinforced for winter with eight- to ten-foot "sealing boards" and completed
with a stick-and-clay tapered chimney for warmth and cooking. His
family farmed a few acres mainly to supply themselves and their herds
with corn. The woods were full of wild game, and a farmer's hogs and
cattle foraged on the surrounding open range. Men hunted and farmed;
women tended gardens, spun cloth, and milked cows.[14]

It was a way of life that many backwoods people did not want disrupted, not by gamblers, and certainly not by a war fought to assert the
right of disunion. As well as a desire to be left alone, their opposition
to secession included a political recognition that slave-based Southern
commerce, empowered by the new Confederate government, threatened that way of life more than did the federal government. This was
not abolitionism; it was rural class consciousness.

I am reminded of historian Eugene Genovese's 1975 article, "Yeoman Farmers in a Slaveholders' Democracy."[15] Genovese argued that
even farmers who lived outside the plantation belt largely supported the
Confederacy because they wished to protect a way of life threatened by
Yankee intrusions. Genovese admitted that these farmers also viewed
commercial planters as a threat to their way of life. But through unend-
ing propaganda, he argued, Southern fire-eaters had convinced backcountry farmers that Yankees were by far the greater threat. There's more
than a little truth in Genovese's argument, and it may well fit Hardin
County, which voted in favor of secession. Yet it has the effect of passing
over the politics, even the historical origins, of Southern Unionism. And
it certainly does not fit the actions of the Big Thicket jayhawkers.

Warren's grandson, Bud Overstreet, remembered what fueled his
grandfather's opposition to the Confederacy. "I heard grandpa say it was
a rich man's war and a poor man's fight," he told interviewers. "That's
the reason they wouldn't fight; they didn't own nothin'." Another East
Texan described the Big Thicket jayhawkers as "just sensible people.
They knew what would happen if the slaves were not freed. . . . Men who
had money to start a business of any kind would buy slaves for his labor
and poor whites would be left out." In other words, it was not just any
outsider who threatened the autonomy of East Texas Unionists, it was
the commercial planter.[16]

And so it had been for a long time. Yeoman farmers like the Collinses who migrated to Texas during the 1850s were not as likely as native Texans to share the dominant Anglo-Texan ethos that made secession appear to be a natural, patriotic progression of that state's history. They participated in neither the state's revolution of 1836 nor the furor preceding its annexation in 1845. In moving to East Texas, yeoman farmers and herders sought a new, unsettled, unspoiled Piney Woods—which many found in Hardin County. To their chagrin, less than a decade after their arrival the Southern secession movement enjoyed widespread support among slaveholding and nonslaveholding citizens alike.[17]

To be sure, there were many Unionists in Texas, as other essays in this volume make clear, especially those by Walter Kamphoefner and Omar Valerio-Jiménez. But with their state's history inextricably tied to the 1850s' sectional crisis, political leaders successfully trumpeted secession as the only means for saving Texans' cherished freedoms and independence from ruin. Dissenters were brutally suppressed. Anyone who disagreed faced harassment, even murder, in the Lone Star State.[18]

The extent of silent support for the Union can therefore never be known. Pro-Confederate vigilantes terrorized pro-Union farmers in North Texas and German-Texans of the Hill Country after they publicly supported the U.S. government. As a result, fewer and fewer people dared to voice—or even vote—their objections. Angelina County was the only East Texas county where voters rejected, by 57 percent, secession. Unlike Hardin County, this cotton-growing plantation region exhibited a significant anti-secession alliance between small farmers and slaveholding planters.[19]

On February 23, 1861, Hardin County voters supported Texas's prosecession referendum 167 to 62. Back in Jones County, Mississippi, from where the Collinses had most recently migrated, it was quite different. By 166 to 89, voters there elected a cooperationist delegate to attend Mississippi's secession convention a month earlier. For evidence of the Collins brothers' political opposition to disunion, the records of Mississippi, the state in which they were born and raised, are considerably more revealing than those of Texas.[20]

In fact, it turns out that the Collins contingent of Texas jayhawkers had more than a passing acquaintance with another anti-Confederate

guerrilla band—Mississippi's Knight Company, located in a region pop-
ularly known as the "Free State of Jones."[21] Newt Knight, the infamous
"Captain" of the Knight Company, and Warren Collins knew each other
personally, having grown up together in Jones County. Even more remarkable, at least fifteen of the fifty-four men who joined the Knight
band were kin to Warren Collins and his wife, Tolitha Eboline Valentine.
One of Eboline's brothers, James "Morgan" Valentine, was Newt's first
lieutenant, and two other brothers were Newt's privates. Likewise, two
of Warren's brothers, Jasper and Simeon Collins, were listed as Knight
Company sergeants, and three of his nephews as privates.[22]

As an old man, Newt Knight himself credited Warren's brother Jasper
with turning him against the Confederacy. When the "Twenty-Negro
Law" was passed in fall 1862, Newt remembered that Jasper Collins
"threw down his gun and started home." "This law," he said, "makes
it a rich man's war and a poor man's fight. I'm through." Newt agreed,
and both men returned to Jones County, where they were sheltered by
Unionist friends and relatives.[23]

The differences between the regions tell the story. Hardin County,
Texas, created in 1858, lacked the intricate, extensive bonds of kinship
and long community histories that characterized the Piney Woods of
southeastern Mississippi. Although people of the two regions shared
similar ancestral roots and class backgrounds, the political context and
social environment in which they experienced the sectional crisis made
all the difference. These differences in turn hampered the emergence
of local leaders (such as Warren Collins) who might have galvanized a
wider anti-secession movement among nonslaveholding citizens.[24]

In Jones County, Collins kinfolk did organize in opposition to pro-
secession forces. The county's cooperationist delegate was John H.
Powell, the father-in-law of Warren Collins's brother Jasper. Another
Collins brother, Riley James, presided over a neighborhood meeting at
which he urged people not to support the cause of secession. The oldest
Collins brother, Vinson (after whom Warren named his first son), was
appointed probate judge in 1865 by Republican provisional governor
William Sharkey. Vinson would also serve as Jones County's delegate to
the Mississippi Constitutional Convention of 1868.[25]

After the war, Newt Knight aggressively petitioned Congress on behalf of the Knight Company for compensation as Unionist soldiers.

Several of Warren and Eboline Collins's kin testified on their behalf. In 1870, for example, Eboline's father, Allen Valentine, vouched for the Unionism of Knight Company men.[26] In 1887 and 1897, after Newt Knight renewed his petitions to Congress, several more Collins relatives testified to having been members of the Knight Company from October 13, 1863, until September 10, 1865, and to having fought numerous battles against Confederate troops. Jasper Collins testified that he had traveled all the way to Memphis in a failed effort to unite the Knight Company with Union forces.[27]

Because the Knight Company was never mustered into the Union army, the burden was on its men to prove they had banded together for the explicit purpose of defending the U.S. government. When asked by his interrogator to explain the men's "real purpose" in "bonding your-selves together," Jasper Collins replied that he could not speak for the others, but that his "object" was to gain protection for families and to remain "loyal to the U.S. government." Eboline Collins's brother, James "Morgan" Valentine, similarly stated that the company was formed "for defense of the Union" and pointed out that its members were conse-quently harassed by the Ku Klux Klan "after the surrender."

Lawyers for the federal government pressed the men to provide the name of the justice of the peace who allegedly administered oaths of al-legiance to the Knight band. Once again, the Collinses were key figures in the debate. Some men testified that Thomas Jefferson "Jeff" Collins had delivered it; others thought that county judge Vinson A. Collins, the oldest Collins brother, had done so. The principal figures could not be questioned, however. Vinson Collins was dead, and Jeff Collins had moved to Polk County, Texas, where he now lived near his uncle—Warren J. Collins.

Federal lawyers interrogated Morgan Valentine about another Knight Company member, Simeon Collins, who had died shortly after the war. During an April 1864 Confederate raid on Jones County by Col. Rob-ert Lowry, Simeon and two of his sons had been captured and forced back into the army. Was it true, the lawyer asked Morgan, that their lives had been spared only after Simeon's wife, Lydia, tearfully interceded on behalf of her husband and sons? This was the same Lydia who moved to Hardin County, Texas, around 1873 to live near her closest Texas relative—her brother-in-law, Warren Collins.[28]

After the war, quite a few Mississippians associated with the Free State of Jones moved to East Texas. Along with Lydia Collins, all four of Simeon Collins's grown sons—three of whom had been members of the Knight Band—likewise moved to Hardin County and neighboring Polk County. And there were others. By the mid-1870s, numerous families from the Mississippi and Texas guerrilla bands had reunited and were living in close proximity in East Texas.[29]

Understanding the political implications of Warren Collins's family connections as well as his Civil War stance helps us also to understand his participation, forty years later, in Texas's vibrant socialist movement.[30] While in his late seventies, Warren joined the effort to defeat the power of the big lumber companies. He ran not only for Congress as a socialist but also as county judge with a socialist slate of candidates from Hardin County. His political views were well known and heartily endorsed by T. A. Hickey of Hallettsville, the editor of the socialist newspaper the *Rebel*. On August 19, 1911, Hickey praised the "old fighter from East Texas" for running for Congress against Democrat Martin Dies. Hickey expressed hope that the Collins clan would "increase and multiply until they cover the earth with the clean, clear water of Socialism." During his 1912 run for county judge, Warren wrote to Hickey that he was "in the fight up to my chin" and optimistically predicted that "six months of [President] Wilson's administration will make more Socialists than [Eugene] Debs could make in four years of public speaking."[31]

In the pages of the *Rebel*, editor Hickey in turn praised the "strain of radicalism" that ran through "the veins" of the Collins family. Perhaps he knew that back in Jones County, Mississippi, not only had many of Warren's kinfolk opposed the Confederacy, but some of them were now socialists too. Of course, most Southern Unionists did not become socialists. A good many more, including Warren's brother Jasper, *did* become populists, and from there, especially in Texas, but also in Winn Parish, Louisiana, they made the transition to socialism. The government, these rural populists and socialists believed, was the best means of countering the power of Big Business (represented by lumber barons in both Texas and Louisiana) and restoring economic independence to the common man.[32]

Back in Jones County, Mississippi, Jasper Collins's grandson, grand-nephew, and son-in-law all ran for office on socialist tickets between 1913 and 1915. Jasper himself, who died in 1913, had founded Jones County's first and only Populist newspaper alongside his son back in 1895. He and two other Collins descendants were elected delegates to Mississippi's Populist conventions in 1895 and 1896. Clearly, the political evolution of Warren's Mississippi kinfolk dovetailed with his own.[33]

One will not discover Warren Collins's political views by reading the family histories published by his descendants. The political career of son Vinson Allen Collins began in 1910 when the forty-three-year-old attorney was elected to the Texas state senate. In order to succeed in Democratic Party politics, Vinson soon deferred to the increasingly popular, pro-Confederate myth of the Lost Cause. Although he began his political career as a progressive Wilsonian Democrat, he ended it as a conservative Democrat who supported the presidential campaigns of two Republicans, Herbert Hoover and Dwight Eisenhower.[34]

Given the political environment in which he lived, it is not surprising that Vinson Collins was mostly silent about his father's political views. Between 1890 and 1930, Southern journalists, historians, and novelists attributed the formation of the Confederacy to Southern statesmen's determination to protect the liberty and independence of state governments—not slavery—against the encroachment of a too-powerful federal government. Erasing economic and cultural differences among whites, and insisting that the issue of slavery was peripheral to the coming of the war, Lost Cause chroniclers envisioned a noble South in which all honorable whites were united in advancing the cause of liberty in the face of Northern invasion.[35]

Lost Cause orthodoxy left little room for white Southerners who opposed the Confederacy—certainly not those, like Warren Collins, who had armed themselves against it. And so, as the 1920s approached, Vinson's political views accordingly shifted. Civil War jayhawkers—and certainly socialist firebrands—were a distinct liability in his quest to build a political career, particularly as that career emerged simultaneously with Lost Cause conservatism.

Perhaps because of the diminished force of Lost Cause history after World War II, Vinson felt freer to discuss his father's Civil War Unionism. In 1949, despite his conservative transformation, he wrote a brief family history that obliquely acknowledged the early Collins's political views. After laying out the genealogical connections between the Texas and Mississippi branches, he described them as "people of convictions; few [of whom] ever held office, because they had opinions and dared to express them. They were all opposed to slavery and to concession [secession]." When he published his final version of the family's history in 1962, however, those final sentences were omitted.[36]

Until now, it appears that the only publication to acknowledge not only the jayhawker past of Warren J. Collins but also his twentieth-century socialism was the Hallettsville *Rebel.* Back in 1911, T. A. Hickey praised Warren Collins, the "veteran fighting Socialist of east Texas," for rejecting mainstream political parties despite his son Vinson's political career. "Neither his son's politics nor prominence in the Dem[ocratic] ranks," he wrote, "have any weight with that brave old Spartan."[37]

Editor Hickey was certainly right about that. Until his death in 1926, Warren himself defended his wartime support for the Union as "the greatest patriotic act" of his long eventful life.[38] Lost Cause orthodoxy, however, followed by the crushing of socialism during World War I and the post–World War II cold war, all contributed to a diminished appreciation of the politics of dissent displayed during and after the Civil War by Warren Jacob Collins and a sizable chunk of Texas's white southern yeomanry.

NOTES

1. On the photographs, culture, and "lifeways" associated with the Big Thicket of East Texas, see esp. Thad Sitton and C. E. Hunt, *Big Thicket People: Larry Jene Fisher's Photographs of the Last Southern Frontier* (Austin: University of Texas, 2008). Stories from the Big Thicket abound. See Francis E. Abernethy, ed., *Tales from the Big Thicket* (Denton: University of North Texas Press, 2002 [1967]); Campbell Loughmiller and Lynn Loughmiller, comp. and eds., *Big Thicket Legacy* (Austin: University of Texas Press, 1977); Robert L. Schaadt, *The History of Hardin County, Texas* (Hardin County Historical Commission, n.d.), 20–21; Dean Tevis, "The Battle at Bad Luck Creek," *Beaumont Enterprise,* October 25, 1931, reprinted in Abernethy, *Tales from the Big Thicket,* 75–92; Macklyn Zuber, "Fire at Union Wells, *Frontier Times,* October/November 1963, 28.

2. Vinson Allen Collins, *A Story of My Parents: Warren Jacob Collins and Tolitha Eboline Collins* (Livingston, Tex.: n.p., 1962); and Carr P. Collins, Jr., *Royal Ancestors of Magna Charta Barons: The Collins Genealogy* (n.p., 1959). Warren Collins obituary, *Beaumont Enterprise,* January 31, 1928, reprinted in Collins, *Story of My Parents.*

3. On such stereotyping, see esp. *Tempo* magazine, May 17, 1970.

4. Schaadt, *History of Hardin County,* 20–21.

5. Account by Lance Rosier in Loughmiller and Loughmiller, *Big Thicket Legacy,* 71.

6. "S" to Editor, *Houston Tri-Weekly Telegraph,* December 21, 1864. My thanks to librarian Vicki Betts of the University of Texas at Tyler for supplying me with this letter.

7. The Burnout tale, here and following, from Ralph A. Wooster and Robert Wooster, "A People at War: East Texas during the Civil War," *East Texas Historical Journal* 28, no 1 (1990): 3–16; Loughmiller and Loughmiller, *Big Thicket Legacy,* 70–72; Schaadt, *History of Hardin County,* 20–21; Aline House, *Big Thicket: Its Heritage* (San Antonio, Tex.: Naylor, 1967).

Warren Collins's military records offer a tantalizing but incomplete record of his Civil War experiences. On June 30, 1862, he enrolled in Company F, Twenty-Second Texas Infantry at Camp Hubbard. By November of the same year, he was AWOL. On July 23 and August 2, 1864, he was reported "in arrest" at Sabine Pass. Just before his record ends in November 1864, he appears as a private in Company H, Twenty-First Texas Infantry, and as a "Regimental Return" to Company D, Spaight's Battalion, Texas Volunteers.

8. Pete A. Y. Gunter, *The Big Thicket: An Ecological Reevaluation* (Dallas: University of North Texas Press, 1993), 3; Harold W. Willis, *A Short History of Hardin County, Texas* (Kountze, Tex.: Hardin County Historical Commission, 1998), 27–29; *Tempo* magazine, May 17, 1970; Anne Bailey, "Twelfth Texas Cavalry," *Handbook of Texas Online,* Texas State Historical Association, www.tshaonline.org/handbook/online/articles/qkt12.

9. Dean Tevis, "Surveyor Nullifies Attempt to Punish Big Time Beaumont Gamblers in 1854," undated newspaper clipping, author's files. Tevis was a feature writer for the *Beaumont Enterprise* during the 1930s.

10. Victoria Bynum, *The Long Shadow of the Civil War: Southern Dissent and Its Legacies* (Chapel Hill: University of North Carolina Press, 2010), 24, 108.

11. Petitions to Congress by Inhabitants East of the Pearl River [referred 14 December 1815], 1814–1815, in *The Territory of Mississippi, 1807–1817,* ed. Clarence Edwin Carter, 569–74, 601–603, Vol. 6 of *The Territorial Papers of the United States* (Washington D.C: Government Printing Office, 1938). For a full history of Stacy and Sarah Collins's migrations west, see Collins, *Story of My Parents,* and Victoria Bynum, *Free State of Jones: Mississippi's Longest Civil War* (Chapel Hill: University of North Carolina Press, 2001), 29–69.

12. U.S. Federal Manuscript Population and Agricultural Censuses, 1850, Jones County, Miss.

13. Stacy Collins died within two years of settling in Texas. See Collins, *Story of My Parents,* 1–7.

14. Thad Sitton and James H. Conrad, *Nameless Towns: Texas Sawmill Communities, 1880–1942* (Austin: University of Texas Press, 1998), 6–9; Vinson Allen Collins, "Settling the Old Poplar Place," in Abernethy, *Tales From the Big Thicket,* 58–68.

15. Eugene D. Genovese, "Yeoman Farmers in a Slaveholders' Democracy," *Agricultural History* 49, no. 2 (April 1975): 331–42.

16. Quoted in Loughmiller and Loughmiller, *Big Thicket Legacy,* 70–71.

17. On the characteristics of the Texas yeomanry, see Richard G. Lowe and Randolph B. Campbell, *Planters and Plain Folk: Agriculture in Antebellum Texas* (Dallas: Southern Methodist University Press, 1987).

18. David Paul Smith, "The Limits of Dissent and Loyalty in Texas," in *Guerrillas, Unionists, and Violence on the Confederate Home Front,* ed. Daniel E. Sutherland (Fayetteville: University of Arkansas, 1999), 133–49; Walter L. Buenger, "The Riddle of Secession," in *Lone Star Blue and Gray: Essays on Texas in the Civil War,* ed. Ralph A. Wooster (Austin: Texas State Historical Association, 1995), 1–26; Ralph A. Wooster, *Civil War Texas* (Austin: Texas State Historical Association, 1999), 35–45.

19. On violent opposition to Unionism in Texas, see esp. David Pickering and Judy Falls, *Brush Men and Vigilantes: Civil War Dissent in Texas* (College Station: Texas A&M University Press, 2000); Dale Baum, *The Shattering of Texas Unionism: Politics in the Lone Star State during the Civil War Era* (Baton Rouge: Louisiana State University Press, 1998); Richard McCaslin, *Tainted Breeze: The Great Hanging at Gainesville, Texas, 1862* (Baton Rouge: Louisiana State University Press, 1994); James Marten, *Texas Divided: Loyalty and Dissent in the Lone Star State, 1856–1874* (Lexington: University of Kentucky Press, 1990); Walter Buenger, *Secession and the Union in Texas* (Austin: University of Texas Press, 1984). On Angelina County, see Richard McCaslin, "Voices of Reason: Opposition to Secession in Angelina County, Texas," *Locus* 3, no. 2 (Spring 1991): 180–94.

20. Willis, *Short History of Hardin County,* 23. Most of the Collins brothers joined the Confederacy before deserting either to the Piney Woods swamps of Mississippi or to the Big Thicket of East Texas. Three died as a result of the war. Edwin Collins of Texas volunteered for service at Galveston and died of typhoid and pneumonia in January 1862. In Mississippi, Riley Collins refused to join the Confederacy. He joined Newt Knight's band and, later, the Union army in New Orleans, where he died of disease. Simeon Collins also joined the Knight band and was wounded and captured during Colonel Lowry's raid on Jones County. The eldest Collins brother, Vinson Allen, was beyond draft age, but his son, Harrison C. Collins, was killed in battle in February 1862. See Bynum, *Free State of Jones,* 115–29; Bynum, *Long Shadow of the Civil War,* 20–36. The death of Edwin Collins was described by Vinson Allen Collins of Mississippi in a letter to his son Harrison, who was killed in action before receiving the letter. Vinson's description was based on a letter he received from Newton Carroll Collins of Texas. Vinson also mentioned that his brothers Simeon and Jasper had joined the Confederacy along with fifteen other relatives "that opposed the war." See Vincent Allen Collins to 2nd Lieut. Harrison Calhoun Collins, February 21, 1862, reprinted in Everett Hammond, ed., *Storm Clouds over Jones County, Mississippi* (Jones County, Miss.: Jones Company Genealogical and Historical Organization, 2001).

21. The literature on Mississippi's Free State of Jones is voluminous. See esp. Bynum, *Free State of Jones;* Rudy Leverett, *Legend of the Free State of Jones* (Jackson: University Press of Mississippi, 1984); Ethel Knight, *Echo of the Black Horn* (n.p., 1951); Thomas Jefferson Knight, *The Life and Activities of Captain Newton Knight*

and His Company and the "Free State of Jones" (n.p. 1935, rev. ed., Laurel, 1946); James Street, *Tap Roots* (Garden City, N.Y.: Sun Dial Press, 1943).

22. Warren and Tolitha Eboline Valentine Collins were related to a multitude of Knight Company members. In addition to those mentioned, Warren's brother, Riley James Collins, was a private in the Knight Company. Privates James Madison, Benjamin Franklin, and James Morgan Collins were Warren's nephews, as was Pvt. Prentice M. Bynum, son of Warren's sister, Margaret. Richard Hampton and John Ira Valentine, brothers of Eboline, were also Knight Company privates, as was Eboline's cousin, William Patrick Valentine. Through her mother, Cynthia Welch Valentine, she was related to four additional Knight Company privates: William M., Timothy L., Harrison R., and R. J. Welch.

Kinship links between the Hardin County, Texas, and Jones County, Mississippi, Collinses were determined by research into U.S. federal manuscript censuses and published genealogies. See esp. Collins, *Story of My Parents*, and Bynum, *Free State of Jones*, 60–62. Military service, desertion, and membership in the Knight Company were traced from Compiled Service Records of Confederate Soldiers Who Served in Organizations from the State of Mississippi, 7th Battalion, Mississippi Infantry (microfilm), and Newton Knight Folder, Box 15, Records of the U.S. House of Representatives, RG 233, National Archives, Washington, D.C. [hereafter Newton Knight Folder].

23. Newt Knight, quoted from interview with Meigs Frost, *New Orleans Item,* March 20, 1921.

24. Baum, *Shattering of Texas Unionism*, 52–56.

25. Bynum, *Free State of Jones*, 88, 92–148. Jones County was temporarily named Davis County by disgruntled pro-Confederates during this year.

26. Newton Knight Folder, 1872.

27. This and following testimony from Claims of Newton Knight and Others, referred to the Court of Claims, U.S. House of Representatives by the Committee on War Claims, House of Representatives, February 4, 1895, nos. 8013 and 8464, National Archives, Washington, D.C.

28. Simeon and son Matt were subsequently captured by Union forces at Kennesaw Mountain, Georgia, and imprisoned. Soon after their release from prison, Simeon died from wounds sustained in Jones County during Colonel Lowry's raid. See Bynum, *Free State of Jones*, 124–25.

29. U.S. Federal Manuscript Population Censuses, Polk and Hardin Counties, Texas, 1870, 1880.

30. James R. Green, *Grass Roots Socialism: Radical Movements on the Southwest, 1895–1943* (Baton Rouge: Louisiana State University Press, 1978); Peter Buckingham, "The Socialist Party of Texas," in *The Texas Left: The Radical Roots of Lone Star Liberalism*, ed. David Cullen and Kyle Wilkison (College Station: Texas A&M University Press, 2010).

31. Hallettsville (Tex.) *Rebel*, August 19, 1911 (first quote), December 14, 1912 (second quote). Martin Dies of Beaumont, Texas, served as house representative from the Second District from 1909 until 1919. Dies was the father of congressman

Martin Dies, Jr. Warren Collins's unsuccessful run for Congress is recorded in Election Returns, 1910, Hardin County, Election Division, Records of the Secretary of State, Texas State Archives and Library Commission. His run for county judge was announced in the *Rebel*, March 23, 1912. On the lumber wars that led to socialist organization, see James Fickle, "the Louisiana-Texas Lumber War of 1911–1912," *Louisiana History: Journal of Louisiana Historical Society* 16, no. 1 (Winter 1975): 59–85.

32. Hallettsville *Rebel*, August 19, 1911. On Mississippi populists, see William D. McCain, "The Populist Party in Mississippi" (M.A. thesis, University of Mississippi, 1931), 16–17; Jackson *Clarion Ledger*, June 20, August 8, September 12, September 28, October 10, 1895, February 27, 1896. On Mississippians who joined third-party movements, see Stephen Cresswell, "Who Was Who in Mississippi's Oppositional Political Parties, 1878–1963," Mississippi Department of Archives and History. On populists and socialists in Winn Parish, Louisiana, see Green, *Grass-Roots Socialism*, 247–48; Grady McWhiney, "Louisiana Socialists in the Early Twentieth Century: A Study in Rustic Radicalism," *Journal of Southern History* 20, no. 3 (August 1954): 137–48; John Milton Price, "Slavery in Winn Parish," *Louisiana History: Journal of Louisiana History Society* 8, no. 2 (Spring 1967): 137–48.

33. On the Collins's role in the populist and socialist movements of Jones County, Mississippi, see Bynum, *Long Shadow of the Civil War*, 114, 139.

34. Collins, *Story of My Parents*. On this era of Texas politics, see Lewis L. Gould, ed., *Progressives and Prohibitionists: Texas Democrats in the Wilson Era* (Austin: Texas State Historical Association, 1992). On the political career of Vinson Allen Collins, see Norman D. Brown, *Hood, Bonnet, and Little Brown Jug: Texas Politics, 1921–1928* (College Station: Texas A&M University Press, 1984), 211–12, 388, 390–91; Ron Tyler, ed., *New Handbook of Texas,* (Austin: Texas State Historical Association, 1996), 2:218; Clarence Ray Wharton, *Texas under Many Flags* (New York: American Historical Society, 1930), 112; Dallas *News*, July 14, 1953.

35. On creation of the myth of the Lost Cause, see esp. Gaines M. Foster, *Ghosts of the Confederacy: Defeat, the Lost Cause, and the Emergence of the New South* (New York: Oxford University Press, 1987); Charles Reagan Wilson, *Baptized in Blood: The Religion of the Lost Cause, 1865–1920* (Athens: University of Georgia Press, 1980); Paul M. Gaston, *The New South Creed: A Study in Southern Mythmaking* (New York: Alfred Knopf, 1970).

36. V. A. Collins, "A Little Sketch of the Descendants of Stacey Collins," unpublished manuscript, 1949, Lauren Rogers Museum of Art History Collection, Laurel, Miss.

37. Hallettsville *Rebel*, August 19, 1911.

38. Schaadt, *History of Hardin County*, 20–21.

5

New Americans or New Southerners?

UNIONIST GERMAN TEXANS

Walter D. Kamphoefner

Throughout role of German Americans in the Civil War era and their stand on issues of slavery, secession, the Union, and emancipation were controversial at the time and continue to arouse controversy to this day. German Unionism was epitomized by the Nueces Massacre, or Battle of the Nueces, if you prefer (actually it was both), and the Treue der Union ("true to the Union") monument in the German Hill Country village of Comfort memorializing the victims and their ideals.[1] The town even saw fit to commemorate the battle's 150th anniversary with a symposium and ceremony. However, a research note in the January 2012 *Southwestern Historical Quarterly*, authored by one of its Germanic residents, Frank Wilson Kiel, casts doubt upon both the uniqueness and the significance of Comfort's German monument.[2] Most of Kiel's debunking is technically correct, but, like the assertion that General Lee came in second at the Battle of Gettysburg, Kiel's analysis misses the main point. It leaves unscathed the fact that the Germans of Comfort (and the Hill Country generally) were unique among inhabitants of the would-be Confederacy and particularly of the Deep South in the degree and outspokenness of their Unionism. Kiel challenges assertions that the Comfort monument is the only one to the Union in the South, that it is the oldest of its kind, that it is the only one inscribed in German, that it was endowed with special rights to fly the U.S. flag at half-mast, and above all that it symbolizes an "overwhelming Unionist solidarity in the Comfort community." All of these, Kiel claims, are "false."

Much depends on one's definition of "South." If it includes all slave state residents, Comfort stands not the least bit apart: Missouri Germans resisted a secessionist governor and practically dragged the state back into the Union. But if one looks for monuments erected in the former Confederacy in the wake of the war by people who were resident there in 1861, Comfort maintains its unique position. When Yankees moved south sometime after the war and erected a monument to the G.A.R. (the Union veterans organization Grand Army of the Republic), that was hardly indicative of the civil courage the Comfort monument represents. The "Great Hanging" of forty-two Anglo Unionists at Gainesville, Texas, does pose certain parallels to the Comfort situation, but even into the twenty-first century there is no historical marker that objectively gives the victims their due.[3] There is an older German-language monument in Kentucky, commemorating the Battle of Rowlett's Station, but it was erected by troops of the Twenty-Third Indiana, only a couple dozen of whom were Kentucky Germans from Louisville and none of whom were "locals." The only other area that produced significant numbers of local Unionists was east Tennessee, but Kiel documents nothing memorializing Unionists there before the twentieth century. He cites a monument in Greeneville, Tennessee, celebrating the Union soldiers from Greene County with an inscription quite similar to that at Comfort, but he seems to have overlooked a Confederate monument on the opposite side of the courthouse square. Moreover, the Union monument was probably dated much later; the courthouse itself was built only in 1916. Similarly, the G.A.R. monument in the east Tennessee town of Cleveland may well commemorate local troops, but it was not erected till 1914. Nearly all the other Union monuments in the South that Kiel lists date from the twentieth century, and few of them involve people local to the area before 1865.

There are two standards one could apply to these issues: German divergence from the Texan majority and German unanimity. If one uses unanimity as the standard, it is easily refuted. Germans were never unanimous on anything except perhaps alcohol and prohibition, and even there with enough effort one could probably find a German teetotaler. That a minority in Comfort voted in favor of the secession referendum is no revelation of Kiel's; it had already been noted in 1930 by Rudolph Biesele and later by Guido Ransleben in his centennial history of Comfort, though the latter attributed the split vote in part to intimidation.[4] As evidence against the "overwhelming support for the Union in Comfort," Kiel also cites the team that recovered the remains of the slain Unionists on the Nueces, which included nine Confederates, several civilians (he lists seven) with no known military service, and two Union soldiers in "deserter" status. Here too, much nuance is lost. Of the nine German Confederates, only two had served in other than local units, one each in the Fourth and Fifth Texas Cavalry. The rest were in county or frontier units, providing home protection and suffering fewer conflicts of conscience than fighting directly against their adopted country. The same would apply to one individual who served as a "Confederate" freighter between San Antonio and Mexico, another form of "alternative service" often sought by Germans for reasons of conscience (including one Nueces survivor). One person Kiel lists merely as "civilian" was Edward Degener. His civilian status is unsurprising given that he was fifty-two years old at the war's outbreak, but Kiel makes no mention of the fact that Degener lost two sons at the Nueces, was tried for disloyalty before the Confederate Military Commission and required to post $5,000 bond, and subsequently served as the first Republican congressman from Texas.[5]

Although Kiel's piece is more interesting from a historiographic than a historical angle, it does illustrate a long-standing dilemma for German Texans: if they wanted to join the mainstream, which one—the national mainstream or its Southern subculture? One gets the impression that some modern descendants try to retrofit their ethnic ancestors into a Southern identity that their forefathers would have denied or even abhorred. For example, on the SPJST[6] Czech fraternal cemetery along Highway 21 west of Caldwell one can find two graves that have their stones supplemented with Confederate veteran markers; what is not commemorated there is the fact that both were deserters.[7] The relationship of other Central European immigrant groups in Texas with the Confederacy appears to have been quite similar to that of Germans.

This essay presents an overview of the actions and reactions of German immigrants to these issues in Texas, with occasional side-glances to other slave states, particularly my native Missouri. These two states were home to the largest concentrations of Germans below the Mason-Dixon Line. The settlement patterns themselves raise an issue: German immigrants largely avoided the slave states, though there were other factors involved besides slavery.[8] In fact, some scholars have questioned whether Germans really avoided slavery at all. A pioneer in this area of research, the late University of Texas geographer Terry Jordan, attempted to place his German ancestors closer to the Texas mainstream. He pointed out significant regional differences in the behavior of Texas Germans in relation to slavery. German settlements in East Texas were older, their inhabitants more acculturated to American values, their climate and soils better suited for plantation agriculture and slavery. The Texas Hill Country west of Austin was settled later and, given its ranching economy, had less need for slaves. Jordan provided a needed corrective to Texas German ancestor worship and demolished the myth that they were unanimously opposed to slavery and true to the Union. But he went too far in characterizing Texas Germans as "unremarkable" in their attitudes toward race and slavery, and he underestimated the degree to which Germans stood apart from their fellow Southerners on issues of the Civil War era.[9]

According to Jordan, lack of capital was the main factor preventing Germans in East Texas from owning slaves, and one that would have been overcome in the course of time had the Civil War and emancipation not intervened. A study of three cotton counties (Austin, Fayette, and Colorado), documenting about sixty Germans who did own slaves between 1840 and 1865, would seem at first glance to confirm this. But upon closer observation, Germans in East Texas still stand apart (see graph). Although they made up one-third or more of the white population of these counties, Germans constituted less than 5 percent of the slaveholders there, owning less than 2 percent of all slaves. Nor was this merely the result of poverty. At every level of wealth from bottom to top, a higher proportion of Anglo-Americans than Germans owned slaves. For example, among people with $3,000–$6,000 worth of property, more than half of the Anglos but hardly 2 percent of Germans were slave owners. Those who came from the servant-keeping class back in Germany were the most likely to become slaveholders, but even in the richest category only half of the Germans but 92 percent of the Anglos owned slaves. To be sure, for Germans the acquisition of slaves required an active decision unless they married into a slave-owning family, whereas many native Texans inherited slaves. But contrasts of this

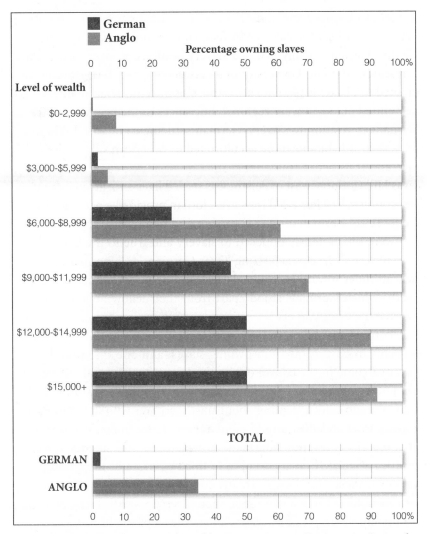

Slave ownership by ethnicity and wealth, Fayette County, Texas, 1860. Drawn by Carol Zuber-Mallison. Copyright © 2016 by the University of Oklahoma Press.

magnitude could have hardly come about without a conscious decision against human property on the part of many Germans.[10] Very similar patterns were observed in three other widely scattered studies of Germans across the slave states: in rural Missouri, in five mid-size cities, and in Charleston. Regardless of where one looks, in matters of slave owning Germans brought up the rear, falling behind every other group including the Irish.[11]

Even the few Germans who did own slaves do not appear particularly wedded to the peculiar institution. One of the rare firsthand accounts is by an immigrant who arrived in Washington County in 1850 and wrote in February 1861 that he had bought a "slave" or "black man," which he explained on purely economic grounds: "When I die, my children will inherit him. So you can be sure that he is worth as much as two hired hands." But even such a German expressed little regret at the demise of slavery, an institution he identified primarily with Anglo-Americans, as he stated in a letter of 1866: "The Americans almost all had Negroes . . . because whoever had a lot of Negroes, he was rich. They had to do all the work, because the Americans, they don't like to work." He did justify slavery with the biblical "Curse of Ham," but he also remarked with a touch of schadenfreude, "The Americans can't get along with the Negroes now, but they don't like to work themselves."[12]

The only German slave owner in New Braunfels, Texas, a prosperous Jewish merchant named Joseph Landa, freed his five slaves immediately in 1863 when he received word of the Emancipation Proclamation, evoking such ill will among his Confederate neighbors that he fled to Mexico and spent the rest of the war there.[13] Ferdinand Flake in Galveston owned a female domestic with three children, but he still edited a German newspaper with the telling name *Die Union,* which because of its "warning voice" was subjected to "threats, intimidations of all kinds, and even open violence," as Flake related when he resumed publication in 1865 after a three-year suspension. Missouri presents similar cases: several Germans who were small-scale slave owners became leading and even radical members of the Republican Party.[14]

The voting record of Germans in the slave states provides additional insights. In Missouri they were among the few supporters of Lincoln, who came in fourth in the state. In fact, the only counties he carried in any slave state were two German counties of Missouri: rural Gasconade County, which has gone Republican in every presidential election since 1860, and urban St. Louis.[15] Texas Germans obviously did not vote for Lincoln; he was not even on the ballot, and just trying to vote for him meant risking life and limb. But Texas was one of the few states that put the issue of secession up to a popular vote, and here too Germans stood

apart from the Texas mainstream, though not always to the same degree. The referendum of February 23, 1861, provides a measure of Texas
German attitudes toward Southern institutions and independence.[16] In
an appeal to ethnic voters, the secession resolution and declaration of
causes had also been published in 2,000 copies of German translation,
and an equal number in Spanish.

But the German copies largely fell on deaf ears. Across Texas, secession won by a landslide, with less than a quarter of the voters opposing. In contrast, two German frontier counties (table 1) in and around
Fredericksburg led the state with a 96 percent margin against secession.[17] San Antonio turned in a razor-thin margin for the Union due
primarily to German voters, with some Tejano help. After the election,
German city councilmen still resisted for several months demands to
turn over seized federal arms to the secessionist state.[18] Even older Texas
German settlements farther east show little evidence of enthusiasm for
secession. The 64 percent support for secession in Colorado County,
for example, masks an internal polarization. Three German precincts
voted 86 percent against, while five Anglo precincts cast all but six votes
in favor. Similarly in Fayette County, where no precinct returns have
survived, some Anglos must have contributed to the narrow majority
opposing secession because less than half of the voters were German,
but a local paper with the telling name *State Rights Democrat* blamed
what it called the "sauer-kraut *dirt-eaters*." It pilloried Texas Revolution
veteran "Benedict Arnold [F. W.] Grassmeyer" for deceiving "the honest Germans of Fayette County" in the election and for his abolitionist
sympathies and friendliness toward free blacks.[19] Only in Austin County
did close to half the Germans vote for Southern independence, still a
rather lukewarm result compared to the 96 percent level in six Anglo
precincts.[20]

The stance of New Braunfels, the only German area of the Hill Country voting strongly in favor of secession, has been widely misunder-
stood. It was largely the work of one man, reflecting trust in the advice
of the venerable Ferdinand Lindheimer and his *Neu Braunfelser Zeitung*.
But Lindheimer seldom attempted to sell his readers on the merits of the
secessionist case, stressing instead the reprisals they might suffer should
they be perceived as opposing it: "When in Texas, do as the Texans do.
Anything else is suicide and brings tragedy to all our Texas-Germans."[21]

Darlegung der Gründe,

welche den Staat Texas veranla[ß]en aus der Föderal-Union zu scheid[en].

Die Regierung der Ver. Staaten schlug durch Resolutionen vom 1. Mär; 1845, der Republik Texas, welche damals eine freie, unabhängige und souveraine Nation war, den Anschluß an die andere, als einen gleichberechtigten Staat, vor.

Das Volk von Texas erklärte sich durch seine in Convention versammelten Abgeordneten am 4. Juli desselben Jahres für die Annahme jenes Vorschlages, und verfaßte eine Constitution für den neuen Staat. Am 29. Dezember desselben Jahres wurde auf Grund dieser Constitution der neue Staat förmlich in die verbindende Union aufgenommen.

Texas gab seine eigene Nationalität auf, und willigte darein einer der verbündeten Staaten zu werden, um innerer Ruhe sicher zu sein, und um seinem Volke die Segnungen der Freiheit und des Friedens dauernd zu sichern. Es wurde mit seiner eigenen Constitution in die Conföderation aufgenommen, damit es sich unter den Garantien der Föderal-Constitution und des Anexations-Vertrages ihrer Segnungen erfreuen sollte. Es wurde aufgenommen, als eine Gemeinschaft, in der das Institut der Neger-Sclaverei bestand, erhalten und beschützt wurde — eine abhängige Dienstbarkeit der afrikanischen von der weißen Race innerhalb seiner Grenzen. Ein Verhältniß welches seit der ersten Ansiedelungen der Wildniffe durch die Weißen bestanden hatte und welches man für alle Zeiten beizubehalten beabsichtigte. Seine Einrichtungen und geographische Lage brachten eine innige Verbindung zwischen ihm und den anderen Sklaven-Staaten der Conföderation hervor. Diese Verbindung ist noch durch die Vereinigung nach und nach erstarkt. Wie war nun das Benehmen der Regierung der

---

The ordinance of secession appeared not only in English but in German and Spanish, the two other major languages spoken in Texas at the time of the Civil War. Everett C Wilkie, *The 1861 Texas printings of the ordinance of secession, A declaration of the causes, and An address to the people of Texas: an illustrated descriptive printing history commemorating the sesquicentennial anniversary of their adoption and the secession of Texas from the United States of America.* Courtesy of Sam Lanham and the DeGolyer Library, Southern Methodist University, Dallas, Texas.

In general, the factor of intimidation must be kept in mind when examining Texas German behavior in the winter of disunion. Only 4 percent voted against secession in Washington County; even if all of them were German, that would amount to only one-third of the German voters—but in this county they were too few and too new to stick their necks out.

Jordan calls New Braunfels a "secessionist hotbed"; in fact it was one of the few places in Texas where Confederate sympathizers were subject to wartime intimidation. Throughout the war, the *Neu Braunfelser Zeitung* exhibited a strongly defensive tone. Editor Lindheimer's pragmatism was not universally appreciated. So incensed were some New Braunfelsers that they threw the press and type into the Comal River—but Lindheimer fished it out of the clear water so that the paper did not miss an issue. On top of that, his windows were stoned in twice, and his dogs poisoned with strychnine.[22] The only homogeneous German county or precinct where German support for secession exceeded the statewide average (New Braunfels fell only a couple of points below) was the settlement of Industry. With respect to Unionism, Jordan states that Texas Germans were split, "just as Anglo-Americans were." Both were indeed split, but there the similarities end. With Anglos there was at least a 3:1 majority for secession, whereas Germans turned in at least a slim majority for the Union and a disproportionate number of stay-at-homes as well.[23]

The tendency toward staying home applied to Confederate military service as well. A comparison of participation rates North and South provides more insight into German ideology and motivation. There is a scholarly consensus that Germans were overrepresented in the Union army, more so than almost any other nationality, though recruitment rates varied considerably from state to state. Missouri presents the best-case scenario, where Germans foiled a secessionist governor and sent him fleeing into exile all the way to Marshall, Texas. However, a German study of immigrants in the Confederacy (now also available in English translation) claims that the rate of military participation of Germans was very similar North and South: 16.1 percent of the German population of the South in uniform, compared to 16.6 percent of those in the North wearing blue. At first glance this would seem to indicate widespread sympathy with the Southern cause, but not upon closer examination. Since a much higher proportion of the military age population

Table 1. County and precinct returns from the 23 February 1861 Texas secession election

Precinct	Ethnicity or % German[1]	N for	N against	% against
Western counties				
Bexar[2]	28	827	709	46
San Antonio				
Pct. 1	Hispanic	227	146	39
Pct. 2	Hispanic	72	160	69
Pct. 3	German	124	186	60
rest of county	Mixed	292	147	33
Blanco	20	108	170	61
Comal (New Braunfels)	88	239	86	26
Gillespie (Fredericksburg)	87	16	398	96
Kerr[3]		76	57	43
Pct. 2 (Comfort)	60	34	53	64
rest of county	11	42	4	9
Mason	55	2	75	97
Medina[4] (Castroville)	43	140	207	60
Eastern counties				
Austin[5]	45	825	212	20
Cat Spring	German	8	99	93
Industry	German	86	2	2
New Ulm	German	36	30	45
Shelby's	German	16	51	76
subtotal	German	146	182	55
rest of county	Anglo	679	30	4
Bastrop[6]	25	335	352	51
Rabb's Creek	German/ Wend	1	56	98
Bastrop	Mixed	158	183	54
rest of county	Anglo	176	113	39

Table 1. Continued

Precinct	Ethnicity or % German[1]	N for	N against	% against
Colorado[7]	35	584	330	36
Frelsburg	German	22	154	88
Mentz/Bernardo	German	10	41	80
Weimar	German	7	37	84
subtotal	German	39	232	86
Columbus	Mixed	201	93	32
rest of county	Anglo	344	6	2
Fayette	37	580	628	52
State of Texas	7	46,153	14,747	24

[1] Ethnic percentages are based on calculations from the 1870 census, multiplying proportion with foreign parentage among whites by proportion of Germans among foreign-born. County-level votes from Joe E. Timmons, "The Referendum in Texas on the Ordinance of Secession," *East Texas Historical Society Journal* 11 (1973), 12–28.

[2] Lawrence P. Knight, "Becoming a City and Becoming American: San Antonio, Texas, 1848–1861" (Ph.D. dissertation, Texas A&M University, 1997), 267–70.

[3] Bob Bennett, *Kerr County, Texas, 1856–1956* (San Antonio: Naylor, 1956), 136, states that Pct. 1 was practically the area that became Kendall County in 1862; thus the exact figures for ethnicity from the 1870 census.

[4] Does not include French, who in this county were primarily German-speaking Alsatians; their inclusion would raise the German proportion to about two-thirds.

5 *Bellville Countryman*, February 27, 1861.

[6] Bill Moore, *Bastrop County, 1691–1900* (Wichita Falls, Tex.: Nortex Press, 1977), 77–78.

[7] L. R. Weyand and H. Wade, *An Early History of Fayette County* (LaGrange, Tex.: LaGrange Journal, 1936), 244–45.

in the South saw service (61 percent as opposed to 35 percent in the North), it is apparent that Germans in the Confederacy were much less enthusiastic than either their Anglo neighbors or their compatriots in the North to support the cause of their section of the country.[24]

One can gain a rough estimate of ethnic loyalties by searching for common Anglo and German names on Union and Confederate muster rolls in Texas. Of every Texas soldier named Smith or Jones on the National Park Service database of Civil War soldiers, one finds that less than 1 percent of them served the Union. But searching for two leading German names, Schmidt and Meyer, in the same data reveals that, of those who rendered military service, one in nine served the Union (table 2). Although their situations were not entirely comparable, people with the common Hispanic names Garcia and Martinez showed much greater Union affiliation, 43 percent. The Latino record cannot simply be written off to mercenary motives, as Omar Valerio-Jiménez demonstrates in another chapter of this volume. But for Hispanics, Union enlistment did not require a perilous journey of several hundred miles to Brownsville as it did for Texas Germans, or Anglos for that matter.[25] Still, this issue bears further investigation, especially the question of how many Germans enlisted in the Rebel ranks before April 1862, when Confederate conscription took effect.[26] The pioneering work of Ella Lonn, and above all her list of ethnic officers and companies in the Rebel army, is long overdue for an update.[27]

Even a German like Capt. Robert Voigt, who raised one of the three German companies in Waul's Texas Legion, showed little zeal in his letters. He does write of doing his "duty" for "our cause" but never elaborates, and he hardly mentions slavery at all in his letters to his wife back in Industry, Texas. But he tells her at one point, "I come first, and then the Confederation, I won't be a fool and ruin myself by destroying my health in the army." It is apparent from his writings that he had considered whether his postmaster's position would exempt him from conscription, and he advised his wife how to avoid being paid in inflated Confederate currency unless she could pay off some of their own debts with it. In the wake of the German draft riot in Industry, he did lament that "it will always remain a blot on the reputation of the entire settlement" and complained that "the Germans in general . . . behave at various times in a manner that makes one ashamed." Even so, after surrendering in the aftermath of the Vicksburg campaign and being confined on Johnson's Island for the rest of the war, he volunteered to take an oath of loyalty to the United States, although not until February 11, 1865.[28]

Voigt was not the only or the earliest German Confederate to become a "Galvanized Yankee"; he mentions several of the men in his command who had become so by the end of 1863. Even earlier, when the Sixth Texas Infantry surrendered at Arkansas Post, 152 of its men, mostly Germans and Poles, "took the oath" of allegiance to the United States. One German captain in the unit resigned his post because his company had virtually disappeared.[29]

Table 2. Frequency of common Anglo, German, and Hispanic surnames on
          Texas Union and Confederate muster rolls

	Total	Union	%	Confederate	%
Smith	1,896	13		1,883	
Jones	1,138	9		1,129	
Total Anglo	3,034	22	0.7	3,012	99.3
Schmidt	84	11		73	
Meyer/Meier	85	8		77	
Total German	169	19	11.2	150	88.8
Garcia	173	77		96	
Martinez/Martines	92	37		55	
Total Hispanic	265	114	43.0	151	57.0
State Total	163,121	4,200	2.6	158,921	97.4

With the end of the war, several Texas German towns, including New
Braunfels and New Ulm, were already celebrating July Fourth in 1865,
when it was otherwise mostly a freedmen's holiday, and Round Top
claims never to have interrupted its Fourth of July parade since 1851. Although Union occupation during Reconstruction is often portrayed as
a military dictatorship, Texas Germans obviously saw things differently.
One immigrant writing from Round Top complained in 1866 of "rowdy
gangs" targeting Germans and blacks and in May 1867 reported, "We are
still under martial law, which is no small irritation to the Americans, but
the 40 soldiers who are stationed here in Roundtop can hardly keep the
peace." Whatever their position during the war, New Braunfels residents
took a distinctly un-Southern view of the occupying federal troops in its
aftermath. When one Anglo Yankee from the Fifty-Ninth Illinois said
good-bye in December 1865, he noted in his diary, "Some of them shed
tears almost. I never felt so bad at leaving any place as that[,] except
home in 1861. Farewell Braunfels." Two days later he noted receiving
presents from New Braunfels friends, and two other Anglo members of
his regiment married local girls and settled permanently in the community. Similarly in Corpus Christi, a bourgeois German woman who had
expressed sympathy for the Confederacy, which her husband served as
a surveyor during the war, was happy to see her eldest daughter marry
a Boston Yankee, U.S. Lt. James Downing, in November 1867. Downing

and another Union officer who apparently also boarded with the family prepared a Christmas tree and gave children "many nice gifts."[30]

One thing that was apparent in my work with German immigrant letters nationwide was the low level of interest in developments in the postwar South once the Civil War was over. The one exception to this was in areas, both loyal and rebel, where there had been slavery. The letters of Georg Schwarting provide a good example. An antebellum immigrant to Texas who happened to be in Germany when the war broke out, he briefly joined the Union army on his return trip in 1864, but as a "bounty jumper" his loyalty was rather ambivalent. His reaction to the war's outcome, however, is unambiguous. He wrote his brother at the beginning of 1866: "The blood was not shed in vain, slavery has ceased. How the Negro will get along as a free laborer, time will tell. . . . anyhow they are free, and the 10 bottles of wine that I bet on it with Lönneker I gave away with no little delight. And when you get a chance, you can drink up some of it to the blessings of freedom and the health of the United States."[31]

An early immigrant slave owner named Bartels from Schwarting's German home town is mentioned frequently in his letters, for example, at Christmas of 1867: "With old Bartels everything is still like before, only their log cabins are increasingly falling into disrepair, and the two old folks now have to work their farm alone, cut off from the world and humanity, enriched from year to year only by a few new wrinkles in their faces." As it turns out, they were neither all alone nor burdened by poverty. A 1930 local history reported the following: The Bartelses were childless and had purchased a slave boy, who had learned their language and loved them like their own child. After Mr. Bartels died and his wife was bedridden with a stroke for two years until her death, she was faithfully cared for by this former slave and his wife. The Bartelses' will left their entire property to this freedman, Henry Williams, who in 1930 was reportedly still in possession of the farm and of a bundle of old German letters, which he greatly treasured.[32]

Stories like this, tinged with the magnolia myth, always evoke skepticism. But then it occurred to me that I had actually read some of Bartels's German letters at the Dolph Briscoe Center for American History in Austin. A brief e-mail exchange confirmed my hunch: "Gift of Annie and Henry Williams, Industry, Texas." Other parts of the story find verification in several manuscript census entries down to 1930, which all show Williams as a mortgage-free farm owner.[33]

During Reconstruction, Germans in the former slave states involved themselves in politics as never before, mostly on the Republican side. They included the familiar Carl Schurz in Missouri and Michael Hahn in Louisiana, but also the more obscure Christoph Barthel, who wrote from Baltimore in 1865: "I am the first German to ever have the honor of being elected to the Maryland Legislature," a Republican, as one might expect.[34] Also in Texas, Forty-eighter Edward Degener, who lost two sons in the Nueces Massacre, was elected as the state's first Republican congressman from a district heavily populated by Germans and Tejanos. But Degener lasted only one term, and the next Texas German elected to Congress, in 1874, was Democrat Gustav Schleicher, who in just a dozen years had undergone a remarkable transformation from communist to Confederate.[35]

The positions taken during Reconstruction by Germans who had worn the gray also give some insight into their wartime motivations. At the outbreak of the war there were some courageous Texas Germans who resisted the Confederacy and sometimes paid for it with their lives, and others such as Robert Voigt who voluntarily joined the Rebel ranks. But one suspects that the majority fell into the category of reluctant Confederates, who had doubts about the cause but could find no way to avoid military service. Louis Lehmann probably spoke for the majority when he wrote to his brother-in-law from his farm near Brenham in 1866: "As much as I hated to, I also had to enter the army and fight for a cause that I had never approved." Returning home after a stint as a Union prisoner, he sat out the last six months of the war with, as he put it, "intentional illness." In general Lehmann appeared pleased with the outcome of the war: "The existence of the United States stands more firmly than ever before, the stumbling block of slavery is cleared out of the way," an opinion that most of his German neighbors shared: "No element of the population rejoiced more about peace than the Germans, since they never had any interest in the cause anyhow."[36]

Lehmann's letters show at best an ambivalence toward blacks, but in the first Reconstruction legislature his county was represented by a freedman, Matt Gaines, in the state senate and in the lower house by a German, Lehmann's comrade Wilhelm Schlottmann, both of course

Republicans, or "Radicals." In the deliberations over a new school law, Schlottmann and a half-dozen other Germans stood united against a clause that would have required segregation in the schools.[37] According to textbooks, Reconstruction ended in 1877, or even earlier in Texas, but Washington County remained under Republican control through 1884, upheld by the majority of blacks, about half of the Germans, and a handful of courageous Anglo-Americans. As long as they held on, blacks continued to serve as deputy sheriffs and jurors and received a relatively fair shake in the local judicial system. The Democratic takeover in 1884 could only be achieved through violence and intimidation, and a Republican revival in 1886 was suppressed by stealing three ballot boxes in Republican precincts, lynching three African American Republicans, and running three white Republican leaders out of the country.[38] At least one of them was German, lawyer and publisher Carl Schutze. Two years after his departure, Schutze wrote to Lehmann's brother Julius, who had helped finance his newspaper: "[I] am afraid the *Mob* will put on the same show in this election that we went through 2 years ago. Violence and intimidation will once again be the main weapons used to intimidate the Negroes and if need be control the *Ballotboxes*. . . . I can imagine that these are just the rascals who are doing their best to play themselves up as friends of the Germans and stir them up against the Negroes, just as they stir up the Negroes against the Germans."[39] And Washington County was not unique; Randolph Campbell documented a similar pattern in neighboring Colorado County, where Republicans maintained local control till 1890, again through a coalition of Germans and blacks.[40]

There is no disputing that the German-black alliance in the Republican Party was to some extent a marriage of convenience, and that German racial idealism eroded over the decades. But in Missouri it persisted to some extent well into the twentieth century. In 1915 when St. Louis introduced by referendum a residential segregation law, Republican mayor Henry Kiel spoke out prominently against it, and most of the white votes in opposition came from Germans, especially socialists. The law was challenged in the courts by Charles Nagel, a Texas German who had fled with his father via Mexico during the Civil War.[41]

Another Missouri Republican, congressman Leonidas C. Dyer, sponsored an anti-lynching bill that actually passed the House in 1923, only to see it fail in the Senate. Although an Anglo-American, he had grown up among Missouri Germans, studied at a German Methodist college, and represented a St. Louis district with a considerable black constituency but an even larger German one. (In fact he was one of only two congressmen in the state who voted against Wilson's declaration of war.) Though not quite a smoking gun, this evidence suggests that the German-black alliance was still alive at this late date, or at the very least that German Americans were not violently opposed to black rights. Not even in Texas: the lone congressman in the Deep South to vote in favor of the Dyer bill was a Texas German Republican from a Seguin-San Antonio district, Harry Wurzbach.[42] But perhaps his Confederate ancestry protected him.

One additional indicator of relatively friendly relations with Germans is the number of blacks who learned the German language. For example, that was what Carl Schurz reported in 1867 when he visited my home town of Augusta, Missouri.[43] There were similar reports from Texas, though in the case of the notorious black Fredericksburger who during World War I was quoted as saying "Mir Deutscha müssa zusammahalta" (We Germans have to stick together), German was literally his mother tongue; he was of mixed parentage.[44] What is more surprising is to find similar patterns farther east in Texas, areas with a larger black population that was not so overwhelmingly German—for example, in Industry, the oldest German settlement in the state, about 15 miles south of Brenham. A woman from Bavaria whose M.A. I supervised at the University of Houston in the early 1990s interviewed an old black gentleman named Woody Williams, born around 1928, who still spoke fluent German.[45]

So when did Texas Germans join the political mainstream? In the 1920s when the Texas Klan was crusading against the German language, New Braunfels defiantly named a new school after Carl Schurz—not just a German but a Yankee general and a Republican politician. In the thirties, the town finally got around to erecting the obligatory Civil War statue on the town square, but rather than portraying a Rebel it was a generic soldier dedicated to both sides. When the Supreme Court passed the Brown decision, New Braunfels integrated its schools immediately in 1954, just like my little German home town in Missouri. Having largely avoided slavery a century earlier, Comal County had a black population of only 2 percent. But New Braunfels clearly stood apart; even ten years later, less than 6 percent of all African Americans in Texas were attending integrated schools.[46]

Maybe Texas Germans never quite joined the mainstream; instead, the mainstream joined them. When the Democrats replaced the Republicans as the party of civil rights in the era of LBJ, Hill Country Germans remained Republican for reasons having little to do with race, soon to be joined by the majority of white Texans, for reasons having a lot to do with race.[47] Normal white Texans at last! Unfortunately!

NOTES

1. The most balanced treatment of this issue is offered by Stanley S. McGowen, "Battle or Massacre? The Incident on the Nueces, August 10, 1862," *Southwestern Historical Quarterly* 104 (2000): 64–86.

2. Frank Wilson Kiel, "Treue der Union: Myths, Misrepresentations, and Misinterpretations," *Southwestern Historical Quarterly* 115 (January 2012): 283–92.

3. Not until a century later, in 1964, was any commemorative marker erected in Gainesville, and its text has a strongly Confederate slant. Since 2007 there has been an annual public commemoration, but no Texas historical marker. E-mail correspondence with Rick McCaslin, January 1, 2012.

4. Rudolph Leopold Biesele, *The History of the German Settlements in Texas, 1831–1861* (Austin: Press of Von Boeckmann-Jones, 1930), 206; Guido Ernst Ransleben, *A Hundred Years of Comfort in Texas: A Centennial History* (San Antonio, Tex.: Naylor, 1954), 80.

5. Alwyn Barr, "Records of the Confederate Military Commission in San Antonio, July 2–October 10, 1862," *Southwestern Historical Quarterly* 73 (1969): 246–68.

6. Slovanska Podporujici Jednota Statu Texas (Slavonic Benevolent Order of the State of Texas).

7. Marek Vlha, a Fulbright doctoral student from the Czech Republic who worked with me, brought this to my attention in 2009. In an e-mail correspondence of February 27, 2014, he provided more detail: There were three Votypka brothers conscripted to the Waul's Texas Legion, which had three heavily German companies. They deserted together with the sons of well-known Czech pioneer Josef Lidumil Lesikar, but two of them were captured. Thomas Votypka was shot and died in prison; his brother Jan was also captured but was lucky enough to escape from the prison. The elder Lesikar of Austin County was harassed for distributing an "abolitionist" Czech Republican newspaper published in St. Louis. *Bellville Countryman*, August 4, 1860.

8. Dennis C. Rousey, "Aliens in the WASP Nest: Ethnocultural Diversity in the Antebellum Urban South," *Journal of American History* 79 (1992): 152–64.

9. Terry G. Jordan, *German Seed in Texas Soil: Immigrant Farmers in Nineteenth-Century Texas* (Austin: University of Texas Press, 1966), 106–11, 180–85; a more succinct statement of the thesis, but without any additional evidence, is found in Jordan, "Germans and Blacks in Texas," in *States of Progress: Germans and Blacks in America over 300 Years,* ed. Randall Miller (Philadelphia: German Society of Pennsylvania, 1989), 89–97, 96 (quote).

10. Cornelia Küffner, "Texas-Germans' Attitudes toward Slavery: Biedermeier Sentiments and Class-Consciousness in Austin, Colorado, and Fayette Counties" (M.A. thesis, University of Houston, 1994), 17–20, 46–68, 110–14, 123–26.

11. Walter D. Kamphoefner, "Missouri Germans and the Cause of Union and Freedom," *Missouri Historical Review* 106 (2012): 115–36; Dennis C. Rousey, "Friends and Foes of Slavery: Foreigners and Northerners in the Old South," *Journal of Social History* 35 (2001): 373–96; the cities he investigates are Baton Rouge, Louisiana; Columbia, South Carolina; Montgomery, Alabama; Natchez, Mississippi; and Savannah, Georgia. Jeff Strickland, "How the Germans Became White Southerners: German Immigrants and African Americans in Charleston, South Carolina, 1860–1880," *Journal of American Ethnic History* 28 (2008): 52–69, table 3.

12. Heinz-Ulrich Kammeier, *"Halleluja, jetzt sehen wir Amerika": Auswanderung aus dem Kreis Lübbecke und Umgebung, 1836–1889* (Espelkamp: Verlag Marie L. Leidorf, 1994), 79–82, letters of February 25, 1861, and July 16, 1866. Kammeier identifies the letter writer as Franz Hinze, who only arrived in 1860, but research in the census and county tax lists confirms that it was more likely his son-in-law Christian Emshoff or the latter's father of the same name, who both arrived in Texas by 1850. Since Hinze later had the pastor write a letter for him, it is possible that Emshoff wrote a letter partially in Hinze's name and voice and partially in his own.

13. Bryan Edward Stone, *The Chosen Folks: Jews on the Frontiers of Texas* (Austin: University of Texas Press, 2010), 48.

14. Kamphoefner, "Missouri Germans," 117–18.

15. Ibid., 119–20.

16. Walter L. Buenger, *Secession and the Union in Texas* (Austin: University of Texas Press, 1984), 26–33, 91–94.

17. Ibid., 67, 151, 174–75.

18. Lawrence P. Knight, "Becoming a City and Becoming American: San Antonio, Texas, 1848–1861" (Ph.D. dissertation, Texas A&M University, 1997), 189–200, 267–81. The rural areas of the county had a slightly lower foreign-born percentage than the city.

19. La Grange *State Rights Democrat,* March 7 and 21, 1861. According to a report of November 13, 1863, in the *Neu Braunfelser Zeitung,* Grassmeyer was arrested as a traitor and taken to Houston, along with four Fayette County Anglos.

20. *Bellville Countryman,* February 27, March 17, 1861. The issue of January 16, 1861, shows that New Ulm, which voted 36–30 for secession in February, had gone 52–1 against in a preliminary election on December 22, 1860, to elect state delegates; countywide, German slaveholder and secessionist Knolle came in last among six candidates, further evidence of Anglo suspicions of Germans. Despite the name,

Shelby's, originally know as Roeder's Mill, was a largely German settlement in the extreme northwest corner of Austin County. See Biesele, *History,* 52–53.

21. Walter L. Buenger, "Secession and the Texas German Community: Editor Lindheimer vs. Editor Flake," *Southwestern Historical Quarterly* 82 (1979): 395–96; Selma Metzenthin-Raunick, "One Hundred Years *Neu Braunfelser Zeitung,*" *American-German Review* 19 (1953): 15–16; Karl J. R. Arndt and May E. Olson, *German-American Newspapers and Periodicals, 1732–1955* (Munich, 1965), 628.

22. Arndt and Olson, *German-American Newspapers,* 628; Metzenthin-Raunick, "One Hundred Years," 15–16; *Neu Braunfelser Zeitung,* June 6, July 3, 1863, for example.

23. Similar patterns show up in a statewide quantitative analysis of the secession referendum. Robin E. Baker and Dale Baum, "The Texas Voter and the Crisis of the Union, 1859–1862," *Journal of Southern History* 53 (1987): 395–420, esp. table 10.

24. Andrea Mehrländer, *The Germans of Charleston, Richmond, and New Orleans during the Civil War Period, 1850–1870* (Berlin: De Gruyter, 2011), 302. Except for this Confederacy-wide estimate, this work explicitly excludes the Lone Star State, because allegedly "Texas was never a part of the Deep South" (6).

25. National Park Service, U.S. Civil War Soldiers, 1861–1865 (Ancestry.com database on-line; original data: National Park Service, Civil War Soldiers and Sailors System, www.itd.nps.gov/cwss). An exact name search was conducted for each of these names, specifying first Confederate and then Union. Some entries in both rolls are duplicates, and there may not be the same degree of preservation of muster rolls from the two sides. So, although the figures may not reflect the exact proportions of a given group that served in one or the other army, there is no reason to believe this would introduce any ethnic biases. Smith is the most common Anglo-American name, and Jones is in fourth place. Schmidt is the most common German name, and Meyer/Meier is the fourth most frequent. Among Mexican names, Garcia is the most common, Martinez/Martines is in second place. All these names also have the virtue that they are not highly prone to misspelling. The same methodology was used in Kamphoefner, "Missouri Germans," 125–26, producing highly plausible results.

26. A nuanced discussion of the dilemmas facing Texas Germans is provided by Charles David Grear, *Why Texans Fought in the Civil War* (College Station: Texas A&M University Press, 2010), 135–55.

27. Ella Lonn, *Foreigners in the Confederacy* (Chapel Hill: University of North Carolina Press, 1940), 482–502. Online indexes to census and military records would greatly facilitate the task of verification. Some of the Texas units listed as ethnic by Lonn show very few German names on their muster rolls, whereas several companies that were almost exclusively German, such as Company I, Sixth Texas Infantry, and Marold's Company E, Sixteenth Texas Infantry, go unmentioned.

28. Robert Voigt, letters of November 12, 1862, February 11, 1863, translated in Walter D. Kamphoefner and Wolfgang Helbich, eds., *Germans in the Civil War: The Letters They Wrote Home* (Chapel Hill: University of North Carolina Press, 2006), 409–10, 417.

29. Voigt, letter of January 12, 1864, in ibid., 422–23; Charles Spurlin, ed., *The Civil War Diary of Charles A. Leuschner* (Austin: Eakin Press, 1992), 12–14, 60, 93–96. This aspect of the regiment's history goes unmentioned by Brett J. Derbes, "Sixth Texas Infantry," *Handbook of Texas Online*, Texas State Historical Association, www.tshaonline.org/handbook/online/articles/qks14.

30. Kamphoefner and Helbich, *Germans in the Civil War*, 447–48; Arnold Gates, ed., *The Rough Side of War: The Civil War Journal of Chesley A. Mosman, 1st Lieutenant, Company D, 59th Illinois Volunteer Infantry Regiment* (Garden City, N.Y.: Basin, 1987), 399–401; Bruce S. Cheeseman, ed., *Maria von Blücher's Corpus Christi: Letters from the South Texas Frontier, 1849–1879* (College Station: Texas A&M University Press, 2002), 122, 168, 170.

31. Kamphoefner and Helbich, *Germans in the Civil War*, 43–44, 446 (quote).

32. Nordamerika-Briefsammlung, Forschungsbibliothek Gotha; C. W. Schmidt, *Footprints of Five Generations* (New Ulm, Tex.: n.p., 1930), 88.

33. Bartels Papers, Dolph Briscoe Center for American History, University of Texas at Austin.

34. *Dictionary of Missouri Biography*, ed. Lawrence O. Christensen et al. (Columbia: University of Missouri Press, 1999), s.v. "Schurz, Carl"; "Michael Hahn," *KnowLA Encyclopedia of Louisiana*, Louisiana Endowment for the Humanities, www.knowla.org/entry.php?rec=940; Kamphoefner and Helbich, *Germans in the Civil War*, 75.

35. Anne W. Hooker, "Degener, Edward," *Handbook of Texas Online*, Texas State Historical Association, www.tshaonline.org/handbook/online/articles/fde28; and Hubert Plummer Heinen, "Schleicher, Gustav," *Handbook of Texas Online*, Texas State Historical Association, www.tshaonline.org/handbook/online/articles/fsc09.

36. Louis Lehmann was born in 1824 in Havelburg, Brandenburg, where he took his Abitur, and emigrated to Texas with his parents and siblings in 1849. By 1860 he was a farmer worth $3,400 and was married with three children. He was one of the founders of a Lutheran parish near Brenham in Washington County, Texas. For letter of January 1866, see Kamphoefner and Helbich, *Germans in the Civil War*, 471–74. Lehmann's translated letters have subsequently been published in their entirety by a descendant: Edmund Louis Burnett, *Civil War Letters of Louis Lehmann: With Alexander Terrell's and James B. Likens' Texas Cavalry Regiments, 1863–1864* (Hillsboro, Tex.: Hill College Press, 2011).

37. Wilfred O. Dietrich, *The Blazing Story of Washington County*, rev. ed. (Wichita Falls, Tex., 1973), 171–74; *House Journals of the 12th Legislature of the State of Texas. First Session. 1870* (Austin, Tex., 1870), 803.

38. *Dallas Herald*, August 20, 1870, identified radical members of the legislature by whether they voted for mixed-race schools. Besides Schlottmann, among the thirty-five voting in favor were men named Prissick, Schlickum, Zapp, and Zoeller; the thirty-three nays included one Germanic name, Schutze. Donald G. Nieman, "Black Political Power and Criminal Justice: Washington County, Texas, 1868–1884," *Journal of Southern History* 55 (1989): 391–420. Gillespie County, where Fredericksburg is located, voted Republican in every twentieth-century presidential

election except 1932 and when local boy LBJ ran in 1964. Walter Dean Burnham, *Presidential Ballots, 1836–1892* (Baltimore, Md.: Arno Press, 1955); E. E. Robinson, *The Presidential Vote, 1896–1932* (Stanford, Calif.: Stanford University Press, 1947).

39. Kamphoefner and Helbich, *Germans in the Civil War,* 475–76, n. 42.

40. Randolph B. Campbell, *Grass Roots Reconstruction in Texas, 1865–1880* (Louisiana State University Press, 1997), 27–62, 220, 222, 229.

41. James Neal Primm, *Lion of the Valley: St. Louis, Missouri, 1764–1980,* 3rd ed. (St. Louis: Missouri History Museum Press, 1998), 410–14. Ward-level election returns are reported in the *St. Louis Post Dispatch,* March 1, 1916, 3. A quantitative investigation based on 1910 census population data shows that, as expected, the strongest opposition was by black voters, but a regression analysis shows that Germans were less inclined than other whites to support segregation. On Nagel, see Kamphoefner and Helbich, *Germans in the Civil War,* 394–403.

42. Jeffery A. Jenkins, Justin Peck, and Vesla M. Weaver, "Between Reconstructions: Congressional Action on Civil Rights, 1891–1940," *Studies in American Political Development* 24 (2010): 66–77. An Anglo-Texan, Hatton Sumners, was one of the main opponents of the law. See also George C. Rable, "The South and the Politics of Antilynching Legislation, 1920–1940," *Journal of Southern History* 51 (1985): 201–20.

43. Joseph Schafer, ed. and trans., *The Intimate Letters of Carl Schurz, 1841–1869* (Madison: Wisconsin Historical Society, 1928), 379–83.

44. Marcus Nicolini, *Deutsch in Texas* (Münster: Lit Verlag, 2004), 63, 217; additional research in manuscript census material, plus e-mail and phone conversations with the late Arthur Rode, Fredericksburg.

45. Küffner, "Texas-Germans' Attitudes," 8–9.

46. Charles David Grear, "'All Eyes of Texas Are on Comal County': German Texans' Loyalty during the Civil War and World War I," in *Texans and War: New Interpretations of the State's Military History,* ed. Alexander Mendoza and Charles David Grear (College Station: Texas A&M University Press, 2012), 133, 140; Gene B. Preuss, "Within Those Walls: The African American School and Community in Lubbock and New Braunfels, Texas," *Sound Historian* (1998): 36–43; U.S. History Transparency Set (Lexington, Mass.: D. C. Heath, 1996), vol. 2, table 43.

47. Andrew Greeley, *Why Can't They Be Like Us? America's White Ethnic Groups* (New York: E. P. Dutton, 1971), 68–69, 73–74, 203, 206, finds that German American college graduates were the least likely among the ethnic groups questioned in 1968 to ascribe racial unrest in the cities to white racism; Catholic Irish came in second only to Jews in the degree of sympathy for blacks expressed, the diametric opposite of the situation in the Civil War era. Not coincidentally, the Irish had the highest Democratic affiliation; Germans the lowest.

6

"Although We Are the Last Soldiers"

CITIZENSHIP, IDEOLOGY, AND TEJANO UNIONISM

Omar S. Valerio-Jiménez

In April 1861 a group of forty Mexican Texans led by Antonio Ochoa seized control of a southern precinct in Zapata County and attempted to prevent county officials from pledging their support for the Confederacy. They claimed to owe no allegiance to the state or to the Confederacy. County judge Isidro Vela, a prominent Tejano landowner, intervened and persuaded the rebels to withdraw.[1] Days later Ochoa and his men presented Vela with a *pronunciamento* (proclamation) against the Confederacy and asked him to forward it to federal officials. Alarmed, Vela and Henry Redmond, an Englishman who had married Tejana Refugia Díaz, requested aid from nearby Webb County. Confederate soldiers from Webb County led by Capt. Matt Nolan joined Sheriff Pedro Díaz and Judge Vela to surprise Ochoa's men at Rancho Clareño, killing combatants and noncombatants alike in what became known as the Clareño Massacre. Tejano Unionists would later seek to avenge these deaths by attacking Redmond's fortified rancho complex. Reporting on this attack, an Anglo-American would claim "not a single citizen of the county came to our assistance." Subsequent news stories confirmed that most Zapata County residents sided with the Union or remained neutral. Their actions were part of the multiple ways that Tejanos expressed resistance and dissent to their county and state officeholders' support for the Confederacy.[2]

Dismissing the Unionists as ignorant criminal opportunists, local Confederates delegitimized Tejano grievances. Politicians and journalists were quick to characterize them as "bandits" and "assassins" from Mexico. According to Judge Vela, Ochoa had "collected all the thieves,

murderers and assassins of Guerrero." Since Guerrero was located in
Mexico opposite Zapata County, Vela's accusation implied that Ochoa's
troops were not Tejanos but rather Mexican nationals. Yet these men
had asked Vela to forward their *pronunciamento* to U.S. federal officials,
whom they believed were "a few miles on the other side of Bexar," according to Redmond. This led Redmond to conclude that it was "hard
to say how far their ignorance will lead them." Ochoa's supporters, however, were far from ignorant; rather, they refused to continue accepting
the patronizing control exercised by the county's political clique, including Judge Vela, Redmond, and Sheriff Díaz.[3]

Several historians have echoed the view that Tejanos were not aware
of the issues over which the Civil War was fought. Throughout Texas,
Tejanos owned sixty slaves in 1860, but most of them were held far from
the border. Only fourteen slaves (all owned by Anglos) lived in the border counties of Cameron, Starr, and Hidalgo in 1860. Such low numbers are not surprising, because slaves could easily escape into Mexico.
These statistics, scholars have argued, demonstrate that slavery did not
play a major part in the daily lives of Mexican Texans. According to one
scholar, Tejanos did not join the Union army for the "same high ideals as
[John L.] Haynes and [Edmund J.] Davis." Instead, this historian argues,
they joined because the "army gave them a sense of self-esteem and an
opportunity to strike back at their old political enemies in Texas."[4]

Scholars have also argued that Tejanos chose sides according to their
socioeconomic class because they lacked an "ideological orientation . . .
towards the conflict." According to this view, the wealthy chose the Confederacy because they had alliances with the Democratic Party and with
white slave owners, whereas the poor chose the Union because of their
resentment against the "growing Anglo-Texan political and economic
dominance of their communities." This resentment was particularly true
for the South Texas border region, where a history of racial antagonisms
fueled the desire of poor Mexican Texans to seek revenge on the largely
pro-Confederate white minority by joining the Union troops.[5] Yet this
explanation for Tejanos' involvement assumes that they were motivated
only by economic factors and political resentments and not by ideology.
It also fails to account for the number of poor Confederate supporters or elite and middling Union backers. Another historian argues that
"the mass of Tejanos could not identify with the philosophical origins

of the war."[6] Speaking of residents of Laredo, yet another scholar states that "most of the townspeople probably did not have any expectations of owning slaves, had never heard of abolitionists, and did not understand the economic and political rivalry between the North and the South."[7]

These interpretations are puzzling. Some might be a result of undue influence by primary sources authored by Anglo-Texan residents who held patronizing views of Tejanos. Other scholars might have offered such historical interpretations after failing to find a significant number of written sources authored by Mexican Texans. Whatever the reasons, these interpretations discount the ability of Tejanos to understand political issues in the United States as well as the reality that many Mexican Texans acted on such beliefs.

Contrary to these interpretations, I argue that Mexican Texans chose to participate in the sectional conflict because they understood the reasons over which the Civil War was fought. In this essay, I focus on the experiences of Tejanos along the South Texas border region (see map). Although slaves were not a large part of the border region's labor force, their actions to seek freedom directly affected local residents. Some Mexican Texans, for example, helped slaves flee across the international border, others captured runaway slaves in Texas, and still others pursued runaway slaves into Mexico and returned them to the United States. After the outbreak of the Civil War, Tejanos and Mexican nationals joined both the Confederate and Union armies. Most of the Union and Confederate recruits were illiterate laborers, farmers, and herdsmen, but their numbers also included shoemakers and masons as well as literate former officeholders and rancheros. Approximately 11 percent of the troops were literate, leading some historians to believe that these recruits failed to understand the ideological motivations for the war.[8] But was literacy necessary to understand the issues that triggered the war? Were poor whites in the backcountry of West Virginia or African Americans in Georgia sufficiently literate? Moreover, did these soldiers need to be literate to understand the intricacies of the conflict? If not, then why do scholars insist on judging Tejanos and Mexican nationals by such standards?

Ochoa's men left few written records, so their motivations are difficult to discern. Nevertheless, their actions offer some clues. Journalists reported that they had allegedly threatened to "kill the gringos" in the

The Lower Rio Grande Valley at the time of the Civil War. Cartography by Matthew Murphy, Department of Geography, Texas State University. Copyright © 2016 by the University of Oklahoma Press.

county. These reports might have been the exaggerated fears of Anglos, who were vastly outnumbered by Mexican Texans in Zapata County and most of the border counties. Yet the Unionists' actions discount the fear of a so-called race war because Ochoa's men also targeted Tejano pro-Confederate officeholders. Rather than seeking to foment a race war, the Unionists were likely venting their frustration at the powerful

political control exercised by the *americano* and Tejano elite. The racial and class divisions along the border during the Civil War era became fittingly demonstrated by the armed conflict in Zapata County.
The county's population (which boasted the largest percentage of Tejanos along the border) consisted of numerous small landowners and
agricultural workers along with a few elite Tejanos allied with wealthy
americano merchants and landowners. Among the elite were Judge
Vela and Redmond, another large landowner. The political elite in the
border counties exercised a strong influence through their control of
local offices. In January 1861 the voters of Zapata County had joined the
citizens of Cameron, Hidalgo, Starr, and Webb Counties in voting overwhelmingly for secession.[9] Zapata County recorded no ballots opposing
secession, confirming the power of elite merchants and landowners to
control elections. This power was manifested in Judge Vela's threat to
fine anyone who did not support secession; he also arrested those who
refused to vote. The vote, however, masked the political divisions within
Zapata County, which were manifested three months later with Ochoa's
rebellion in support of the Union.[10]

The rebels led by Ochoa had also threatened to hang Sheriff Díaz and
to seize the county's funds. According to a local *americano*, "Fifty men
of this county had armed themselves, and organized for the avowed
purpose of keeping the county officers from taking the oath of office
prescribed by the Convention. They had declared that they owed no allegiance to the State or Confederate States, and that they would not obey
or respect the authorities holding office under either." Had these Unionists merely been displeased with the county's political machine, Ochoa's
men would have little reason to mention local officeholders' support for
the Confederacy. A more nuanced reading of the Unionists' proclamation and actions reveals that they understood the ideological issues involved in the secession vote. Ochoa's men opposed the county's vote for
secession and wanted to avoid fighting for a cause they did not support.
Given the proclamation's various demands, the Unionists' motivations
were more complicated than merely striking back at Zapata County's
political elite.[11]

After Ochoa's uprising, local recruits swelled the Union ranks. Some
joined as a result of Union recruitment; others enlisted for complex
reasons. Among the Union supporters were Teodoro Zamora, a former

Hidalgo County judge, Octaviano Zapata, a small landowner in Zapata County, and several men allied with Juan Cortina. Some of these men were based in Mexico; others lived in Texas. Zamora had joined Juan Cortina's troops in 1859 during a six-month rebellion to protest various injustices and the denial of civil rights to Mexican Texans. Afterward, he joined other Tejanos who abandoned the United States because they believed that its government could not guarantee their rights as citizens. When the American Civil War broke out, Zamora lived on his mother's ranch in Tamaulipas and continued to support Cortina (who had similarly left Texas for Mexico). Unionists were soon harassing Confederate cotton shipments and engaging in cross-border raids. In December 1862, two hundred Tejano Unionists demonstrated their resentment against Zapata County's political elite by capturing Judge Vela at his ranch and hanging him from a tree. They left a note warning others not to remove the body unless they wished to suffer the same fate. The political divisions embodied in these conflicts reflected the Tejano community's economic fissures, resentment over political subordination, and ideological differences over slavery.[12]

Tejanos did understand the ideological reasons for the Civil War, but like other participants they did not have a uniform reason for taking sides or remaining neutral. Tejano participation on the Confederate side was at least partly driven by the circumstances of Texas's economic, political, and military roles in the Confederacy. In part, Mexican Texans' reactions to the Civil War were rooted in the relationships Mexicans had established with African Americans in the *villas del norte* (northern towns along the Rio Grande) during the Spanish and Mexican periods. These relationships continued to develop and strengthen after U.S. annexation in the mid-nineteenth century. Ultimately, Mexican Texans who supported the Union army did so for various reasons including anti-slavery sentiment, opposition to pro-Confederate local politicians, and as expressions of U.S. citizenship. Tejanos also invoked their military service as a claim to U.S. citizenship throughout the war, and though they endured hardships as soldiers they were not politically rewarded afterward.

During the Civil War, the South Texas border region became important economically because the Confederacy began exporting cotton across the Rio Grande—one of the few areas that Union forces did not blockade. Cotton initially flowed out of a Texas port near Brownsville, but Confederate officials subsequently shifted operations to Matamoros because of pressure from federal forces. The Confederacy used the port of Bagdad, along the beach in Matamoros, to export cotton from Texas, Louisiana, and some states east of the Mississippi River and to import manufactured goods and war supplies.[13] The population of Matamoros, which had decreased to about 5,000 from 25,000 because of Mexico's war against French occupation, rose quickly as cotton exports to England and New York increased. Bagdad also grew in the economic boom, its population reaching approximately 15,000.[14]

The strategic importance of the Rio Grande area encouraged both the Confederacy and the Union to recruit and draft ethnic Mexican men regardless of their citizenship status. The recruitment occurred on both sides of the international boundary as Confederate and Union agents attempted to obtain as many able-bodied men as they could from the ethnic Mexican communities along the border. An estimated 2,550 Mexican Texans joined the Confederate troops and approximately 960 became Union soldiers. More ethnic Mexican men joined the Confederate army than the Union army because Texas sided with the Confederacy and the state implemented a draft law. The forced conscription of Mexican Texans and Mexican nationals increased so much that it depleted the number of cart men and seriously threatened to curtail trade between Texas and Mexico. Many of the Civil War soldiers came from the South Texas border region, with Bexar, Refugio, and Webb Counties supplying the most ethnic Mexican Confederate troops and Cameron, Hidalgo, and Nueces Counties contributing the majority of Tejano soldiers for the Union.[15]

The first armed action in favor of the Union by Mexican Texans occurred on April 12, 1861, when Ochoa's men rebelled in Zapata County. Union soldiers, unaware of the Civil War's end, also fought one of the last battles of the war, on May 13, 1865, near Brownsville over one month after the Robert E. Lee had surrendered in Virginia. Although most of the soldiers were concentrated in South Texas, ethnic Mexican troops fought battles throughout the state, in neighboring Louisiana and New Mexico, and as far away as Virginia and Georgia.[16]

Relations between Mexicans and escaped African American slaves in the Lower Rio Grande border region dated to the early nineteenth century. African American slaves began escaping into New Spain's sparsely settled northern borderlands before the Adams-Onís Treaty (1819) formalized the boundary between the United States and New Spain. The flow of fugitive slaves into Tamaulipas increased after President Vicente Guerrero's decree outlawing slavery in 1829, which exempted Texas. Their flight into the interior of Mexico and the state legislature's moves toward abolition undermined slavery in Texas and motivated slave-owning Texans to support separatist rebellion in 1835.[17]

After the successful Texas rebellion in 1836, tensions increased as Mexico refused to recognize the independence of Texas and made several unsuccessful military attempts to retake control of the separatist republic. Moreover, tensions were further increased when Mexican government and military officials encouraged runaway slaves to flee to Mexico. In the ensuing years, prominent Anglo-Texans, including the Texas Republic's president Sam Houston, learned that their runaway slaves were enjoying life in the *villas del norte*. The efforts of bondsmen and bondswomen to flee, according to historian Sean Kelley, indicate that Texas's slave communities had gradually associated Mexico with nonslavery and had invested the border with "liberationist significance." In the ensuing years, reports about runaway slaves enjoying life in Mexico confirmed this view. A prisoner in the aftermath of the ill-fated Mier Expedition, Gen. Thomas J. Green, encountered Tom and Esau, the former bondsmen of President Houston. He bore witness to the respected status of these two well-known runaway slaves. They had acculturated to Mexican society and gained wide acceptance, as evident by the Mexican army general who served as godfather at one of their weddings. Both criticized their former master and clearly appreciated the freedom they now enjoyed.[18]

Fugitive slaves living in Mexico nurtured positive relations with Mexicans. They lived, worked, and appeared in public throughout various Mexican border towns. Several former slaves married Mexican nationals and used their skills to obtain financial security. This positive relationship with Tejanos' relatives and friends in Mexico undoubtedly fueled anti-slavery feelings. African Americans, including some who had been former slaves in the United States, became part of the skilled labor force of the *villas del norte* in the early nineteenth century. In an 1832 judicial dispute in Matamoros, for example, municipal officials charged one African American immigrant, Enrique Viudy, with murder for shooting and killing another, his brother-in-law José Jorge Orr. Viudy was a thirty-five-year-old barber from New York who had assumed the name Antonio Guadalupe Refugio after being baptized in Matamoros. He subsequently married a local non-elite *mexicana*, as did Orr, who was a local craftsman. In the court testimony, their Mexican in-laws and friends described their acculturation to and acceptance within local society.[19]

Although a few Mexican Texans captured runaway slaves in Mexico, most border residents did not cooperate with slave owners despite bounties of $200–$500 on runaways. Opportunities to collect such bounties occurred regularly; local newspapers routinely carried notices posted by slave owners who suspected that runaways were traveling toward the Mexican border. For Southerners who visited the border region, the friendly relationship between ethnic Mexicans and African Americans, including fugitive slaves, was unsettling and led several Anglo-Americans to comment disapprovingly. "This admiration for negroes somewhat disgusted me with the Mexicans," wrote newcomer Teresa Vielé while visiting Rio Grande City, "for in spite of philanthropy, Christian charity, and liberal views, I do not believe that the colored and white races can ever by any possibility amalgamate to an equality!"[20]

Slaves continued to arrive in the *villas del norte* during the U.S. Army's buildup for the U.S.-Mexican War. Officers in Gen. Zachary Taylor's army reported that three slaves had fled in 1845 as the army marched toward the Rio Grande because "every inducement is offered by the enemy."[21] Runaway slaves owned by army officers continued to escape into Mexico in subsequent months. Moreover, the aid Mexicans provided to runaway slaves created resentment among Anglo-Americans. The appraiser general summed up the hostility between Anglo-Texans and Mexican nationals as a result of the asylum provided to runaway slaves: "The frequent escape of slaves from the American side of the Rio Grande into Mexico, and the folly of any attempt to recapture them—although you often met your own property in Matamoros—has been one of the excitants of bad feeling between the citizens of Mexico and those on the frontier; consequently, all the household drudgery and menial services are performed by Mexican servants."[22]

Like Mexican employers whose indebted laborers fled into the United States, Anglo-American slave owners became frustrated with the lack of an extradition treaty that would return runaway slaves from Mexico. Laborers who fled across the river dismantled labor controls in each nation. Along the U.S.-Mexico border, indebted laborers and runaway slaves shared a desire to obtain a better life by crossing an international boundary that was meant to contain them.[23] Fleeing across the Rio Grande was one of the "weapons of the weak" available to some of the most downtrodden workers on each side of the international boundary.

Elsewhere in Texas, Tejanos' sympathies for African Americans were manifested in various ways. On some plantations, Mexican Texans developed friendships while working alongside African American slaves. Others took considerable risks in assisting runaways or rescuing slaves and transporting them to Mexico for safety. Incensed at Tejanos' aid to runaway slaves, *americanos* in Guadalupe County passed a resolution prohibiting "Mexican peons" from entering the county "because of their alleged sympathy with bondspeople."[24] Because slave flight to Mexico was a prominent worry for the state's slave owners, as Andrew Torget explains in his essay in this volume, Tejanos' possible aid to runaways was particularly unsettling. Commenting on Anglo-Americans' punitive measures against Tejanos, Frederick Law Olmsted wrote: "Wherever slavery in Texas has been carried in a wholesale way, into the neighborhood of Mexicans, it has been found necessary to treat them [Mexican Texans] as outlaws. Guaranteed by the Treaty of Guadalupe Hidalgo, equal rights with all other citizens of the United States and of Texas, the whole native population of county after county has been driven, by the formal proceedings of substantial planters, from its homes, and forbidden, on pain of no less punishment than instant death, to return to the vicinity of the plantations."[25]

Along the South Texas border, Tejanos' sympathies for African Americans were most evident in Hidalgo County, where intermarriage became common. In the 1850s, Matilde Hicks, of French and Cherokee ancestry, and Silvia Hector, a former slave, arrived in Hidalgo County accompanying their husbands, Nathaniel Jackson, a Cherokee, and John F. Webber, a white man who settled in the area. Their ranches became refuge communities for escaped and freed slaves before the Civil War. As more African Americans arrived, the number of mixed-race and black offspring increased, augmenting the community's *mestizaje* (racial intermixture). From 1852 to 1888, the community witnessed eleven unions between African Americans and Mexican Texans (five women and six men) and five marriages between African American women and Anglo-American men. In addition, there were ten marriages of mixed-raced individuals and five endogamous unions of African Americans. Unlike marriages between *americanos* and Tejanas, the marriages between African Americans and Tejanos did not involve the elite. Although some unions violated the state's anti-miscegenation laws, the spouses' class background partly explains why local authorities did not prosecute them. Poor couples were likely not prone to inheritance disputes, which triggered appeals to anti-miscegenation statutes. Additionally, Anglo-Americans considered poor Tejanos to be nonwhite and therefore not subject to enforcement. Moreover, local officials were unlikely to apply anti-miscegenation prohibitions to marriages that local residents readily accepted as part of Mexican cultural tradition. Finally, there is no recorded instance of the reenslavement of the former slaves who lived in Hidalgo County, which suggests that they had become strongly integrated into local society.[26]

In addition to their anti-slavery and racial views, some Tejanos were surely motivated to oppose the Confederacy by their experience of being treated as second-class citizens by local and state pro-Confederate officeholders. Anglo-Americans' political views were consistent with their positions on citizenship. They distinguished the residents whom they believed belonged in their communities from those who did not belong through their use of the term "citizen." References in newspaper advertisements and editorials described "meetings of citizens" for purposes of holding elections, organizing militias to defend towns, and promoting commerce.[27] The implied meaning of "citizen" was white male resident. The selective use of this term to refer to Anglo-American residents racially marked Mexican Texans as *noncitizens* and denied them membership in the local community and the nation.[28] In written observations, *americanos* rarely distinguished Mexican nationals with Mexican citizenship from Mexican Texans with American citizenship. Instead, they referred to both groups simply as Mexicans. It seems that Anglo-Americans found it convenient not to distinguish between the two groups, leaving Mexican Texans' citizenship ambiguous and allowing *americanos* to respect or deny Tejanos' citizenship on a case-by-case basis. Occasionally Anglo-Americans nominally acknowledged Tejanos as citizens when a particular action convinced them an individual provided a service to their community. For example, *americanos* accepted Mexican Texans as U.S. citizens when the latter defended white supremacy by upholding slavery. Only a few qualified for this distinction, so the majority of Tejanos could be conveniently suspected of being citizens of Mexico.

Like Civil War soldiers elsewhere in the United States, Tejanos were undoubtedly influenced to join the Confederacy or Union by the decisions of their family and friends as well as by the promised soldiers' pay. Laredo's Benavideses, large landowners and perennial politicians, were fervent slavery supporters who recruited others for the Confederacy. Cortina, Ochoa, and Zapata were equally crucial in recruiting family and friends to the Union cause. The political ties that Tejanos had established with prominent Anglo-American Unionists also played a role. John L. Haynes and Edmund J. Davis nurtured social and political ties to Tejanos during their political and military careers along the South Texas border. Both Haynes and Davis opposed secession and crossed into Mexico after Texas joined the Confederacy.

Haynes and Davis were instrumental in persuading President Abraham Lincoln to allow the Union to recruit along the U.S.-Mexican border.[29] As Carl Moneyhon's essay in this volume explains, Davis underwent an unlikely transformation from a Democratic Party stalwart to an active Unionist and supporter of African American suffrage. After moving to the border region in the aftermath of the U.S.-Mexican War, Davis served as inspector and deputy collector of customs at Laredo between 1849 and 1853. Beginning in 1853, he served as a district attorney in Brownsville and later received an appointment as judge of the Twelfth Judicial District, also in Brownsville. Relying on his prewar contacts, Colonel Davis recruited several influential Tejanos and *mexicanos* into the Union army and led the First Texas U.S. Cavalry.[30]

Haynes was a veteran of the U.S.-Mexican War who served as Starr County clerk before becoming a state legislator. Subsequently, he joined the Union forces and rose to the rank of colonel in the Second Texas U.S. Cavalry. Haynes depended on longtime acquaintances such as Antonio Abad Díaz and George Treviño to recruit *mexicanos* such as Cesario Falcón and José Lino Hinojosa to his command.[31] The U.S. consul in

Matamoros, Leonard Pierce, assisted Davis and Haynes in establishing contact with Union leaders in New Orleans and in enlisting troops. Their success led the Confederate commander stationed at Fort Brown to complain bitterly to Mexican officials in an unsuccessful attempt to stop Union recruiting in Mexico.[32]

As in civilian life, *mexicanos* faced discrimination once in the Confederate or Union army. The Union's signing bonus of land and money undoubtedly attracted some recruits from both sides of the border, but it was not the deciding factor in motivating enlistments. Although Tejano Confederates included volunteers and draftees, the promised soldiers' pay was probably an initial inducement. For Unionists, the signing bonus was one hundred pesos in gold and 50 acres of Texas land for single men or 150 acres for married men. Nevertheless, while serving in segregated units under Anglo-American commanding officers, recruits suffered from insufficient clothing, ammunition, and armaments. Language barriers magnified their problems. In an effort to remedy their mistreatment, some Mexican Unionists objected to the appointment of a monolingual English-speaking officer to their regiment, but they were unsuccessful. The mistreatment included each army's failure to compensate soldiers. Confederate officials neglected to pay one local unit for nine months. This problem exacerbated Tejanos' existing poverty-stricken conditions. Many families, for example, had crossed into Mexico to escape the violence associated with the war. With their lands on the Texas side unattended, these refugee families had little recourse but to sell their small herds of livestock to obtain money for necessities.[33] Both Tejano Confederate and Union troops suffered for months from lack of payment and inadequate supplies throughout their service, so money could not have been the sole motivating factor for their enlistments. Moreover, why would Mexican Texans continue to enlist if other recruits were not receiving payment for their military service and suffering other hardships?

Mexican Texans' claims to U.S. citizenship provided an additional motivation for their decision to support the Union. As U.S. citizens, some undoubtedly felt a desire to support the nation during the Civil War. Moreover, Tejanos might have been motivated by the frequent attacks on their citizenship from local Anglo-American officeholders and journalists. Generally, Tejanos were subject to having their loyalty suspected and their understanding of democratic values—the Southern version, at any rate—dismissed as lacking.

One of the rare times Anglo-Americans lavished praise on Tejanos was when they helped return runaway slaves. On these occasions, *americanos* depicted Mexican Texans as good citizens who had respect for the law. In 1860, for example, the Brownsville *Ranchero* described two captures of runaway slaves by Tejanos, whom the newspaper recognized as "our Mexican citizens" and congratulated by observing that their actions were "deserving of merited praise." It also offered qualified praise for Mexican Texans, arguing that "all must admit that *some* of our Mexican population *are of service* to the community at large, as well *as being law-abiding citizens.*"[34] A year later four slaves escaped from the custody of Maj. S. Peters, who lived on Padre Island in the vicinity of Corpus Christi. Peters offered a $250 reward for their capture. This time, an unnamed Mexican man captured the runaways near the town of Carricitos and received congratulatory praise from the local newspaper.[35] Similar admiration was offered by an Anglo-American Laredo resident who wrote a letter to the editor describing the exploits of Santos Benavides, a wealthy Tejano landowner. Benavides had crossed into Mexico to retrieve runaway slaves. The letter sought to correct the false impressions, the writer explained, "so generally entertained regarding the portion of our fellow-citizens of Mexican origin." Instead, some Tejanos were good citizens, he argued, since they were devoted to upholding "the interests of the country and the welfare of its citizens."[36] Ironically, Mexican Texans "won" acceptance as legitimate American citizens when they denied freedom to African American slaves who had no similar recourse to citizenship.

Given the treatment they generally received as second-class citizens, it is not surprising that Tejanos attempted to avoid being conscripted into an army supported by local and state politicians who were responsible for their disfranchisement. In 1863, after Texas instituted the Confederate draft for all "white men between the ages of eighteen and thirty-five," conscription agents scoured the countryside looking for able-bodied men. Casting aside their concerns about Mexican Texans' racial status and eligibility for citizenship, Confederate recruiters had no misgivings about considering them "white" citizens for draft purposes. Alerted to the recruiters' intentions, many Tejanos fled to Mexico. Despite this large-scale departure, agents managed to conscript over three hundred men (including some Mexican nationals). Others avoided conscription by using an excuse that manipulated Anglo-American prejudices. Frustrated about not finding any eligible recruits in areas that had previously polled many Mexican Texan voters, a conscription agent wrote, "Nearly every other man I met claimed to be a citizen of Mexico, and therefore exempt from conscription." To avoid the draft, Tejanos strategically denied their membership in a society that often did not uphold their citizenship rights. Not only did Mexican Texans cross the physical international border to escape conscription, but they also intentionally blurred the figurative border of citizenship. Like people living in national borderlands elsewhere, Tejanos employed their ambiguous national identity to their advantage.[37]

Mexican nationals who supported the Union also had a variety of reasons for doing so. Their Tejano friends and relatives who were Unionists undoubtedly motivated some *mexicanos* to enlist in the Union army or in other ways provide support. The complexity of the situation is illustrated by the case of Teodoro Zamora. In 1863, Col. Edmund Davis met Zamora at the mouth of the Rio Grande and offered him a commission as a lieutenant in the Union army. Several years earlier, Zamora had served as a judge of Hidalgo County, but later he had escaped to Mexico after joining Juan Cortina's rebels in 1859. After pondering Davis's offer, Zamora refused to become a Union soldier because he would have to renounce his allegiance to Cortina and accept the U.S. annexation of Texas. Zamora subsequently wrote a letter to President Lincoln in which he explained his decision not to become a Union soldier. According to historian Alice Baumgartner, Zamora did not want to renounce his allegiance to Cortina and he would not join an army that had conquered his people in a war of territorial expansion. He wrote that Tejanos remembered "what we should have forgotten: when those men (americanos) came to assault, murder, hang, rape, burn, and rob us . . . to make us disappear from our homes and lands until we were conquered." Although Zamora acknowledged that Lincoln was trying to obtain the support of Cortina and his followers by inviting them to join the Union army, he could not accept such an offer because his "cause was not motivated by money, nor caprice, nor grievance, but by the justice that God gave to

Among the Tejanos who served in the Union's Second Texas Cavalry were Quarter-master Sgt. José Lino Hinojosa and his brother-in-law Sgt. González, circa 1863–64. Courtesy of Margaret H. McAllen Memorial Archives, Museum of South Texas History, Edinburg, Texas.

all civilized nations."[38] Zamora, like some Mexican government officials, believed that the American Civil War was the United States's just punishment for its annexation of Mexico's northern territory. Such elegant rhetoric and logic do not support the characterization that *mexicanos* and Tejanos were devoid of ideology and did not understand the war's causes. Nevertheless, although neither Zamora nor Cortina would officially join the Union army, they both supported the Union by attacking Confederates and allying with Tejano Unionists.

Mexican Texans who supported the Union were undoubtedly influenced by the negative characterization of the Tejano community that appeared in English-language newspapers published along the border. Staffed by pro-Confederate journalists, the local press was extremely partisan and racist in its coverage of political developments. During the Civil War, the press denounced Tejanos in Webb County as pro-Union even though many had risked their lives for the Confederacy. Post-election comments reveal deep-seated racist views that excluded many Tejanos from political participation. In 1863, after Laredo provided the swing votes to defeat the state representative candidate favored by *americanos,* editors expressed hostility toward local voters. The predominantly Mexican Texan electorate voted for Charles Callaghan instead of Sommers Kinney, who was supported by *americanos* in Corpus Christi. After serving as a Confederate lieutenant among troops commanded by Laredo's Santos Benavides, Callaghan was well known to Tejanos. When he defeated Kinney, newspaper editors unleashed a vitriolic attack against the Laredo electorate. Brownsville's *American Flag* portrayed Laredo's "lower order" of Mexican Texans as "not only abolitionists but amalgamationists" who married blacks and "always assist a runaway slave to escape from his master."[39]

Unacknowledged by these editors was a widely known fact: Laredo supplied a disproportionately high number of Tejano Confederates compared to other regions of the state. The Brownsville *Ranchero* disregarded this strong Confederate support, choosing instead to argue against the electoral rights of Mexican Texans. "The returns of the election show that Mr. S. Kinney is the choice for representative over Mr. Callaghan by fifteen voters out of every sixteen in every place where the English language is spoken; but, over yonder, where the Mexican language is spoken, the tables were turned, and Mr. Callaghan is the choice

almost unanimously. We have no objection to Mr. Callaghan; nevertheless, we think American men in an American country should have
a fair showing in shaping the destinies of the country, by their votes."
The term "American men" implied Anglo-American males. To explain
the election results, the *Ranchero* trotted out the age-old allegation of
imported voters from Mexico. The *American Flag,* in strong objection
to Mexican Texans' political participation, wrote, "We affirm that it is
inconsistent with our laws or our institutions that Mexicans should have
the same political rights in this state as Americans."[40]

Faced with such fervent opposition, Tejanos pursued avenues that
would guarantee their rights. In April 1863, Hamilton Bee, the Confederate brigadier general stationed at Fort Brown and an antebellum legislator who had supported Tejano rights, decided against enforcing the
conscription law. The enforcement of the draft, Bee argued, would drive
Mexican Texans across the border and convert them into enemies of the
Confederacy. Instead, he implemented a "course of policy toward the
Mexicans on this frontier by which I seek to protect them in their rights
and immunities as *citizens* and thereby attach them to our cause." Bee
concluded, "This plan is meeting with success."[41] His alternative recruitment plan contained a veiled acknowledgment of a common problem
facing Tejanos—the denial of their rights. The plan's success suggests that
some Mexican Texans joined the Confederate military to obtain protection for their citizenship rights. But Bee was the exception to the rule.

Like African Americans who expected to be rewarded for their patriotic Civil War service to the Union with full citizenship rights, Tejanos
considered their military service as proof of their loyalty. In an 1864
petition to their superiors, George Treviño and several Mexican Texan
Union officers alluded to this loyalty. They asked that "the Government
may take into consideration our patriotic desires, and that we may, in
future as in the past, have the pride of increasing the ranks of the Army
of the United States, although we are the last soldiers."[42] Among the reasons that Tejanos joined the Union army, as was the case with some of
their Confederate brethren, was their belief that military service would
act as a future guarantee of their citizenship rights.

In the postwar period, Mexican Unionists derived fewer benefits
from their military service than did Anglos. Reconstruction governments rewarded Union officers and soldiers with political posts, land,

and other benefits. Edmund Davis became governor in 1870 under the Radical Reconstruction government, and John Haynes became collector of customs for Galveston and later for Brownsville and Brazos Santiago. Mexican Texans did not fare as well. One subsequently became justice of the peace in Zapata County, and several served as Cameron County constables. Most Tejano Unionists, however, did not reap political or economic benefits. Mexican nationals who obtained an honorable discharge from the Union army became eligible for naturalization after a year of residence. Despite their military service, however, these newly naturalized Americans were accused of voter fraud by *americanos* intent on limiting their electoral rights. Additionally, several Union veterans fell victim to a rash of racially motivated violence between 1865 and 1870 that resulted in over one hundred murders in the border region.[43] Other parts of Texas also witnessed anti-Unionists violence, so the violence in South Texas was not unique. Yet Tejano Unionists had to confront increased racial tensions undoubtedly aggravated by the Confederate-Union divide among the populace while having few prominent state-wide leaders to draw attention to their plight. Like the post–Civil War violence against African Americans, as described by Rebecca Czuchry in this volume, the attacks in South Texas served to disfranchise Tejano Unionists and to keep them in a politically subordinate position.

After the Civil War, the ex-Confederates' view of Mexican Texans underwent a metamorphosis. The Reconstruction Congress passed laws disfranchising former Confederates. Most Tejanos were not affected by this legislation because few had been officeholders who supported secession. Subsequently, both Radical Republicans and ex-Confederates courted Mexican Texans. A *Daily Ranchero* editorial illustrates *americanos'* changing notion of citizenship based on new political circumstances. In sharp contrast to their prewar position, ex-Confederate editors acknowledged Tejanos' American citizenship in a front-page appeal to "the Citizens of the United States, of Mexican origin, in Cameron County." Mexican Texans had a choice "between confiscation, negro equality and your ultimate extinction," the editors declared, "and on the other hand, liberty, rights of interest, and social distinction." In their most dramatic statement, the editors portrayed Tejanos (irrespective of class) as "freeborn white citizens" and urged their "fellow-citizens" to register and vote against the Republican program. This dramatic reversal demonstrates how Anglos socially constructed citizenship to suit their needs. Tejanos had also socially constructed their citizenship, or sense of belonging to the nation, but with less freedom and political power.[44]

The Civil War brought several unresolved issues, such as slavery, citizenship, and political participation, to a head in Texas. Although these issues had different salience along the border than in other regions, they nevertheless motivated residents to take sides. Like other ethnic groups throughout Texas and the nation, Mexican Texans displayed sharp divisions during the Civil War and had complex, and often contradictory, reasons for participating in the conflict. Clearly, many Tejanos knew the conflict's causes and significance and made conscious choices about whether or not to participate. By soldiering in the Civil War for the Union, they staked a claim to American citizenship at the same time that they reflected the reality of life in the *villas del norte*.

NOTES

1. To distinguish between Mexicans with different citizenship, I use "Mexican nationals" for Mexican citizens and "Mexican Americans" for American citizens. When the records fail to note citizenship, I use *mexicanos* or "Mexicans" to refer to people of Mexican descent regardless of nationality. After 1848, Mexicans in Texas border counties gradually accepted the regional identity of fellow Tejanos, so I use this term for the postwar period. The term "Mexican Texan" refers to Mexican Americans living in Texas with U.S. citizenship.

2. Brownsville *Ranchero*, April 27, June 8, 1861 (quote); Arnoldo De León, *They Called Them Greasers* (Albuquerque: University of New Mexico Press, 1982), 55–56; Jerry D. Thompson, *Mexican Texans in the Union Army* (El Paso: Texas Western Press, 1986), 3; Thompson, *Vaqueros in Blue and Gray* (Austin: Presidial Press, 1977), 15–17; Jerry D. Thompson and Lawrence T. Jones III, *Civil War and Revolution on the Rio Grande Frontier: A Narrative and Photographic History* (Austin: Texas State Historical Association, 2004), 35–36.

3. Thompson, *Vaqueros in Blue and Gray*, 16, (fourth quote), 18–19 (third quote); Brownsville *Ranchero*, May 18, 1861 (first and second quote); Thompson, *Mexican Texans in the Union Army*, 8, 17; Jerry D. Thompson, *Cortina: Defending the Mexican Name in Texas* (College Station: Texas A&M University Press, 2007), 97–99.

4. Jerry D. Thompson, *Mexican Texans in the Union Army*, viii, 17 (quote). Thompson states that all fourteen slaves were owned by recent Anglo-American immigrants to the border area. These slaves were undoubtedly domestic servants since almost all of them were female servants or children. Three counties accounted for this small slave population, with seven in Cameron County, six in Starr County,

and one in Hidalgo County. De León, *They Called Them Greasers,* 49–52; Sean Kelley, "'Mexico in His Head': Slavery and the Texas-Mexico Border, 1810–1860," *Journal of Social History* 37 (Spring 2004), 714.

5. Thompson, *Mexican Texans in the Union Army,* viii, 17.

6. Arnoldo De León, *Mexican Americans in Texas: A Brief History* (Arlington Heights, Ill.: Harlan Davidson, 1993), 47.

7. Gilberto M. Hinojosa, *A Borderlands Town in Transition* (College Station: Texas A&M University Press, 1983), 81, 83.

8. Thompson, *Mexican Texans in the Union Army,* 17.

9. Given Tejanos' subsequent actions in favor of the Union, these skewed votes in favor of secession are suspect. Local political elites (both Anglo-Americans and Mexican Texans) often manipulated election results by offering voters liquor and other incentives. In other cases, the political elite issued threats to make sure that the electorate voted in favor of the candidates or policies favored by the elite. For more information on electoral manipulations, see Omar S. Valerio-Jiménez, *River of Hope: Identity and Nation in the Rio Grande Borderlands* (Durham, N.C.: Duke University Press, 2013), 237–40.

10. Jerry D. Thompson, *Warm Weather and Bad Whiskey: The 1886 Laredo Election Riot* (El Paso: Texas Western Press, 1991), 22; Thompson, *Civil War and Revolution,* 31, 34–35; Virgil N. Lott and Mercurio Martínez, *The Kingdom of Zapata* (Austin: Eakin Press, 1953), 43.

11. Brownsville *Ranchero,* April 27, 1861 (quote); Thompson, *Cortina,* 97–98.

12. Hinojosa, *Borderlands Town in Transition,* 82–86; Thompson, *Civil War and Revolution,* 36–39, 46–48; Thompson, *Mexican Texans in the Union Army,* 1–5, 9; Thompson, *Vaqueros in Blue and Gray,* 49; Thompson, *Warm Weather and Bad Whiskey,* 22–24.

13. Robert A. Calvert and Arnoldo De León, *The History of Texas* (Arlington Heights, Ill.: Harlan Davidson, 1990), 123.

14. LeRoy P. Graf, "The Economic History of the Lower Rio Grande Valley, 1820–1875" (Ph.D. dissertation, Harvard University, 1942), 489–91.

15. Thompson, *Vaqueros in Blue and Gray,* 26, 56–57; Thompson, *Mexican Texans in the Union Army,* 43.

16. Thompson, *Mexican Texans in the Union Army,* 3; Thompson, *Vaqueros in Blue and Gray,* 27, 92–93, 123.

17. Along with protecting slavery in Texas, additional motivations included opposition to centralism and cultural conflict between Anglo-Texans and Mexicans. Among the supporters of the Texas separatist rebellion were Tejanos of various social classes. Randolph Campbell, *An Empire for Slavery: The Peculiar Institution in Texas, 1821–1865* (Baton Rouge: Louisiana State University Press, 1989), 14–49; Andrés Reséndez, *Changing National Identities at the Frontier: Texas and New Mexico, 1800–1850* (Cambridge: Cambridge University Press, 2004), 153–70; Raúl A. Ramos, *Beyond the Alamo: Forging Mexican Ethnicity in San Antonio, 1821–1861* (Chapel Hill: University of North Carolina Press, 2008), 134–53.

18. W. H. Chatfield, *The Twin Cities (Brownsville, Texas; Matamoros, Mexico) of the Border and the Country of the Lower Rio Grande* (New Orleans: E. P. Brandao,

1893; repr., Brownsville: Brownsville Historical Association, 1991), 12; Rosalie Schwartz, *Across the Rio to Freedom: U.S. Negroes in Mexico* (El Paso: Texas Western Press, 1975), 16, 24–54; Frederick Law Olmsted, *Journey through Texas: A Saddletrip on the Southwestern Frontier,* edited by James Howard (Austin: Von Boeckmann-Jones Press, 1962), 323–34; Kelley, "Mexico in His Head," 709 (quote), 712–16; John Hope Franklin and Loren Schweninger, *Runaway Slaves: Rebels on the Plantation* (New York: Oxford University Press, 1999), 26, 115–16.

19. On foreign workers and former slaves, see Archivo Histórico de Matamoros, Judicial (Casa Mata, Matamoros, Tamaulipas) [hereafter AHM-JUD] 2:6, 30 noviembre 1823; Justicia [hereafter AHM-JUS] 2:3, 4 septiembre 1832, 12 octubre 1832; AHM-JUS 3:13, 10 octubre 1836, 13 junio 1836; AHM-JUD 4:30, 7 mayo 1834; AHM-JUD 2:18, 9 agosto 1826; AHM-JUD 2:6, 30 noviembre 1823; Thomas J. Green, *Journal of the Texian Expedition against Mier* (Austin: Steck, 1935), 122–24; Schwartz, *Across the Rio to Freedom,* 26–27, 32–38, 43–46; Teresa (Griffin) Vielé, *"Following the Drum": A Glimpse of Frontier Life* (New York: Rudd and Carleton, 1858; repr., Lincoln: University of Nebraska Press, 1984), 157–58; and AHM-JUD 3:44, 5 marzo 1832.

20. Brownsville *Ranchero,* May 21, 1863, June 8, 1861; Vielé, *"Following the Drum,"* 156–58.

21. Captain Henry quoted in Paul S. Taylor, *An American Mexican Frontier: Nueces County, Texas* (Chapel Hill: University of North Carolina Press, 1934), 33.

22. Reyburn to Hatch, November 21, 1859, quoted in Taylor, *American Mexican Frontier,* 33.

23. James Scott, *Weapons of the Weak: Everyday Forms of Peasant Resistance* (New Haven, Conn.: Yale University Press, 1986), 28–30; Michael Baud and Willem Van Schendel, "Toward a Comparative History of Borderlands," *Journal of World History* 8 (Fall 1997), 216.

24. De León, *They Called Them Greasers,* 49–50; Olmsted, *Journey through Texas,* 106, 163, 256–59, 271–72, 331–34; Ana Cristina Downing de De Juana, "Intermarriage in Hidalgo County, 1860–1900" (M.A. thesis, University of Texas-Pan American, 1998), 59–61, 99.

25. Olmsted, *Journey through Texas,* 456.

26. Various scholars, including Downing de De Juana, identify Jackson as Nathaniel, but the U.S. Census identifies him as Mathew Jackson. U.S. Census of Population, Hidalgo County, 1860; Downing de De Juana, "Intermarriage in Hidalgo County," 59–61, 76–77, 99; Armando C. Alonzo, *Tejano Legacy: Rancheros and Settlers in South Texas, 1734–1900* (Albuquerque: University of New Mexico Press, 1998), 164; David Mycue, "Jackson Ranch Church," McAllen (Texas) *Valley Town Crier,* January 21 and 28, 1987; Frances W. Isbell, "Jackson Ranch Church" (Typescript, December, 1982), Museum of South Texas History, Hidalgo County Historical Commission, Edinburg, Tex., 3–5; Mark M. Carroll, *Homesteads Ungovernable: Families, Sex, Race, and the Law in Frontier Texas, 1823–1860* (Austin: University of Texas Press, 2001), 68–70; Neil Foley, *The White Scourge: Mexicans, Blacks, and Poor Whites in Texas Cotton Culture* (Berkeley: University of California Press, 1997), 208.

27. Brownsville *Ranchero,* May 19, 1860.

28. For a description of "racial marking," see Lise Lowe, *Immigrant Acts: On Asian American Cultural Politics* (Durham, N.C.: Duke University Press, 1996), 8.

29. Thompson, *Cortina*, 111–12.

30. Carl H. Moneyhon, "Davis, Edmund Jackson," *Handbook of Texas Online,* Texas State Historical Association, www.tshaonline.org/handbook/online/articles/fda37; Thompson, *Civil War and Revolution,* 67.

31. Alwyn Barr, "Haynes, John Leal," *Handbook of Texas Online,* Texas State Historical Association, www.tshaonline.org/handbook/online/articles/fhabk; Thompson, *Cortina,* 118; George Treviño et al. to Col. Juan L. Haynes, February 26, 1864, Regimental Papers of the Second Regiment [hereafter RG94], National Archives, Washington, D.C.

32. Thompson, *Vaqueros in Blue and Gray,* 52, 81–83; Thompson, *Mexican Texans in the Union Army,* 10–18.

33. Col. John L. Haynes to Col. E. J. Davis, March 11, 1864, and George Treviño et al. to Col. Juan L. Haynes, February 26, 1864, RG94; Thompson, *Vaqueros in Blue and Gray,* 6, 47, 90–91, 121–22.

34. Brownsville *Ranchero,* March 17, 1860 (emphasis added).

35. Brownsville *Ranchero,* June 8, June 29, July 6, 1861.

36. Brownsville *Ranchero,* November 17, 1860.

37. *Corpus Christi Ranchero,* April 23, 1863 (quotes); Thompson, *Vaqueros in Blue and Gray,* 56; Peter Sahlins, *Boundaries: The Making of France and Spain in the Pyrenees* (Berkeley: University of California Press, 1989), 165.

38. Alice L. Baumgartner, "Teodoro Zamora's Commission," *New York Times,* January 6, 2014.

39. Thompson, *Vaqueros in Blue and Gray,* 58–59; *American Flag* quoted in Brownsville *Ranchero,* September 3, 1863.

40. Brownsville *Ranchero,* August 13, 1863; *American Flag* quoted in Brownsville *Ranchero,* September 3, 1863.

41. H. P. Bee to Edmund P. Turner, April 27 1863, in *The War of the Rebellion: A Compilation of the Official Records of the Union and Confederate Armies* (Washington, D.C.: Government Printing Office, 1880-1901), Series I, Vol. 15, 1056–57 (emphasis added).

42. George Treviño et al. to Col. Juan L. Haynes, February 26, 1864, RG94.

43. Randolph B. Campbell, *Grass-Roots Reconstruction in Texas, 1865–1880* (Baton Rouge: Louisiana State University Press, 1997), 198–99, 221–22, 226–27; Thompson, *Mexican Texans in the Union Army,* 36–38; *Daily Ranchero,* November 23, 1869, April 23, 1870.

44. Campbell, *Grass-Roots Reconstruction,* 18; De León, *They Called Them Greasers,* 56; *Daily Ranchero,* July 2, 1867.

7

A Texas Reign of Terror

ANTI-UNIONIST VIOLENCE IN NORTH TEXAS

Richard B. McCaslin

Capt. George A. Custer, recently decommissioned as a major general of volunteers, sat before the Joint Committee on Reconstruction in March 1866 holding a bloody flag in his lap. He told the congressmen that North Texas Unionists remained under siege, and that the blood on the flag was from Frederick W. Sumner of Sherman in Grayson County. Sumner had been shot, and lost an eye, when he raised the banner over his home. Custer asserted that many Unionists were killed in North Texas during the war, an assertion corroborated by journalist Ben C. Truman. Oran Milo Roberts, senator-elect from Texas, recalled that when he arrived in Washington, the question he was most often asked was whether his home state was safe for loyal men.[1] The plight of Unionists and other dissenters in North Texas, especially in the counties that opposed secession, had become horrific during the war, but it was quickly forgotten soon afterward outside the bitterly divided region. A consideration of what happened, and why, can help put aside the popular mythology of the Lost Cause and provide a more useful insight into the total experience of Texans in the Civil War.

At the time of the Civil War, the eight North Texas counties that voted against secession definitely lay within a frontier region. Though settlers had come as early as 1815, most of the western communities were not established until the 1850s. Fannin and Lamar Counties were created in 1837 and 1840, respectively, and Collin, Cooke, Grayson, Jack, Montague, and Wise Counties were organized during the next two decades. Trails had to be blazed, and lawsuits settled, before farmers arrived and began to develop the land. The lack of good roads or navigable rivers hindered the hauling of heavy cargo, so, although almost all of the settlers came from the South, few men came with large numbers of slaves to raise market crops such as cotton. The arrival of the Butterfield Overland Mail route did bring some changes. David J. Eddleman recalled, "In 1859 there came to Texas a flood of emigration from the north such as had never been known before." The new arrivals increased the preponderance in North Texas of Upper Southerners, who generally owned fewer slaves and grew less cotton than their counterparts from the Lower South. Most came from Tennessee and states contiguous to it, bringing with them the divided opinions of that region on slavery and, ultimately, secession.[2]

North Texas settlers may not have agreed on slavery and cotton, but they all shared one fear: Indians. Much of the area was the ancestral home of the Wichitas, settled farmers who, as the white frontier infringed on customary hunting grounds, often allied with more warlike intruders such as Comanches and Kiowas. Comanches were the most numerous of the nomadic raiding groups, and Kiowas were noted for their ferocity. These three groups attacked North Texas settlers with alarming regularity until after the Civil War, and they were often joined by raiders from tribes relocated to the Indian Territory across the Red River. The federal government provided some protection by erecting forts, but this was only partly successful. White Texans took matters into their own hands, and militia units as well as Rangers patrolled alongside army regulars or operated independently. In 1858, Indians attacked a Cooke County farm, killing everyone but one small boy. Ranger companies mustered under William R. Bourland and his brother, James G. Bourland. The latter, a veteran of almost two decades of Indian battles on the frontier, was already well known for his expertise and, though his troopers failed to find their enemy, many believed that his efforts had prevented other attacks. It was a model that would be remembered.[3]

Persistent rumors of white renegades riding with Indians in raids fostered angry suspicions regarding the newcomers who poured down the Butterfield Overland Mail route. Not a few were reviled as outlaws, and they became the target of the same violence used against the Indians. An 1858 raiding party in Jack County that killed several settlers included four white men; they were lynched after being acquitted by the district court. Sadly for those who sought peace, among the new arrivals in the late 1850s were abolitionists, including some "fanatic preachers, preaching the antislavery question." The latter were often ministers of the Methodist Episcopal Church, North, who refused to recognize the schism in their church over slavery and continued to preach abolition in areas claimed by the southern branch of the church. North Texas was the only part of the state in which Northern Methodists organized in defiance of their southern brethren. Because many white Texans, slave owners and non–slave owners alike, feared insurrection as much as a raid by Indians or outlaws, the ministers and their followers became the targets of vigilantes in North Texas.[4]

Reports of abolitionist activity began almost as soon as the new wave of immigration reached North Texas. In June 1858, at the plantation of widow Ann D. Black in Grayson County, several slaves revolted. Two were shot to death by the overseer and James G. Bourland's son William. The editor of the Sherman *Patriot*, E. Junius Foster, himself a recent immigrant, blamed abolitionists for the uprising and warned that anyone caught tampering with slaves "would require a super-natural imposition to save them from the lynch code." On December 15 editor Charles Pryor of the Dallas *Herald,* a radical Democrat who would push for secession, reported that thirty vigilantes had been acquitted by a district judge in Collin County. They had warned two "suspicious characters" to leave or be dealt with "according to Judge Lynch's code." The two fled, then had the vigilantes arrested. Pryor applauded the decision of the judge to dismiss the case. Suspicion focused on Northern Methodist ministers. The 1859 convocation of the Arkansas Conference of the Northern Methodist Church met in a schoolhouse near Bonham in Fannin County. One week earlier, at Millwood in Collin County, an assembly had condemned the Northern Methodists and organized a vigilance committee to prohibit the dissemination of abolitionism. This committee sent fifty men to tell the intruders that they were not welcome. The group swelled to several hundred, and their leader told the Northern Methodists that unless they ceased to operate in Texas violence would ensue. The conference adjourned the next day, and they did not meet again in Texas before the Civil War.[5]

John Brown's raid on Harper's Ferry in October 1859 further increased tensions in North Texas and the suspicions among outsiders about the

region. Tempers flared when mysterious fires in the summer of 1860 destroyed portions of several towns. On July 8, a fire in Dallas destroyed
every store, both hotels, and the office of Pryor's *Herald*. Fires subsequently erupted in six North Texas county seats, including Collin, Cooke,
and Grayson. In Collin County, a large flour mill burned in Millwood,
a loss estimated to be $10,000. As the destruction spread south and east
into the more populated areas of the state, leaders such as Gov. Sam
Houston tried to offer rational explanations for the blazes, such as the in-
stability of newly introduced phosphorous matches. But the editor of the
Austin *Texas State Gazette*, John Marshall, printed a letter from Pryor,
who wrote that the fires were evidence of a "deep laid scheme of villainy
to devastate the whole of Northern Texas" among abolitionist ministers.
Pryor claimed that every county in North Texas had white agents awaiting a signal to lead a slave uprising. He concluded, "I write in haste; we
sleep upon our arms, and the whole country is most deeply excited."[6]

Many fled North Texas during the hysteria after the fires, fearing the
wrath of vigilantes, but others were not so fortunate. William H. Crawford was hanged less than a mile from Fort Worth on July 17, 1860, the
day after a town meeting had warned all abolitionists to leave at once.
He was posthumously accused of being an agent of the underground
railroad, of trying to hire a slave to kill another white man, and of distributing revolvers to slaves to be used during an insurrection. Nearly a
hundred slaves were corralled in Dallas, and three were hanged on July
24, 1860, after being tried by a vigilante committee. Northern Methodist
minister Anthony Bewley was pursued to Missouri by Texas vigilantes,
brought back to Fort Worth, and hanged in September 1860. Editors
such as Pryor and Marshall kept North Texas aflame, and thus an object of great suspicion, by reprinting every rumor that surfaced, linking
unrest in the region to the violence in Kansas, abolitionist agents, and
Indian conspirators. Committees for "public safety" organized in several
towns, and patrols mustered in Cooke and Grayson Counties.[7]

While the battle over slavery in North Texas became violent, and outsiders increasingly regarded the area with concern or even hostility, voters there consistently rejected the Democrats' push for secession. Like
many Texans, they returned a strong vote for Houston in the 1859 race for
governor, despite his increasingly clear stand for the Union. Some North
Texas leaders and their followers became known as "Unionists" even

before the Civil War began, a distinction that would become dangerous when those who favored secession became a majority. Robert H. Taylor of Fannin County and Benjamin H. Epperson of Red River County campaigned actively in favor of the Constitutional Unionists. Epperson was one of four Texas delegates who attended the national convention at Baltimore in 1860. They nominated Houston, who ran second in the presidential balloting behind John Bell. Epperson was nominated to be an elector for the Constitutional Union Party in the eastern district of Texas at a caucus in Fannin County, then toured North Texas along with fellow delegate Lemuel D. Evans. They spoke at Dallas, Sherman, and Weatherford but were hounded by Democrats who told the crowds that the Constitutional Unionists were proponents of disunion and insurrection. Despite such efforts, a public meeting at McKinney in September 1861 voted to endorse Bell for president. And though Bell's Texas vote, 24 percent, was the smallest in the South, most North Texas counties returned a Constitutional Union percentage equal to or higher than the state as a whole.[8]

After the election of Republican Abraham Lincoln as president, secession gained some momentum in North Texas. John R. Diamond chaired a rally at Whitesboro in Grayson County on November 23, 1860, and his brother James J. Diamond—who had been a member of the Texas delegation to the national convention of the Democratic Party in 1860—served as chairman of the steering committee. Most of those present endorsed a resolution declaring that Lincoln's election on a "platform of principles in violent opposition to Southern interests and Southern institutions" demonstrated that the states could no longer coexist peacefully. They raised a Lone Star flag and forwarded a petition to Houston for a state convention, declaring the time had come for Texas to consider severing its ties to the Union. At the same time, they organized a company of a hundred men from Grayson and Cooke Counties to defend "Southern interests and Southern equality in the Union, or out of it." A second caucus at Preston in Grayson County in late December 1860 went a step further. Planter James G. Thompson, a South Carolina native who had been on the steering committee at Whitesboro, directed the raising of another Lone Star flag and the adoption of a more belligerent resolution that called for immediate independence. James J. Diamond also served on the steering committee for a caucus chaired by James G. Bourland in

Gainesville in mid-December 1860. Again, prominent community leaders met to debate secession, including William C. Young, a former U.S.
marshal who had attended the annexation convention in 1845, and district attorney William T. G. Weaver. Young and Weaver hotly opposed
a resolution for disunion, but Diamond and Bourland prevailed, and
most voted in favor of disunion.[9]

The North Texas meetings had little effect on Houston, who stead-
fastly opposed secession and refused to cooperate with those who demanded a convention. Secessionists circumvented him by issuing a
call for the election of delegates in prominent newspapers. This proved
effective. Of the 122 organized counties in Texas, ninety-two sent delegates to the Secession Convention. Secessionist representatives were
often elected because of the "studied indifference" of Unionists, or from
misguided efforts to invalidate the effort by not participating. A correspondent in Collin County told Pryor that Unionists in his county had
decided to follow the example of the Free Soilers in Kansas and boycott
the makeshift election, hoping to see the movement collapse by default.
Apparently that was not entirely true. Instead, two opponents of secession, Samuel A. Bogart and James W. Throckmorton, were elected to
represent Collin County in the convention. They were encouraged by
the adoption of resolutions that endorsed compromise and union at a
December 1860 meeting in McKinney and not dissuaded by a larger
meeting at the same place one month later that called for disunion. In
Lamar County, three Unionists dominated the polls: William H. Johnson, Lemuel H. Williams, and George W. Wright. Montague, Wise, and
Jack Counties sent no delegates. These counties were lost to the secessionists through a grassroots Unionist campaign that rallied support for
compromise. Secessionists adopted a resolution in favor of disunion at
Decatur, the seat of Wise County, but they failed to elect a convention
delegate. Secessionists carried only three of the eight North Texas counties that later voted against disunion: Cooke, where James J. Diamond
allegedly won although the returns were apparently misplaced; Fannin, carried by A. J. Nicholson and Gideon Smith; and Grayson, which
was won by Thompson, Jesse Marshall, and William W. Diamond, the
younger brother of John R. and James J. Diamond.[10]

The triumph of the secessionists in Grayson County sparked a coun-
terattack by at least one outraged Unionist. Editor Foster of the Sherman

Patriot disseminated a proposal for the separation of many counties on the Red River from Texas. They would join with nations in the Indian Territory to petition for admission into the Union as a new state. Many settlers signed a petition endorsing this scheme as an alternative if the convention did not submit a secession ordinance to a popular vote. Both the plan and the petition were sent to editor Anthony B. Norton of the Austin *Southern Intelligencer*. Norton staunchly opposed secession and published the proposal, although not the attached list of signatures, in his newspaper in January 1861. The reaction was predictably hostile. Marshall of the Austin *Texas State Gazette* wrote, "Every honest man should trample under foot this mischievous development of Helperism, and treat its authors as public enemies."[11]

Hoping the legislature would refuse to recognize the Secession Convention, Houston did call a special session in January 1861. In spite of a valiant effort by Taylor of Fannin County in the house and Throckmorton in the senate, the legislators endorsed the convention. Taylor was passionate in his denunciation, asking, "In this new *Cotton Confederacy what will become of my section, the wheat growers and stock raisers?*" He answered, "I fear they will hang, burn, confiscate property and exile any one who may be in the way of their designs." The only restriction the legislators imposed was that a secession ordinance had to be approved in an election. The few anti-secessionist delegates in the convention found themselves at a further disadvantage. Bogart was clearly their leader, but he was ill at home and would die on March 11. Throckmorton thus became their spokesman. When the final vote was taken on the ordinance of secession on February 1, he ignored rules requiring that he say only yes or no, saying, "Mr. President, in view of the responsibility, in the presence of God and my country, and unawed by the wild spirit of revolution around me, I vote no." When spectators hissed in the gallery, he added, "Mr. President, when the rabble hiss, well may patriots tremble." Only seven other delegates—including Williams, Wright, and Johnson of Lamar County—joined him in voting against secession. The overwhelming majority, 168 in all, approved the ordinance.[12]

Throckmorton and the Unionists tried to rally Texas voters against the secession ordinance. Eighteen legislators—including Taylor, Epperson, Norton, William A. Ellet of Cooke County, John E. Henry of Grayson County, and M. L. Armstrong of Lamar County—and convention delegates Throckmorton, Williams, Wright, and Johnson signed a petition against disunion on February 6 and presented it at an anti-secession meeting in Austin three days later. Bogart pledged his support from his deathbed, and local leaders such as farmer Abraham McNeese and blacksmith John M. Crisp of Cooke County campaigned at home against secessionists such as James J. Diamond and Bourland. In Collin County, secessionist John H. Brown spoke at McKinney during an extensive speaking tour, and "General Good" and William Gates, both former Union leaders, also spoke in favor of secession. Gates claimed that he was a Unionist until William H. Seward, "arch-angel of Black Republicanism," was appointed as secretary of state, an action that to him indicated Lincoln's intention to attack the South. But the secession vote revealed the impact of local Union leaders such as Ebenezer L. Dohoney and Armstrong. They were, respectively, an attorney and a legislator in Lamar County, and Armstrong had signed Throckmorton's petition. They stumped persistently and stymied the secessionists in their county. The state as a whole returned a majority of more than three to one in favor of disunion. Only nineteen counties voted against secession; eight were in North Texas. The latter—Collin, Cooke, Fannin, Grayson, Jack, Lamar, Montague, and Wise Counties—endorsed the Union, returning a majority against secession that ranged from 51 percent in Wise to 84 percent in Jack.[13]

Unionism in North Texas persisted after secession. James W. Thomas, Unionist editor of the McKinney *Messenger*, pledged on March 1, 1861, to fight "tyrants and usurpers . . . so long as freedom of opinion is tolerated." To the north, Unionist J. P. Whitaker resumed publication of his Sherman *Journal*. A Confederate informant wrote that Wise and Cooke Counties were "all right," but Grayson and Collin were "almost hopeless" because the people there saw "nothing objectionable in Mr. Lincoln and his doctrine." On April 27, in McKinney, many boycotted a meeting after learning that it was only for those who supported the Confederacy. They organized their own caucus and adopted an angry resolution that condemned the Secession Convention for annexing Texas to the Confederacy without a popular vote. They asserted that war "might have been averted if prudent counsels had prevailed" but stopped short of sedition, asserting that although they were "more and more convinced of the ruinous policy that has been forced upon the people," they recognized that it was their "duty and the duty of all good citizens to stand forth united as one man in defense of the country." Such caution was wise as opposition to Unionists became violent. This became clear in Sherman, where Sumner had raised a U.S. flag over the courthouse on New Year's Day in 1861. When secessionists protested, a Lone Star banner was flown alongside it until after secession, when his flag was removed. But in May 1861, vandals ruined the press of Unionist editor Foster. Someone retaliated by removing the Confederate banner from over the courthouse, whereupon more than a hundred armed men occupied the town. Violence erupted on May 25, when two Sherman Unionists were attacked by two Collin County Confederates. One Unionist was killed, and the other was badly wounded. Both Confederates, one of whom had his finger shot off, were acquitted by a justice of the peace. Another Confederate flag was raised, guarded by a secessionist with a rifle. At the same time, vigilante committees organized in Collin, Cooke, Grayson, and Montague Counties to watch for Unionists and other "suspicious persons."[14]

In the face of such intolerance, many opponents of the Confederacy chose to leave North Texas, but most preferred to remain. They were joined by an increasing number of deserters; with the Federals gone, many North Texans saw no need to stay in the Confederate army. When units from Texas were ordered east of the Mississippi River, the trickle of deserters became a flood. The area also became a refuge for people from states that had become battlefields. The newcomers further disrupted the racial composition of North Texas by bringing slaves, reinforcing a perception of an unwelcome invasion in the minds of many earlier settlers. In 1860, slaveholders in Cooke County, for example, paid taxes on 360 slaves; by 1862, after a year of war, the number had swelled to 500. Similar or even greater increases in the slave population were recorded in neighboring counties during the same period, and this trend continued through the end of the war.[15]

Many settlers, old and new, did join local defense units in North Texas, at first to defend against Indians and later perhaps to avoid the draft imposed by the Confederacy. The legislature approved the creation of the Frontier Regiment in December 1861. Its companies were to remain in state service and be stationed on the western border. One company was enlisted in Montague, Cooke, and Wise Counties, and the others mustered in the counties along a line south to the Rio Grande. Another act on Christmas Day 1861 divided Texas into thirty-three militia districts, each led by a brigadier general. William R. Hudson commanded the Twenty-First District, which included Cooke, Jack, Montague, and Wise Counties; Hugh F. Young was assigned to the Fifteenth District, which encompassed Grayson and Collin Counties; A. E. Pace led the Four-teenth District, which included Fannin County; and Alexander Smith commanded the Ninth District, in which Lamar County lay. Unfortu-nately for the peace in North Texas, these new organizations would both carry out reprisals against Unionists and themselves become suspected of harboring dissenters.[16]

Efforts by the Confederate government to prosecute the war further increased the tension. President Jefferson Davis in August 1861 had is-sued a proclamation requiring all free white males over the age of four-teen who did not support the Confederacy to leave the new nation or be treated as enemy aliens. Three weeks later he signed a bill providing for the confiscation of property from "alien enemies" and anyone who offered them aid. Thousands of such cases were filed in the Confederate courts of Texas. War taxes and impressment also caused great concern. Although the Confederate Congress did not officially authorize the lat-ter until March 1863, Texas county commissioners endorsed the first lev-ies in the summer of 1862, and these slowly increased. Tax collectors, like court-appointed receivers, became hated men. Finally, the Confed-erate government adopted the first conscription act in the history of the United States. Signed by Davis on April 16, 1862, it mandated the enlistment of all able-bodied white males from eighteen to thirty-five years of age. Very few were exempt from their military obligation. Led by Governor Lubbock, who asked only that men living on the frontier be exempted for defense against Indians, the state government of Texas gave full support to this draft.[17]

Maj. Gen. Paul O. Hébert imposed martial law in Texas to enforce the draft on May 30, 1862, just four days after he took command of the Department of the Trans-Mississippi. Provost marshals directed local conscription operations. They primarily served as enrolling officers, with whom all males over the age of sixteen had to register and pledge to support the Confederacy. They also could arrest and examine any-one whose activities they judged to be "injurious to the interests of the country." If sufficient evidence of guilt was found, prisoners were to be forwarded to a military commission for trial. All provost courts were to be conducted "as far as practical" in accordance with the procedures for civilian courts, but "no unnecessary delays" for "strict and technical compliance" were allowed. Provost marshals thus could select guidelines they deemed "conducive to the ends of justice" and ignore others. To assist them, partisan Ranger units, theoretically enlisted from that portion of the male population not subject to conscription, were organized in the late summer of 1862 and assigned to chasing deserters and draft dodgers. Many previously neutral Texans became irrevocably alienated from the Confederate cause. Some joined the Frontier Regiment, which was exempt from the draft, but others stayed at home or took to the brush. The state militia provided a safe haven for some refugees. Hudson earlier had complained that he could not enlist men into his companies; now his task was much easier, but a new problem arose. As Hugh F. Young wrote, "Our families, our property, our all is now comparatively in the care and keeping of strangers."[18]

By the late summer of 1862, Confederate officials in North Texas believed Unionists to be a real threat. The Federals advanced in the Indian Territory in September, forcing the outnumbered Confederates to retreat. Rumors abounded of an uprising by Unionists to facilitate an invasion of Texas itself. Some provost marshals, such as George W. Wright of Lamar County, who had voted against disunion as a delegate to the Secession Convention, focused on stockpiling military resources to meet the threat. When evidence of a plot to seize militia arsenals in North Texas was uncovered in Gainesville, seat of Cooke County, vigilantes led by provost marshal James G. Bourland decided to eradicate the local "Peace Party," believed to be seditious. They asked Gov. Francis R. Lubbock, who had accompanied James J. Diamond to the national Democratic convention in 1860, for troops, but neither he nor Hébert could spare any. Instead, Lubbock gave Bourland permission to use the militia of the Twenty-first District. A "Citizen's Court" organized under Bourland's direction in October 1862 tried and executed seven suspects in Gainesville. A mob hanged fourteen more, then, after the murder of William C. Young, the prosecutor for this court, hanged yet another nineteen, bringing the "Great Hanging" as it became known to an end.[19]

Bourland ordered the arrest of many more suspected Unionists within the Twenty-first Militia District. Testimony in Gainesville had implicated residents in Prairie Point, a community in Wise County. Bourland sent a list to John W. Hale, commander of the Twenty-first Brigade troops stationed at Decatur. Hale arrested many men and took them to a trial commission of two dozen of the "best known and quali- fied men of the county," which convened in a makeshift courtroom on the second floor of the store that served as Hale's headquarters. Some of the prisoners enlisted in the Confederate army, but five were sentenced to hang. Sheriff Robert G. Cates was the executioner for the condemned men. Sitting on their coffins in wagons, the prisoners were taken from Hale's headquarters to a tree, where they were hanged from the wagon beds on October 18.[20]

Some of those tried at Gainesville asserted that guards at the arsenal in Sherman had joined the Peace Party and supplied its members with weapons and ammunition. Sixteen were arrested in Grayson County and tried by a commission of two dozen jurors, but they were spared through the timely intervention of district judge R. L. Waddill and Throckmorton, who had resigned his commission in the Sixth Texas Cavalry in May 1862 and returned to Collin County. Throckmorton had become the focus of suspicion when Lincoln, in an unsolicited assign- ment, appointed him tax collector for the "Rebel District of Texas," but he demonstrated that he still enjoyed popular support at Sherman. He and Waddill spoke to the crowd, convincing them to send their prison- ers to the Confederate district court at Tyler. Unionist editor J. P. Whita- ker and Sherman jeweler Frederick W. Sumner, alleged to be the leader of the Peace Party in Grayson County, fled the state—a wise choice; an observer wrote that the military intended to send the latter "up salt river sure." Several companies of Confederate cavalry did arrive in Gaines- ville during the Great Hanging, along with at least one company of mi- litia from Grayson County. On October 13, 1862, Maj. John L. Randolph led his Ninth Texas Cavalry Battalion into Sherman with twenty-seven prisoners, all of them men in his command accused of being Unionists. Randolph presided over a court-martial that condemned three men sent to him from Cooke County at their own request. But they never reached Sherman. They left Gainesville with Capt. James D. Young, the son of William C. Young, and he hanged them at his father's plantation. Young also later hanged the man who had shot his father. His campaign of retribution concluded with the shotgun killing of editor E. Junius Foster of Sherman, who had imprudently declared that the death of the elder Young was one of the best things that had happened in North Texas in a long time.[21]

The Confederate courts condemned the violence in North Texas. The district judge at Tyler, William P. Hill, rejected the assertion that the prisoners from Grayson County posed a threat and set their bail at a paltry $200. All the accused men quickly posted bond and scattered; only two came to their trial on November 13, and they were acquitted. This action was paralleled by that of Waddill as judge of the Twentieth Judicial District of Texas. A staunch supporter of the Confederacy, he was also known as an "incorruptible and inflexible Judge" who protested against the "reign of terror, the Pryor raid and the vigilance committee bullyism" in the summer of 1860. He refused to "let the Constitution and Laws be trampled under foot by a reckless gang without rebuke." His opportunity to condemn the Great Hanging came when Joel F. DeLemeron was arraigned in November 1862, charged with treason for aiding some of the fugitives from Cooke County. DeLemeron had been indicted two days earlier by a Cooke County grand jury that included three members of the Citizens Court. The evidence was strong against him, but Waddill was careful in his directions to his jury, pointing out that, if they had a "reasonable doubt," then they had to acquit DeLemeron because it was "better that ninety and nine guilty men should escape, than that one innocent man should suffer"—an obvious rebuttal to the assertion of the Fort Worth vigilantes who hanged William H. Crawford in July 1860. When the jury convicted the prisoner, Waddill, rather than sentence him to death, sent him to the state penitentiary in Huntsville, whence he was released after the war.[22]

Davis did not publicly respond to the Great Hanging and the related violence; Lubbock actively condoned it. In response to claims by Bourland and others that North Texas was still in danger, Maj. Gen. John Bankhead Magruder, Hébert's successor, in May 1863 assigned Brig. Gen. Smith P. Bankhead to command the Northern Sub-District of Texas. Bankhead had already proven quite effective against German dissenters in Central Texas in 1862; after appointing him, Magruder confided to another officer that he knew of "no other officer whom I consider capable." Bankhead arrived in June 1863 and by mid-August had enlisted a new Frontier Battalion commanded by Bourland. The campaign

Rebel barbarities in Texas, from sketches by Frederick Sumner. Library of Congress, LC-DIG-pga-04181.

of terror against Unionists and other dissenters began anew, but raids by Indians and white outlaws made Bankhead's troops restless. He had to disarm a company that threatened to desert and return home, telling them that if they left he would "follow them up and shoot down every man I caught." He ordered Bourland to sweep the frontier and told Magruder that the region harbored "large numbers of deserters and disaffected men from all parts of the State." Realizing that a majority supported the dissenters, Bankhead asked Magruder to transfer him from "this God-forsaken country."[23]

At Lubbock's request, Henry E. McCulloch, a brigadier general with his own reputation for crushing dissent in Central Texas, returned to North Texas to command the sub-district. Pursuant to a policy promulgated by Lt. Gen. Edmund Kirby Smith, McCulloch offered amnesty to all of the "shirkers" who would enlist. He asked North Texas leaders who had opposed secession, such as Throckmorton and Taylor, to persuade dissenters to join the Confederate army. He promised the recruits would stay in North Texas, but he tempered his offer of amnesty with a violent threat. If they did not surrender voluntarily, he would "force them in by the strong arm of military power," by occupying their homes, taking their families hostage, and destroying all their property if necessary. By January 1864 as many as fifteen hundred men enlisted in the region, but many of them were unruly, and they rebelled when told they would serve under Bourland. Frustrated, McCulloch wrote to Magruder that "the best thing that could happen for the country would be to kill them." He repeatedly threatened to resign, but both Kirby Smith and Magruder insisted that he stay. The latter was especially adamant, agreeing that renegades "should be shot without hesitation or mercy" and asking Mc-Culloch to "stick to the ship and do your best, for God's sake; destroy these men whilst you have the means." McCulloch remained in command of the Northern Sub-District through the end of the war.[24]

Under McCulloch, Bourland became a lieutenant colonel in the Confederate service and operated independently in much of North Texas. However, he received support from a variety of state and Confederate units sent to North Texas on temporary duty to aid him in his primary task, which was to assist in the return of deserters to their units and arrest those who refused to join the Confederate army. John R. Baylor returned to the western frontier in the fall of 1863 after being removed from command in New Mexico and serving in the Confederate Congress. In December, Baylor and a small group of Rangers attacked a Unionist camp in Jack County led by Uel D. Fox, a refugee from the Great Hanging. Fox escaped to Wise County, but eight of his men were killed in hand-to-hand fighting. Protests from local authorities led to Baylor's departure one month later. At about the same time, William C. Quantrill, whose Missouri guerrillas had established a winter camp in Grayson County, was enlisted to combat Unionists and other dissenters. Quantrill and his men engaged in several bloody reprisals in Grayson and Collin Counties. Among their victims were James Read and J. M. McReynolds, the former sheriff and chief justice, respectively, of Collin County. Fortunately Quantrill did not feel compelled to use violence when he was asked to confront a mob of hungry women who attacked a commissary in Grayson County. Allegedly he shamed them into going home. The death of Maj. George N. Butts, a Confederate recruiter, precipitated a conflict between Quantrill and McCulloch, and the raiders left North Texas.[25]

Bourland received support as well from Brig. Gen. Samuel B. Maxey, a graduate of West Point and a combat veteran of the Mexican War. Maxey warily assumed command of all of the Confederate troops in the Indian Territory in December 1863 and soon realized that North Texas was his greatest handicap, since unrest there kept McCulloch from supporting his operations. Too, units mustered along Red River leaked a steady stream of deserters into the region. Consequently, Maxey sent troops to aid in chasing conscripts and deserters, and he sent spies to infiltrate Unionist organizations. In late January 1864, responding to reports that a conspiracy was afoot, he assigned Jefferson Mears, a Choctaw scout, to infiltrate a group in the Five Corners area of Collin County. Convinced that the recruit was trustworthy, conspirators gave him enlistment papers for the Union army and told him that they would soon ride north. Instead, they were attacked by Confederates. About thirty fled to the Indian Territory, where Maxey's troopers killed seven, captured ten, and scattered the rest. Maxey had four prisoners executed as deserters. He boasted to DeMorse that a "fiew more such hauls will intimidate the traitors in North Texas, make them afraid of attempting to run the gauntlet in this direction, and thus give security to our rear which at one time bid fair to be as troublesome as our front."[26]

The next alarm came from within the ranks of the state troops. Persistent disaffection and low enlistments plagued the militia in North Texas, as well as elsewhere. Several solutions were tried before the thirty-three districts were reorganized into six in March 1864. Throckmorton took charge of District Number 3 and established his headquarters at Bonham, although he was later posted at Decatur. The new organization was intended to serve as a reserve for the regular army of the Confederacy, but the state troops also had to chase deserters and protect the region against any attacks. Ironically, Throckmorton found it difficult to recruit men and resorted to measures that encouraged violence in his home county of Collin. Avowed Unionist and abolitionist Hugh Boyd, a seventy-five-year-old farmer who had two sons in Union forces, was accused of being a spy, taken from his home between McKinney and Sherman, and hanged on March 20 by a handful of soldiers. Militia captain W. R. Bellew, a veteran of the Ninth Texas Infantry who bitterly protested such acts, fled the state when his friends warned him that he was targeted for assassination. The legislature abolished the militia in May 1864, after many men had been sent to Louisiana for the Red River campaign, but the violence continued. Legislator David Stiff mustered an independent company to patrol the county and arrest those "yet in the *Brush* evading the service." Deputy William W. Warden and a posse of thirty men, which included some Confederates from nearby units, ambushed deserters near Sister Grove in October 1864. Twenty renegades were shot to death, and five more were caught and killed, eradicating organized dissent in Collin County.[27]

Suspicions about Unionists within the state units did not dissipate with the disbanding of the militia. The Frontier Regiment was reorganized as the "Mounted Regiment of Texas State Troops." Many Confederate officials, such as Bourland, disparaged this outfit and tried to have its members sent elsewhere. He accused the troops of being draft dodgers and conspiring with Indians or the Federals. Transfer of the regiment to Confederate service did allay some outside concerns, but those within the ranks worried that they might be removed from the frontier, despite assurances otherwise. The solution for them lay in joining the companies assigned to the new First Frontier District, which was created in December 1863 and included Cooke, Jack, Montague, and Wise Counties. Its commander was William Quayle, formerly the chief justice of Tarrant County and lieutenant colonel of the Ninth Texas Cavalry. Confederate officials constantly tried to draft the men serving in the First Frontier District, but the state government stoutly resisted their attempts to do so. The officers and men of the organization were bound by oath to arrest and turn over to Confederate authorities all draft dodgers and deserters. Many members of the First Frontier District did not like this duty, but Quayle frequently assured his superiors, including Bourland, that he was not enlisting deserters but returning them to their original units.[28]

While preparing for the Red River campaign in the spring of 1864, military officials in North Texas cast a wary eye to the rear. The suspicions of many were confirmed when Capt. James M. Luckey of the First Frontier District told Quayle that he was a Unionist and that pro-Confederate vigilantes were hunting him. He asked Quayle to help him establish communications with Federals and named others who would help to undermine the Confederacy's hold on North Texas. Quayle agreed and then sent John W. Hale to report the conspiracy to Bourland, who in turn informed McCulloch. McCulloch's response to Quayle was to "pounce on them and kill or capture the whole of them," adding "better kill than capture them." Bourland assisted in a covert investigation and sent John R. Diamond to arrest the conspirators in Parker and Jack Counties, admonishing Quayle to "manage this affair in the same way we did in Cooke," an obvious reference to the Great Hanging. Many Unionists escaped, but Luckey and others were captured. Quayle refused to execute them, despite the recommendation of Texas adjutant general David B. Culberson; instead, he sent them to Houston for a trial, where most, including Luckey, were released. Furious, Bourland issued shoot-on-sight orders for some of the refugees, but Quayle ignored him. John R. Diamond, at Bourland's direction, did attack a camp of Bourland's own troops in Montague County, killing some before the rest fled for Kansas or Mexico.[29]

Maxey pronounced himself satisfied with the results of Bourland's efforts and predicted that the arrests, together with Confederate successes in Louisiana and Arkansas, had destroyed organized dissent in North Texas and "effectually scotched that snake." McCulloch disagreed; he and Bourland still distrusted the state troopers. The former wrote Culberson that, if Confederate troops left the Northern Sub-District, "then would commence an indiscriminate robbery of our citizens, and a general desertion to the enemy." To a fellow officer, McCulloch confided that what he actually wanted was a "good regiment . . . under an energetic, fighting, hanging man," to send to the frontier "with orders to attack and kill all who are assembled to resist the authorities, and arrest all others who owe service to the country or are disloyal." He found his man in Bourland, whose command was increased to a regiment with him as colonel and John R. Diamond as lieutenant colonel. Bourland redoubled his efforts during the summer of 1864, dispatching troops to operate in conjunction with Quayle and others. Frequent reports of prisoners being killed led McCulloch to admonish his new commander, but the lynching of the hapless Luckey and subsequent chaos in Jack County, focused on one of Bourland's companies, led McCulloch to restrict Bourland from chasing dissenters. On October 15, 1864, twenty-eight officers and enlisted men in Bourland's regiment, including James

J. Diamond, signed a petition protesting his methods and asking for his removal. Instead, McCulloch expanded Bourland's command to include all Confederate troops in eleven North Texas frontier counties, although he was still to fight Indians, not chase deserters and Unionists.[30]

The reelection of Lincoln in the fall of 1864 was greeted with dismay by Confederates in North Texas. They responded with yet another reorganization of their frontier defenses. The legislature had authorized the assignment of brigadier generals to command the frontier districts, and so Throckmorton superseded Quayle in December 1864. Throckmorton came to his new job directly from the Texas senate, where he had again won notoriety as a defender of Unionists and other dissenters. During a debate on the possibility of a negotiated peace, he was chastised by a senator who said that "any man who talked of reconstruction would be hanged." Throckmorton retorted with the assertion that the draft had caused citizens to be "hunted down like wild beasts & forced into the ranks of the army with the bayonet thrusting them along." Mocking those who advocated fighting to the last ditch, he painted a vivid verbal portrait of Confederate armies reduced to elderly men. Even then, if a ragged veteran expressed his desire for negotiation to end the carnage, he would "be set upon by a mob of fanatics . . . and be treated to a rope & limb because he dared to express himself as a freeman." He sat down in what he recalled as "deathlike stillness." To his chagrin, the senate adopted a resolution opposing a negotiated peace.[31]

Throckmorton assumed command of the First Frontier District at a difficult time. Indians and white raiders worked together to strip North Texas of cattle and horses, often selling them to the Union army, whose scouts were often sighted south of the Red River. Deserters from Confederate units haunted every remote corner, sheltered by a disaffected populace. Many believed, as one observer in Grayson County wrote, that "nothing but bayonets" could impose order, and an order from McCulloch in late December provided that anyone who resisted arrest would be shot where they were found. Bourland's regiment seemed to be on the verge of a mutiny; among those arrested by McCulloch was James J. Diamond, who subsequently resigned and went home. Throckmorton regarded the approach of spring in 1865 with great apprehension. If the Federals invaded North Texas, he wrote to a friend, "scenes of atrocity such as you little dream of, will be enacted by men who claim to fight under our banner." He sent Lt. Col. John R. Diamond and others in pursuit when as many as one hundred deserters assembled in Wise County and marched through Montague County on their way to Kansas or California. Diamond found his quarry, then became their prisoner when he unwisely agreed to a parley. Quick negotiations resulted in the release of Diamond and the arrest of the deserters, who were sent to Galveston about the time that the war ended.[32]

The surrender of Confederate forces in the late spring of 1865 spawned chaos in North Texas. McCulloch, with his command in ruins, asked for volunteers to escort him to Dallas. In McKinney, a crowd of "jayhawkers" gathered to prevent his passage. Undaunted, he organized his bodyguard of thirty men and advanced, and the challengers broke ranks. Bourland remained in the region and ironically was appointed to issue federal paroles to the surrendered Confederates.[33] Within a year Throckmorton became governor of Texas and pressed for forgetting wartime atrocities, apparently abandoning his commitment to his fellow Unionists. These episodes all exemplify the legacy of the North Texas experience in the Confederacy. Just as legislator Robert H. Taylor had predicted, and George A. Custer reported, the ruthless persecution of McCulloch, Bourland, and others had depleted and divided the populace. Ironically, even in victory, when a principal tormentor turned to flee, they could not muster enough strength to avenge themselves.

NOTES

1. Report of the Joint Committee on Reconstruction, House Report 30, pt. 4, 39th Cong., 1st Sess., 72–74, 136–137 (Ser. Set 1, 273); Report of Benjamin C. Truman Relative to the Condition of the Southern People and the States in Which the Rebellion Existed, Senate Ex. Doc. 43, 39th Cong., 1st Sess., 3, 6, 12-13 (Ser. Set 1,238); Jay Monaghan, *Custer: The Life of General George Armstrong Custer* (Boston: Little, Brown, 1959), 264; O. M. Roberts, "The Experiences of an Unrecognized Southern Senator," *Southwestern Historical Quarterly* 12 (October 1908), 138.

2. The first chapters of two books provide detailed information on the early settlement of this region: David Pickering and Judy Fall, *Brush Men and Vigilantes: Civil War Dissent in Texas* (College Station: Texas A&M University Press, 2000), and Richard B. McCaslin, *Tainted Breeze: The Great Hanging at Gainesville, Texas, October 1862* (Baton Rouge: Louisiana State University Press, 1994). This chapter relies heavily on Ron Tyler et al., eds., *The New Handbook of Texas*, 6 vols. (Austin: Texas State Historical Association, 1996), the updated online version of which can

be found at *Handbook of Texas Online,* Texas State Historical Association, www
.tshaonline.org/handbook/online. The David J. Eddleman quotation is from his
"Autobiography of the [illegible]," typescript, 1914, Archives Division, University of
North Texas Library, Denton.

3. Hardin R. Runnels to James G. Bourland, October 1858, and Muster Roll of
James G. Bourland's Company, n.d., James G. Bourland Papers, Manuscript Division, Library of Congress, Washington, D.C. [hereafter LC]; H. S. Woodward et al.
to Runnels, September 18, 1858, Manuel W. Estes et al. to Runnels, October 14, 1858,
Memorials and Petitions File, Texas State Library and Archives Commission, Austin [hereafter TSLAC]; Runnels to John B. Floyd, November 2, 1858, in Dorman H.
Winfrey and James M. Day, eds., *The Indian Papers of Texas and the Southwest,* 5
vols. (Austin: Texas State Library, 1960–66), 3:302–303; H. P. N. Gammel, comp.,
The Laws of Texas, 1822–1897, 10 vols. (Austin: Gammel Book, 1898), 4:949–50, 1138–
83, 1421; Austin *Texas State Gazette,* October 9, 1858; Dallas *Herald,* October 20, 27,
November 3, 1858; Dallas *News,* March 23, 1924, January 1 and 2, 1955; Gainesville
Register, August 30, 1948; Averam B. Bender, *The March of Empire: Frontier Defense
in the Southwest, 1848–1860* (Lawrence: University of Kansas Press, 1952), 9–10,
27–37, 131–34, 138–46; Josiah W. Wilbarger, *Indian Depredations in Texas* (Austin:
Hutchings Printing House, 1889), 320–33, 379–418, 429–39, 514–22, 534–39.

4. Eddleman, "Autobiography," 24 (quote); Petition from Wise County, January 9, 1860, and William C. Dalrymple to Sam Houston, Texas Governor's Office,
Records, TSLAC; Austin *Texas State Gazette,* June 30, July 21, 1860; Dallas *Herald,* January 2, 1861; Ida L. Huckaby, *Ninety-Four Years in Jack County, 1854–1948*
(Austin: Steck, 1949), 35–38; Rupert N. Richardson, *The Comanche Barrier to South
Plains Settlement* (Glendale, Calif.: Arthur H. Clark, 1933), 259–66; Wilbarger, *Indian Depredations,* 334–39, 538–40.

5. Austin *Southern Intelligencer,* July 15, 1858; Dallas *Herald,* December 15, 1858;
Charles Elliott, *Southwestern Methodism: A History of the M. E. Church in the Southwest from 1844 to 1864* (Cincinnati, Ohio: Poe and Hitchcock, 1868), 127–31, 137;
Macum Phelan, *A History of Early Methodism in Texas, 1817 to 1866* (Dallas: Cokes-
bury Press, 1924), 442–52; Wesley Norton, "The Methodist Episcopal Church and
the Civil Disturbances in North Texas in 1859 and 1860," *Southwestern Historical
Quarterly* 68 (January 1965), 323–28.

6. The definitive work on the North Texas fires in the summer of 1860 is Donald E. Reynolds, *Texas Terror: The Slave Insurrection Panic and the Secession of the
Lower South* (Baton Rouge: Louisiana State University Press, 2007). For the Pryor
quotations, see Austin *Texas State Gazette,* July 28, 1860.

7. Eddleman, "Autobiography," 25; Austin *Texas State Gazette,* July 14, August
11 and 18, September 22, 28, and 29, October 6, 1860; Dallas *Herald,* December 26,
1860, May 15, 1861; Houston *Telegraph,* July 21, 1860; San Antonio *Ledger and Texan,*
August 18, 1860; Reynolds, *Texas Terror,* 83–84, 148–55; Elliot, *Southwestern Methodism,* 21–31, 34, 45, 79, 91, 109, 150–54, 161–73, 181–86; Phelan, *History,* 440–41, 452–
56; Norton, "Methodist Episcopal Church," 333–36; William E. White, "The Texas
Slave Insurrection of 1860," *Southwestern Historical Quarterly* 52 (January 1949),

264–67, 277–85; Frank H. Smyrl, "Unionism in Texas, 1856–1861," *Southwestern Historical Quarterly* 68 (October 1964), 30–35, 50–74.

8. Clarksville *Standard*, September 29, October 27, November 3, 1860; McKinney *Messenger*, September 14, 1860; Walter L. Buenger, *Secession and the Union in Texas* (Austin: University of Texas Press, 1984), 35–38, 76–77, 96–101, 106, 112, 184–86; Dale Baum, *The Shattering of Texas Unionism: Politics in the Lone Star State during the Civil War* (Baton Rouge: Louisiana State University Press, 1998), 9–38; James A. Baggett, "The Constitutional Union Party in Texas," *Southwestern Historical Quarterly* 82 (January 1979), 240–57; Smyrl, "Unionism in Texas," 177, 180, 194–95.

9. Austin *Texas State Gazette*, January 12, 1861; Clarksville *Standard*, June 1, 1861; Dallas *Herald*, January 9, 1861; John E. Wheeler Diary, manuscript, 1850–1880, Morton Museum, Gainesville, Tex. [hereafter Morton Museum]; *Ancestors and Descendants: Grayson County, Texas* (Dallas: Taylor, 1980), 58; Graham Landrum and Allen Smith, *An Illustrated History of Grayson County, Texas*, 2nd ed. (Fort Worth: Historical Publishers, 1967), 63; Martha D. Lucas and Mita H. Hall, *A History of Grayson County, Texas* (Sherman: Scruggs Printing, 1936), 99–101 (quotes); Michael Collins, *Cooke County, Texas: Where the South and the West Meet* (Gainesville, Tex.: Cooke County Heritage Society, 1981), 10; A. Morton Smith, *The First 100 Years in Cooke County* (San Antonio, Tex.: Naylor, 1955), 29–30.

10. Dallas *Herald*, January 9, 23, and 30, 1861; Ernest W. Winkler, ed., *Journal of the Secession Convention of Texas, 1861* (Austin: Texas Library and Historical Commission, 1912), 119, 191, 405–408, 425–34; John E. Wheeler Diary, Morton Museum; Buenger, *Secession in Texas*, 2, 116, 125, 143; Cliff D. Cates, *Pioneer History of Wise County* (Decatur, Tex.: privately printed, 1907), 114, 120; Kenneth W. Howell, *Texas Confederate, Reconstruction Governor: James Webb Throckmorton* (College Station: Texas A&M University Press, 2008), 62–63.

11. Annie H. Abel, *Indians as Slaveholders and Secessionists* (Cleveland, Ohio: Arthur H. Clark, 1915), 67–79; Austin *Texas State Gazette*, February 2, 1861; Marshall *Texas Republican*, February 23, 1861; Claude Elliot, "Union Sentiment in Texas, 1861–1865," *Southwestern Historical Quarterly* 50 (April 1947), 449; J. Lee Stambaugh and Lillian J. Stambaugh, *A History of Collin County* (Austin: Texas State Historical Association, 1958), 62. "Helperism" is a reference to Hinton R. Helper, a North Carolina native who was denounced by Southerners after he published an anti-slavery book in 1857.

12. Winkler, *Journal*, 14, 48–56, 119, 191, 405–408; Buenger, *Secession and the Union*, 3, 148; Howell, *Texas Confederate*, 2, 64, 197; James A. Marten, *Texas Divided: Loyalty and Dissent in the Lone Star State, 1856–1874* (Lexington: University Press of Kentucky, 1990). Robert H. Taylor's speech was printed as a broadside, which can be found in the Robert H. Taylor Papers at the Dolph Briscoe Center for American History, University of Texas at Austin [hereafter Brisco Center]. It was also published in the McKinney *Messenger* on March 1, 1861. James W. Throckmorton's defiant outburst was reported in the LaGrange *True Issue*, February 7, 1861, and has been reprinted many times. The other four who voted against secession were

John D. Rains and A. P. Shuford of Wood County, Thomas P. Hughes of Williamson County, and Joshua Johnson of Titus County.

13. Austin *Southern Intelligencer,* February 13, 1861; Austin *Texas State Gazette,* February 23, 1861; Dallas *Herald,* February 20 and 27, 1861; McKinney *Messenger,* March 1, 1861; Winkler, *Journal,* 14, 21, 85; John M. Crisp, Jr., to George M. Crisp, October 20, 1921, photocopies of typescript, Morton Museum; *Members of the Texas Legislature, 1846–1980* (Austin: Texas Legislature, 1981), 31–34; Joe T. Timmons, "The Referendum in Texas on the Ordinance of Secession, February 23, 1861: The Vote," *East Texas Historical Journal* 11 (Fall 1973), 16; Howell, *Texas Confederate,* 65–67; Pickering and Fall, *Brush Men and Vigilantes,* 35–39; Baum, *Shattering of Texas Unionism,* 42–80.

14. Otis G. Welch to Oran M. Roberts, March 24, 1861, and W. E. Saunders to Edward Clark, May 7, 1861, Governor's Office Records, TSLAC; Cooke County Commissioners Court, "Minutes, 1857–1858," 1:35, 82, sheet 2, typescript, n.d., Works Progress Administration Historical Records Survey, Briscoe Center; Dallas *Herald,* March 13, May 27, June 12, 1861; McKinney *Messenger,* March 1, 1861; Clarksville *Standard,* May 11, June 29, July 13, 1861; Thomas Wilson, *Sufferings Endured for a Free Government* (Washington, D.C.: privately printed, 1864), 258–59; Martha D. Lucas, "Interview with William Walsh, November 1928" (Typescript), Martha D. Lucas Papers, and Frederick W. Sumner, "Written by F. W. Sumner during the Civil War" (Typescript), both in Sherman Municipal Library, Sherman, Tex.; Landrum and Smith, *Illustrated History,* 63; Lucas and Hall, *History,* 112; Smith, *First 100 Years,* 32.

15. Mark W. Delahy to Andrew Johnson, June 25, 1866, Andrew Johnson Papers, LC; William C. Young to Clark, May 2, 1861, Governor's Office Records, TSLAC; John E. Wheeler Diary, Morton Museum; Clarksville *Standard,* June 7, 21, and 22, July 5, 20, and 26, November 23, 1861; Austin *Texas State Gazette,* May 4, November 2, 1861; Dallas *Herald,* October 16, 30, November 6, 27, 1861; *The War of the Rebellion: A Compilation of the Official Records of the Union and Confederate Armies,* 130 vols. (Washington, D.C.: Government Printing Office, 1880–1902) [hereafter *OR*], Series I, Vol. 8, 728, 776, Vol. 13, 659, Series IV, Vol. 1, 323–25.

16. Francis R. Lubbock, *Six Decades in Texas,* ed. C. W. Raines (Austin: Ben C. Jones, 1900), 359; List of Brigadier Generals of the State Troops, Nathaniel Terry to Jeremiah Y. Dashiell, January 1, 1862, Hugh F. Young to Dashiell, January 13, 1862, Dashiell to William R. Hudson, February 14, 1862, Hudson to Dashiell, March 4, 1862, Dashiell to William H. Hoard, March 28, 1862, and Dashiell to Young, May 26, 1862, Texas Adjutant General's Office Records, TSLAC; Gammel, *Laws of Texas,* 5:455–56; David P. Smith, *Frontier Defense in the Civil War: Texas Rangers and Rebels* (College Station: Texas A&M University Press, 1992), thoroughly explains the intricate history of the many units assigned to the Texas frontier during the war.

17. Austin *Texas State Gazette,* October 1, 1862; Houston *Telegraph,* October 6, 1862; Washington *National Intelligencer,* October 5, 1862; Cooke County Commissioners Court, "Minutes," 1:98, *OR,* Series I, Vol. 53, 828–30; Lubbock, *Six Decades,* 379; *The Supreme Court of Texas on the Constitutionality of the Conscript Laws* (Houston: Telegraph Book and Job Establishment, 1863), 527; Mary S. Estill, ed.,

"Diary of a Confederate Congressman," *Southwestern Historical Quarterly* 38 (April 1935), 277–78; T. R. Havins, "Administration of the Sequestration Act in the Confederate District Court for the Western District of Texas, 1862–1865," *Southwestern Historical Quarterly* 43 (January 1940), 295–322; J. G. de Roulhac Hamilton, "The State Courts and the Confederate Constitution," *Journal of Southern History* 4 (November 1938), 425–35; Albert B. Moore, *Conscription and Conflict in the Confederacy* (New York: Macmillan, 1924), 13, 163–67; William M. Robinson, Jr., *Justice in Grey: A History of the Judicial System of the Confederate States of America* (Cambridge: Harvard University Press, 1941), 420–36, 448–96; Jonnie M. Megee, "The Confederate Impressment Acts in the Trans-Mississippi States" (M.A. thesis, University of Texas at Austin, 1915), 6–46, 135–59.

18. Young to Dashiell, March 10, 1862, Adjutant General's Office Records, TSLAC; Richmond *Enquirer*, October 28, 1863; Clarksville *Standard*, September 13, 1862; Lubbock, *Six Decades*, 382; *OR*, Series I, Vol. 9, 713–17, 732; Florence E. Holladay, "Powers of the Commander of the Confederate Trans-Mississippi Department, 1863–1865," *Southwestern Historical Quarterly* 21 (January 1918), 280.

19. McCaslin, *Tainted Breeze*, 60–94.

20. Stephen P. Beebe to Holton White, July 26, 1865, Great Hanging File, Wise County Heritage Museum, Decatur, Tex.; Austin *Texas State Gazette*, October 29, 1862; Cates, *Pioneer History*, 81, 117–18, 131–35; Catherine T. Gonzalez, *Rhome: A Pioneer History* (Burnet, Tex.; Eakin Press, 1979), 5–7; Mary C. Moore, *Centennial History of Wise County, 1853–1953* (Dallas: Storybook Press, 1953), 38, 43–44; Phelan, *History*, 335, 482.

21. Jonathan H. Weidermeyer to Dashiell, October 14, 1862, Adjutant General's Office Records, TSLAC; John D. Young to Betty Gunter, February 7, 1917, Cooke County History File, Morton Museum; Sumner, "Written by F. W. Sumner during the Civil War"; John H. McLean, *The Reminiscences of the Reverend John H. McLean* (Nashville, Tenn.: Smith and Lamar, 1918), 103; Wilson, *Sufferings*, 261; Sherman *Journal*, August 21, 1862; Austin *Texas Almanac Extra*, October 25, November 13, 1862; Dallas *Herald*, September 20, 1862; Clarksville *Standard*, November 1, 1862; Houston *Telegraph*, November 7, 1862; San Antonio *Express*, May 8, 1867; McKinney *Courier-Gazette*, August 24, 1906; Landrum and Smith, *Illustrated History*, 65, 125; Howell, *Texas Confederate*, 83–84.

22. Houston *Telegraph*, November 7, 22, 26, 28, 1862; Dallas *Herald*, April 24, 1863; Cooke County Commissioners Court, "Minutes," I, 109, Cooke County District Clerk, Criminal and Civil Minutes, Sixteenth, Twentieth, and Seventh District Courts, 1857–1871, Cooke County Courthouse, Gainesville, Tex., 186, 199–203; Texas Supreme Court, Austin Docket, 1860–1864, Archives Division, TSLAC, 442–43; *OR*, Series II, Vol. 8, 659; J. W. Boyer and C. H. Thurmann, *The Annals of Elder Horn* (New York: Richard R. Smith, 1930), 43, 55–56; Sam Acheson and Julia A. H. O'Connell, eds., *Diamond's Account of the Great Hanging at Gainesville, 1862* (Austin: Texas State Historical Association, 1963), 92–98.

23. James G. Bourland to Andrew Johnson, September 18, 1865, United States Adjutant General's Office, Case Files of Applications from Former Confederates

for Presidential Pardons 1865–1867, Record Group 94, National Archives, Washington, D.C.; Francis R. Lubbock to Bourland, June 24, 1863, Governor's Office Records, TSLAC; William C. Twitty to Lubbock, August 17, 1863, and William Steele to Smith P. Bankhead, July 11, 1863, Adjutant General's Office Records, TSLAC; *OR,* Series I, Vol. 22, 977, Vol. 26, 13, 20–21, 25, 38, 80, Vol. 53, 888–91; San Antonio *Herald,* August 10, 1863; Clarksville *Standard,* September 17, 1863; Dallas *Herald,* August 19, 1863.

24. Henry E. McCulloch to Benjamin H. Epperson, September 29, 1863, Benjamin H. Epperson Papers, Briscoe Center; McCulloch to Bourland, November 22, 1863, Bourland Papers, LC; Lubbock to Edmund Kirby Smith, August 31, 1863, Lubbock to McCulloch, September 2, 1863, Governor's Office Records, TSLAC; Kirby Smith to McCulloch, January 4, June 7, 1864, McCulloch Family Papers, Briscoe Center; Eddleman, "Autobiography," 39–40; *OR,* Series I, Vol. 9, 704–705, Vol. 26, 352–53, 401, pt. 2, 285, Vol. 34, pt. 2, 909 (quote), 925–26 (quote) pt. 3, 814; Vol. 53, 923–25; Lubbock, *Six Decades,* 503; Austin *Texas State Gazette,* October 23, 1863; Clarksville *Standard,* October 3, November 7, 1863, March 26, 1864; San Antonio *Herald,* September 12, 1863.

25. John T. Darnall to Epperson, June 15, [1864], Epperson Papers, Briscoe Center; Bourland to James T. McCord, October 30, 1863, James B. Barry Papers, Briscoe Center; McCulloch to Bourland, December 1, 1863, Bourland to John R. Diamond, December 13, 1863, and Bourland to John R. Baylor, January 4, 1864, Bourland Papers, LC; Henry F. Bone to Dashiell, November 20, 1863, and William Quayle to Murrah, December 27, 1863, Adjutant General's Office Records, TSLAC; Bourland to Lubbock, October 23, 1863, Governor's Office Records, TSLAC; Uel D. Fox to Alex Wilson, November 10, 1862, photocopy, Great Hanging File, Morton Museum; *OR,* Series I, Vol. 22, 1036–37, 1042, Vol. 26, 382, Vol. 34, 969, pt. 2, 911, 932, 942, 945, 1107; Dallas *Herald,* September 9, 1863; Houston *Telegraph,* November 25, 1863, January 15, 1864; San Antonio *Herald,* January 23, 1864; Carl W. Breihan, *Quantrill and His Civil War Guerrillas* (Denver: Sage, 1959), 119–34, 137–44; Albert Castel, *William Clarke Quantrill: His Life and Times* (New York: Frederick Fell, 1962), 122–49, 155, 160–68; William E. Connelly, *Quantrill and the Border Wars* (New York: Pageant, 1956), 421, 436–45; Roy F. Hall and Helen G. Hall, *Collin County: Pioneering in North Texas* (Quanah, Tex.: 1975), 296; Stambaugh and Stambaugh, *History of Collin County,* 68–69; Lucas and Hall, *History,* 35–37, 118–21; Landrum and Smith, *Illustrated History,* 2–8, 67–69; *Ancestors and Descendants,* 13.

26. Samuel B. Maxey to William R. Boggs, December 26, 1863, May 29, 1864, Tom P. Ochiltree to Leonidas M. Martin, April 2, 1864, Maxey to William L. Cabell, January 29, 1864, Maxey to Charles DeMorse, February 13, 1864, Maxey to Douglas H. Cooper, February 15, 1864, and Maxey to S. S. Anderson, February 27, 1864, Samuel B. Maxey Papers, TSLAC; *OR,* Series I, Vol. 26, 382, Vol. 34, 945, pt. 2, 958–59, Vol. 41, pt. 4, 1132, Vol. 53, 923–25; Houston *Telegraph,* January 15, 1864; Louise W. Horton, "General Sam Bell Maxey: His Defense of North Texas and the Indian Territory," *Southwestern Historical Quarterly* 74 (April 1971), 507–18; Boyer and Thurman, *Annals of Elder Horn,* 46 (quote); Louise W. Horton, *Samuel Bell Maxey: A Biography* (Austin, Texas, 1974), 39.

27. Hudson to Dashiell, June 19, July 22, 1863, J. P. Hopson to Dashiell, May 26, 1863, J. B. Wilmeth to Dashiell, July 24, 1863, Young to Dashiell, October 4, 1863, Terry to Dashiell, August 4, 1863, Thomas W. Toler to Dashiell, August 4, 1863, G. W. Wooten to Culberson, March 31, 1864, and David Stiff to Culberson, July 5, 1864, Adjutant General's Office Records, TSLAC; Lubbock to John S. Ford, September 11, 1863, Terry to Lubbock, August 12, October 25, 1863, Terry and Richard M. Gano to John B. Magruder, August 12, 1863, Murrah to McCulloch, November 18, 1863, Throckmorton to Murrah, March 28, 29, 1864, and W. R. Bellew to Andrew J. Hamilton, July 13, 1865, Governor's Office Records, TSLAC; OR, Series I, Vol. 22, 1036–37, Vol. 26, 159–60, Vol. 34, 1011; Gammel, Laws of Texas, 5:698–99; Dallas Herald, December 31, 1862, June 24, 1863; Ila M. Myers, "The Relation of Governor Pendleton Murrah, of Texas, with the Confederate Military Authorities" (M.A. thesis, University of Texas at Austin, 1929), 37–54; Mamie Yeary, ed., Reminiscences of the Boys in Gray, 1861–1865 (Dallas: Wilkinson Printing, 1912), 250–51; Bradford K. Felmly and John C. Grady, Suffering to Silence: 29th Texas Cavalry, C.S.A., Regimental History (Quanah, Tex.: Nortex Press, 1975), 133–38; Stambaugh and Stambaugh, History of Collin County, 69; Hall and Hall, Collin County, 58; Howell, Texas Confederate, 86–89.

28. William Quayle to Culberson, February 4, 1864, and Quayle to McCulloch, February 20, 1864, William Quayle Papers, Special Collections Division, University of Alabama Library, University, Alabama [hereafter UA]; Bourland to McCulloch, November 10, 1863, Barry Papers, Briscoe Center; Quayle to Lubbock, July 20, 1863, Terry to Lubbock, August 15, 1863, Lubbock to McCulloch, September 2, 1863, Magruder to Murrah, November 20, 1863, Murrah to Quayle, January 8, 1864 [dated as 1863], Quayle to Murrah, January 15, 1864, and Smith to Murrah, January 18, 1864, Governor's Office Records, TSLAC; Quayle to Murrah, December 27, 1863, Quayle to Culberson, January 22, February 10, March 31, 1864, and Throckmorton to Jonathan Burke, January 29, 1865, Adjutant General's Office Records, TSLAC; Lubbock, Six Decades, 475; Gammel, Laws of Texas, 5:607–608, 677–79, 828, 856–61; Marshall Texas Republican, October 25, 1862; Dallas Herald, October 16, 1861, July 12, 1862; OR, Series I, Vol. 8, 5–10, 18–19, Vol. 26, 166, Vol. 53, 890–91, Vol. 41, pt. 3, 986–87, Vol. 48, 1373–79.

29. McCulloch to Bourland, October 29, 1863, Bourland Papers, LC; Terry to Dashiell, January 31, 1863, Adjutant General's Office Records, TSLAC; Quayle to Culberson, February 4, April 27, 1864, McCulloch to Bourland, April 15, 1864, Jonathan P. Hill to Quayle, April 2, 1864, Bourland to Quayle, March 26, April 14, 16, 18, 20, and 22, 1864, McCulloch to Quayle, April 14, 15, and 16, 1864, Throckmorton to Quayle, April 4, 12, and 15, 1864, Special Orders No. 99, HQ, Northern Subdistrict of Texas, April 15, 1864, Culberson to Quayle, April 28, 1864, and Quayle to Elkanah J. Greer, August 25, 1864, William Quayle Papers, UA; Maxey to Gano, March 16, 1864, and Maxey to McCulloch, March 18, 1864, Maxey Papers, TSLAC; affidavit of T. J. Stanfield, December 19, 1864, affidavit of Charles Adare, December 19, 1864, affidavit of F. A. Leach, May 25, 1867, McCulloch to Murrah, March 20 and 28, 1864, A. J. Hunter to Murrah, May 22, 1864, Throckmorton to Murrah, December 20, 1864, and Henry J. Thompson to Hamilton, August 9, 1865, Governor's

Office Records, TSLAC; U.S. District Courts, Western District of Texas, Confederate Court Case Files 1895 and 1918, Confederate States of America vs. John Shields and James M. Luckey, Record Group 21, Federal Records Center, Fort Worth, Tex.; *James M. Luckey v. The State of Texas*, in *Reports of Cases Argued and Decided in the Supreme Court of the State of Texas*, 65 vols. (St. Louis: Gilbert, 1848–86), 26:362–65; Austin *Texas State Gazette*, May 18, 1864; San Antonio *News*, May 28, 1864; *OR*, Series I, Vol. 34, pt. 2, 1103–1104, pt. 3, 726–27, 771–83, 792, pt. 4, 634–35; Lemuel D. Clark, ed., *The Civil War Reminiscences of James Lemuel Clark* (College Station: Texas A&M University Press, 1984), 78–88.

30. Maxey to Boggs, May 29, 1864 (first quote), Maxey Papers, TSLAC; J. H. Earle to Culberson, June 4, 1864 (second quote), Quayle to Culberson, July 21, 1864, E. M. Crick to Quayle, September 27, 1864, and George Isbett to Culberson, October 9, 1864, Adjutant General's Office Records, TSLAC; Quayle to Culberson, n.d., Governor's Office Records, TSLAC; John T. Rowland to James B. Barry, May 28, 1864, Special Orders No. 5 and No. 20, HQ, Dist. of Texas, New Mexico, and Arizona, September 15, September 30, 1864, Special Orders No. 266, HQ, Northern Sub-District of Texas, October 10, 1864, Special Orders No. 67, Bourland's Regiment, October 15, 1864, and Special Orders No. [?], Bourland's Regiment, October 16, 1864, Barry Papers, Briscoe Center; H. A. Whaley to John R. Diamond, n.d., McCulloch to Bourland, March 4, July 14, 1864, Bourland to James J. Diamond, July 19, 1864, Bourland to Quayle, July 19, 1864, Affidavit of Mrs. J. H. Hancock, September 26, 1864, Affidavit of Nancy Speer, September 26, 1864, Affidavit of Mrs. N. E. Hancock, September 27, 1864, and General Orders No. 64, HQ, Northern Sub-District of Texas, October 9, 1864, Bourland Papers, LC; Bourland to Quayle, April 26, May 7, July 20, 24, August 26, September 8, 1864, Isbett to Quayle, May 11, 1864, Bourland to James Ward, May 20, 1864, Quayle to Culberson, August 19, 1864, James S. Moore to Quayle, n.d., Quayle to Moore, September 4, 1864, McCulloch to Bourland, September 12, October 7 and 8, 1864, and Charges and Specifications preferred against Jas Bourland Col Comdg Border Reg, P.A.C.S., October 15, 1864, William Quayle Papers, UA; *OR*, Series I, Vol. 34, pt. 3, 794–95, 813–16, pt. 4, 630–35 (third quote); Tom Bomar, *Glimpses of Grayson County from the Early Days* (Sherman, Tex.: Privately published, 1894), 25; Lucas and Hall, *History*, 87, 128; Wilbarger, *Indian Depredations*, 449–52; James B. Barry, *A Texas Ranger and Frontiersman: The Days of Buck Barry in Texas, 1845–1906*, ed. James K. Greer (Dallas: Southwest Press, 1932), 174–83.

31. Throckmorton to Epperson, November 3, 1864 (quote); Epperson Papers, Briscoe Center; Throckmorton to Bourland, March 31, 1865, Bourland Papers, LC; Culberson to Quayle, September 26, 1864, McCulloch to Quayle, March 22, 1865, William Quayle Papers, UA; Quayle to Culberson, October 7, 1864, Adjutant General's Office Records, TSLAC; General Orders No. 1, First Frontier Dist., Texas State Troops, December 13, 1864, Murrah to Kirby Smith, April 18, 1865, and Murrah to John W. Lane, April 18, 1865, Governor's Office Records, TSLAC; Gammel, *Laws of Texas*, 5:771–72; Howell, *Texas Confederate*, 90–91; Marten, *Texas Divided*, 36–37.

32. General Orders No. 33, HQ, Northern Sub-District of Texas, December 29, 1864, Samuel B. Maxey Papers, TSLAC; McCulloch to Barry, February 16, 1865,

Bourland to Rowland, February 17, 1865, and Post Returns for Texas Frontier Battalion . . . March and April 1865, Barry Papers, Briscoe Center; Charles L. Roff to Bourland, February 7, 1865, Whaley to S. J. McKnight, February 12, 1865, Barry to Bourland, February 15, 1865, Special Orders No. 58, HQ, Northern Sub-District, March 14, 1865, Throckmorton to Bourland, March 31, 1865, and McCulloch to Bourland, April 5, 1865, Bourland Papers, LC; Throckmorton to Epperson, March 12, April 6, 1865, and Throckmorton to Josiah F. Crosby, March 19, 1865, Epperson Papers, Briscoe Center; Throckmorton to William C. Walsh, February 23, 1865, Throckmorton to Dashiell, March 30, 1865, Hill to Walsh, April 4 and 5, 1865, and F. M. Totty to Bourland, April 20, 1865, Adjutant General's Office Records, TSLAC; Throckmorton to Murrah, December 9 and 20, 1864, and C. R. Breedlove to Murrah, November 19, 1864, Governor's Office Records, TSLAC; *OR*, Series I, Vol. 48, pt. 1, 1381; Horton, *Samuel Bell Maxey*, 41–42; Howell, *Texas Confederate*, 91–95.

33. Throckmorton to Epperson, April 6, 1865, Epperson Papers, Briscoe Center; Lucas, "Interview with William Walsh"; McCulloch to Bourland, May 23, 1865, Bourland Papers, LC.

8

In Defense of Their Families

AFRICAN AMERICAN WOMEN, THE FREEDMEN'S

BUREAU, AND RACIAL VIOLENCE DURING

RECONSTRUCTION IN TEXAS

Rebecca A. Czuchry

I mmediately after the Civil War in 1865, African Americans in the former Confederacy faced extremely brutal violence perpetrated by whites. This was particularly true in Texas, a state known during the period for both violence and racial intolerance. Although nominal rights had been guaranteed with passage of the Thirteenth Amendment to the Constitution, the majority of former slaves in Texas found themselves at the mercy of whites—in their homes, their places of work and recreation, their churches, and even the courts. For them, this "freedom" was a far cry from reality, as violence against them increased throughout the period. This was particularly true for black women, whose ambiguous legal status left them particularly vulnerable to racist violence that was most often sexual in nature and almost always perpetrated against them with impunity. Just as they had resisted their enslavement and the violence and brutality inherent in that institution, however, freedwomen did what they could to resist their mistreatment after emancipation in Texas. Although civil authorities and even Freedmen's Bureau agents did little to alleviate the violence against them, black women repeatedly risked their lives by reporting acts of violence that they experienced personally, and also those experienced by family and community members. In testifying to federal officials, not only did black women make white authorities "bear witness to black people's suffering," but they actively participated in claiming their rights as citizens and forged a sense of black communal identity through their shared experiences.[1]

Although historians over the past several decades have produced significant works on Texas during the Reconstruction period and on the racial violence that existed in the state, most of these studies have either ignored or paid only slight attention to the issue of gender. Violence against black women in particular is an aspect of Reconstruction history that has long been neglected by historians, whether because of an apparent paucity of source material or possibly the reluctance of scholars in the past to acknowledge the significance of black women's experiences. Although the scholarship on violence against black women in general has grown over the past thirty years, few scholars have focused specifically on the Reconstruction period, and fewer still on the experience of black women in Reconstruction-era Texas.[2]

As conceptualized here, the extremely violent atmosphere that existed in Texas during the early years of Reconstruction is viewed as an extension of the Civil War: a race war in which violence perpetrated against former slaves—men, women, and children—was a central component in the overall strategy of racial dominance and control. In this context, the use of gendered violence to provoke fear and guarantee racial subordination becomes apparent.

Just the notion of freedom had considerably distinctive gender implications for black women and men. Whereas "freedom" and "manhood" were nominally synonymous during the period, "freedom" and "womanhood" were anything but. Because a large proportion of Southern white society was unwilling to expand its prewar definition of womanhood to include former slaves, they stringently denied black women the protections implied by the status of "lady." In addition, postwar racist mythology defined every black woman as "loose" and immoral, so to assault her physically or sexually was not considered a reprehensible act. Black women were, thus, "prepackaged as bad women within cultural narratives about good women who could be raped" and bad women who could not.[3] With white and black women differentiated in this way, white women's bodies became the "sacred territory" over which white male Texans battled during Reconstruction, "re-fighting the war and re-exerting regional and race pride." Black women's bodies became the literal battlefield in this war.[4]

As mothers and wives, black women endured the trauma of separated families, the forcible apprenticeship of their children, and the injury and death of family members at the hands of resentful, bitter whites. Black men certainly endured vicious and deadly attacks by whites during the period, but black women were, by virtue of their gender, peculiarly susceptible to racist violence and doubly victimized—once as blacks and again as women. As victims of both racism and sexism, black women in Texas faced incredible obstacles in the transition from slavery to freedom with little recourse.[5]

Black women were not, of course, passive victims. On the contrary, many risked their lives resisting their own abuse, and especially protecting their children from cruelty. For some, the Freedmen's Bureau served as a beacon in this difficult transition from slavery to freedom, inasmuch as it kept records of offenses perpetrated upon former slaves and tried to make the transition as smooth as possible. Between 1865 and 1868, freedpeople in Texas reported 1,681 incidents of racial violence to the Freedmen's Bureau. Of these incidents, 13 percent (281) involved black women as the victims of violence.[6]

Although black women put their lives at great risk in reporting violence to civil authorities and the Freedmen's Bureau, neither seemed to have placed much value on black women's lives. Of the reported incidents of violence against black women, local authorities acted in a mere 14 percent (38) of the cases. The Bureau's track record is hardly better for the period, having acted in only 19 percent (54) of the cases.[7] To be sure, the hands of Bureau officials were tied in many ways; local citizens and civil authorities for the most part did not support them, and the agency itself was severely understaffed and underfunded with very little, if any, power. But their inaction also raises the question of whether the white male agents' own philosophies on race and gender, seemingly similar to that of Southern whites generally, dictated their responses to some of these crimes.

Bureau officials and civil authorities implicitly condoned the violence against black women by their outright failure to protect them in many cases, regardless of the degree of barbarity. For example, a freedwoman named Susan Goosely reported to officials in Davis County the names of a group of men who dragged her out of bed, raped and pistol-whipped her, knocked her teeth out, strung her up by the thumbs, and choked her. When the authorities failed to take any action against the perpetrators, Ms. Goosely was forced to flee the county for her life, even though she had also alerted Bureau agents. Likewise, the family of Emily Granes reported to civil authorities that James Wise whipped her and gouged out one of her eyes. Wise gave no reason for the crime that almost cost the victim her life. In Limestone, after John Fogarty cut Minerva Ward's ears off and burned her arms "to a crisp," she reported the brutality to the county Freedmen's Bureau agent, who recorded no explanation for the crime and took no action on behalf of Ms. Ward. The inaction of law enforcement officers was often related to their direct participation in the most heinous atrocities committed against black women. For example, in Harrison County, Deputy Sheriff Warnell took Rose Campbell from her home, claiming that she was being arrested; he then raped her. Ms. Campbell had no recourse but to report the incident to Bureau agents who, it appears, did nothing.[8]

Violence took many forms during Reconstruction, and physical assault, especially whipping, was a common practice. Whipping not only served as a psychological reminder for freedwomen of the institution of slavery but also demonstrated the fact that many whites viewed blacks merely as animals.[9] Black women were frequently strapped up and whipped as they had been as slaves and struck with implements ranging from pistols, bricks, hammers, saws, and chairs to metal whip handles, animal bones, and clubs. In most cases, the justifications given for such abuses, whether or not they resulted in death, reflected ingrained antebellum ideas of what had previously constituted appropriate disciplinary action against slaves.

Whipping offenses were the most commonly reported to the Bureau by black women. Julie Gardner, for example, reported being whipped almost to death by her white employer, R. H. Wren, after she had the audacity to disagree with him. Likewise, two black women in Upshur County reported being given one hundred lashes each by their boss—one for not hoeing fast enough and the other for hoeing up a single cotton stalk. This was not the first time these women reported the perpetrator for the same offense, yet there is no record of him ever having been questioned

For many Texas freedwomen, emancipation changed little in
their relationship with whites. From *Aunt Sally; Or, The Cross the
Way to Freedom: A Narrative of the Slave-life and Purchase of the
Mother of Rev. Isaac Williams, of Detroit, Michigan* (Cincinnati,
1860), 153.

by law enforcement. An unnamed freedwoman reported Frank Waller
for knocking her to the ground and whipping her repeatedly because he
considered the bread she baked for one of his meals unsuitable, and a
woman in Harris County reported being brutally beaten across the face
with a paddle for being "lazy."[10]

In over 50 percent of the 131 cases of whipping and similar physical assaults reported to the Bureau against women, agents recorded no
explanation for the crimes and described civil authorities as refusing
to act, even when given evidence. It appears that many white Texans,

civilians and local officials alike, believed that the physical assault of black women, clearly reminiscent of the days of slavery, was their prerogative and certainly not a crime. On the contrary, when a black woman in Walker County reported a white woman for assaulting her, local authorities heard the case but fined the injured woman for court costs totaling $23. This, no doubt, reassured the white populace that the physical assault of black women was acceptable social behavior in the eyes of the law.[11]

Because of such maltreatment, many women were forced to steal in order to survive, even though such "crimes" could likely result in lengthy prison sentences. Of the fourteen black women incarcerated at the Texas State Penitentiary at Huntsville in 1867, thirteen had been convicted of stealing from their employers and were serving sentences ranging from two to five years.[12] Landowners did not always report theft to the authorities, however; it seems many preferred to take the law into their own hands. A woman in Bastrop reported being shot through the thigh by her employer for "stealing peaches," and a woman in Bowie County was whipped severely, pounded with a stick, and then tied up by one thumb for allegedly taking some flour. May Oglesby planned to report Mr. Shaw to the Bureau for "detaining her forcibly" in his service and keeping her in deplorable living conditions. In retaliation, Shaw shot at Oglesby four times. Likewise, a woman in Dallas County was "whipped and kicked" for "trying to procure her freedom" from her employer. Many black women, thus, reported being in a state of virtual slavery as their "employers" controlled not only their labor but their movement as well.[13]

Very few freed black women fit white ideas of the "true" woman, an ideal within which domesticity, piety, purity, and submissiveness were central. Women who worked outside the home, in particular, were thought of as unnatural and unfeminine. The fact that the overwhelming number of black women in Texas performed "double duty in both home and field" weakened their role in white eyes as mothers and wives and came to symbolize "the low esteem in which [they were] held in society." Like white women, black women suffered the same restrictions of their male-enforced gender roles; unlike their white counterparts, however, black women were denied the protections of these gender roles and thus were vulnerable to white violence with little recourse.[14]

Whereas nineteenth-century ideals of womanhood and femininity subjected white pregnant women to chivalry and special protection, it seems that black women in the same condition faced the opposite circumstances and were, in fact, more harshly abused. White Texans showed little restraint in dealing with pregnant black women and in some cases seem to have accelerated the brutality of violence against them specifically because of the pregnancy. During the antebellum period, some slaveholders probably gave slave women the benefit of the doubt when they claimed to have pregnancy-related aches and pains, if only because they realized the economic benefit of a full-term pregnancy and birth. But in just as many cases, it seems, not only were pregnant slaves forced to continue carrying their normal workload in the fields, they often found themselves beaten or otherwise harshly treated for failing to meet their quotas.[15]

One common punishment for such offenses entailed beating a woman's entire backside with a whip or other implement while she lay flat on the ground, her protruding stomach shoved into a hole. Although this type of beating would certainly be excessively painful for the mother and dangerous to the pregnancy, the practice of lying over a hole may have actually been a means of protecting the fetus and, thus, the slave owner's investment. Circumstances seem to have been worse for freedwomen in Texas when they became pregnant, however, for they and their unborn children were no longer seen as investments to be protected. Like the pregnant woman in Fort Bend County who reported receiving 150 lashes from a white man for no reported reason, pregnant black women throughout the Reconstruction period were whipped, raped, shot, and brutally murdered with little regard or respect for their physical or maternal state.[16] Commonly viewed by whites as carriers of the "despised" race, it seems that pregnant black women frequently reported violence they believed to have been directed against their wombs specifically.[17]

Protecting their children outside the womb was even more difficult for freedwomen, for motherhood in many ways intensified their vulnerability to white violence. Women not only faced the daily risk of physical and sexual abuse personally but were also confronted with a white population that continued to control and abuse their offspring. As they had during slavery, whites often used the threat of violence against children as a weapon to keep black women submissive. Isolated from the many parental protections granted their white counterparts in law, black women in Texas frequently saw their children indiscriminately beaten by whites or stripped from them under the guise of apprenticeship. As in slavery, the law in Texas during Reconstruction seemed to conspire against black women and their ability to maintain familial control.[18]

The apprenticeship statute, part of the Texas Black Code enacted by the Eleventh Legislature in 1866, sought specifically to "enslave the rising generation" by allowing so-called orphans to be bound out to white families for long periods of time, most until they reached the age of twenty-one. Because of the institution of slavery and its total disregard for black parental rights, all slave children were basically defined as orphans with no legal connection to their biological parents. After emancipation, free black children in Texas found themselves in an equally ambiguous position; Texas law still considered them orphans primarily because of the legislature's refusal to sanction marriage between black men and women.[19] The Black Code specifically sanctioned the binding out of children without parents as well as those "whose parent or parents could not support them." Texas courts further defined any "fatherless child" as an orphan, regardless of the ability of the mother to care for that child. This made it relatively easy for whites to secure the cheap labor of their young former slaves by making legal arrangements to become "guardians" of black children, whether or not they had living parents. Prospective white guardians had to meet only minimum requirements, including providing "sufficient food and clothing" and administering medical attention as needed. They also had the authority to "inflict such moderate corporeal chastisement as may be necessary and proper." Some agents apparently believed that the binding out of black children to white families was best for the child, given the dire economic condition of the former slaves. Most, however, realized that apprenticeship was simply a legalized form of child slavery and forced labor, and Bureau offices were constantly flooded with desperate requests by mothers whose children had been taken from them. Bureau agent John Dix summed up the situation for Texas when he declared, "I never apprentice colored children to white people, for the reason that colored children would be generally treated as slaves." Even so, until 1870 when the statute was repealed by the Republican-dominated legislature, black children in Texas were bound out to whites in large numbers while their parents could do little to protect them.[20]

As an important means of eliminating white control over their lives after emancipation, it became important for the black family unit, restricted under slavery, to assert itself. There had been no greater pain for mothers than the helplessness and humiliation they suffered watching whites abuse their children during slavery. One of the most profound consequences of emancipation was the hope that black families could live free from the authority of whites. Unfortunately, freedom from slavery did not give black mothers the authority to protect their children from violence.[21]

Often children suffered as an indirect result of their parents' testing the bounds of freedom. For example, Bureau officials concluded that a group of "desperados" who set fire to a house in Leon County were most likely targeting the parents for their "assertiveness," not their small child who burned to death in the flames. Frequently mothers were assaulted and some even killed for trying to protect their children from abuse by whites and for reporting such crimes to authorities. A black woman and her children were "cruelly beaten" for no reason by a group of white men who threatened to hang her if she lodged a complaint with the Grimes County Bureau office. After trying to prevent two white men from whipping her child for no reason, Patsy was "struck over the head with a pistol" and severely injured. Lizzy was assaulted by G. W. Moore simply because she said Moore should not whip her child for misbehaving on the job and threatened to report him for doing so.[22]

Freedmen's Bureau records for Texas show a total of only twenty-five black children reported as injured or killed by whites during the period. This number is deceiving, however; not all of these youngest victims of violence are immediately recognizable in the records, because agents frequently failed to list incidents of violence against children separately.[23] Even so, black women did report outrages against their children to the Freedmen's Bureau, but many acts against them probably went unreported for fear of violent reprisals. Although statistics from the period are scarce, the Freedmen's Bureau records at least give some inkling as to the extent of violence perpetrated against children, violence that manifested itself in forms similar to adult violence. African American males and females, toddlers, and adolescents all suffered at the hands of whites in Texas during Reconstruction. Children were held in a state of quasi-slavery, raped, beaten, mutilated without provocation, and murdered indiscriminately. In most cases, civil authorities failed to charge or successfully prosecute the perpetrators.

Freedwomen in Texas faced a particularly difficult task in trying to protect their daughters from the added threat of sexual violence that had been commonplace during slavery. Because the institution sanctioned the ownership of human beings as property, by extension it gave white men ownership of black women's sexuality and their children. With emancipation, the legal institution as such was outlawed, but many of the advantages of ownership, particularly with regard to the female body, remained in place for white men.[24] Sexual violence against young black girls, thus, continued after the Civil War, while mothers risked and, at times, even lost their lives trying to protect their daughters from vicious attacks by both white and black men. When a black woman begged her employer Mr. Baird to protect her daughter from the "constant ravishing of [his] favorite black man" on the plantation, Baird did nothing about the rapes but proceeded to tie up the mother and give her one hundred lashes for her insolence. After two white men broke into a home and attempted a rape on a young black girl, the girl's mother was beaten severely for coming to her defense.[25] Although the risks were certainly enormous, these examples of bravery demonstrate that black women continually fought to define the terms of their freedom, for themselves and their children.

Although physical violence and intimidation were used regularly against black communities in every part of the state, this was just one tactic used by whites. As recent studies of ethnic cleansing and genocide in twentieth-century conflicts have shown, violence against the women and children of a defeated enemy, particularly rape and other sexualized forms of abuse, can serve the additional purpose of emasculating men.[26] In fact, raping the women of a conquered enemy has been seen as "the ultimate expression of contempt for a defeated foe" and has been used in every culture and world region throughout history.[27] Racial violence in postwar Texas can be viewed through a similar lens. The sexual exploitation and abuse of black women and girls by whites served indirectly as a "weapon of terror" against the entire race, in addition to traumatizing the victims directly. In being prevented from defending their wives and children from violence, especially sexualized violence, black men were "symbolically castrated and assaulted in their essential dignity." In this way, black women were "doubly instrumentalized." Not only were they the objects of forcible rape, but in the act itself they became "instruments in the degradation of their men." The sexual assault of black women and girls during Reconstruction, then, was an important part of the "reinforcing structure" that upheld a "system of racial and economic exploitation," victimizing African Americans of both sexes.[28] This most invasive form of abuse, though serving multiple purposes, was used widely as a tool for instigating terror and guaranteeing racial subordination of the entire black community.

The sexual exploitation and rape of black women and girls was just as widespread, if not more so, after emancipation.[29] Because freedom from slavery meant that black women were no longer the legal property of a particular white man, they became, to a great degree, "sexually available to all white men."[30] Most white Southerners and probably Northerners, both civilians and law enforcement officials, forcefully rejected the idea that a black woman could actually be raped. As was the case in most of the violent incidents perpetrated against black women, white perpetrators were unlikely to be charged with or convicted of rape or sexual assault when their victims were black; neither were black men likely to be charged with or convicted of raping black women.[31] Three black women in McLennan County reported being raped, beaten, and robbed by William Killum, J. Tubbs, and Parish Johnson. These same three white men continued their rampage the following day, sexually assaulting seven-year-old Dolla Jackson and robbing her of twenty-five cents. Even though they were all identified by name to authorities, none of these men were questioned or charged with these atrocities. A Bureau agent commenting on the Jackson assault merely wrote "Chivalry???" in his record of the event, implicitly acknowledging that black women and girls did not enjoy the same basic protections granted to whites of the same gender, or perhaps indicating disdain at Southern concepts of chivalry.[32]

Officials rarely took accusations of rape by black women seriously and seldom levied charges. When they were charged, however, white men were typically acquitted and their black victims blamed for provoking the act. On the very rare occasion that a white man was actually convicted of sexually assaulting a black woman, the racist stereotype of black female promiscuity was likely the main justification for the relatively lighter punishments he received. Texas Bureau agents recorded only one case of a white man charged and convicted of a crime involving the rape of a black woman. Emily Reed reported E. A. Bingham of Red River County for "assault and battery," an assault which, according to Bureau agents, included rape. Because he claimed to be financially unable to make his court-ordered payment, however, Bingham's fine was subsequently reduced to a mere $35. That the perpetrator in this case received a fine in the first place is highly notable, perhaps speaking either to the singular violence of his crime or to his general unpopularity among his peers, since Texas statutes provided specific penalties for rape that did not include monetary fines.[33] The records are unclear, however, as to whether the rape was actually recognized as part of the formal charge. That Bingham not be charged with raping a black woman would certainly reflect nineteenth-century gender conventions regarding who could and could not be raped. It is also likely that Ms. Reed, being black and female, was unable to furnish corroborating evidence and witness testimony to the court's liking (by an upstanding white, preferably male, witness), resulting in less than a preponderance of the evidence necessary to sustain such a charge. Nonetheless, and despite the rarity of both the conviction and the punishment, the court devalued the victim in this case by reducing the fine to an amount agreeable to the criminal rather than impose the sanctioned jail time for the assault.[34]

Black women did not just have to fear the threat of rape itself and retaliation for reporting such abuses; they additionally had to deal with their accusations likely being met with disbelief by civil authorities and, unfortunately, by Bureau officials in many instances. Although most Bureau agents probably did their best to protect black Texans from violence, their records indicate that they, like whites generally, did not recognize the rape of black women as a serious crime. Often Bureau agents failed to note rape as an actual crime committed against black women. Descriptions of circumstances in the records are rife with euphemisms, such as "ravishing" or "maltreatment," but agents then seem to move on to emphasize what they apparently believe to be crimes of a more serious nature.[35] For example, when a black woman reported being brutally beaten and raped by a group of white men, the Bureau described the crime as "hanging by thumbs and striking over the head with a pistol," even though being "ravished" was part of a litany of abuses reported by the woman. Likewise, when a young girl successfully resisted an attempted rape by a group of white men and reported the incident to the Harrison County Bureau office, the agent listed the offense as "whipping and threatening to kill."[36] Although "attempted rape" is mentioned as part of the lengthier description of the offense, it is clear that the agent in this case, like many others, did not view this type of violation as severe enough to be predominant in the record. This fact is especially disturbing when one considers that in 34 percent (96) of all cases of violence perpetrated against black women, agents failed to describe incidents at all, aside from listing the crime that was alleged to have been committed or the law that was violated (e.g., "homicide" or "assault and battery"). This certainly begs the question as to whether at least some of these crimes perpetrated against black women were not also sexual assaults.

Often Bureau agents only allude to sexualized forms of abuse in their records, using terms such as "unmercifully" or "shamefully" to describe physical violence that is implicitly sexual. According to one historian, it is this implied sexuality, rather than the violent act itself, that is thought of as shameful by agents. This same implicit sexual undertone is evident in the many cases where partially or totally naked victims are further degraded by "bucking" or being whipped on their "private" or "bare" parts.[37] Black women, then, faced the humiliation associated with such "unspeakable" acts and were further subjugated by their induced silence.

Black women in Texas did retaliate, albeit infrequently, against their attackers. Usually, however, retaliation could be met with even more severe violence, and in many cases resistance could lead to death. Bureau records indicate that it was quite common for abuses by whites to accompany threats of more severe harm. Instead of risking the physical fallout from retaliation, most black women sought justice by taking their cases of abuse to local authorities. But public apathy combined with prejudiced officials made it virtually impossible to secure convictions against whites for crimes against black women during Reconstruction in Texas. Civil authorities contributed to the violence against freedwomen by their outright failure to protect them. Not only did they submit to the influence of white community members, but many local officials actively participated in racist violence.[38]

During Reconstruction in Texas, then, violence against black women became an essential means of reasserting racial control and helped to perpetuate the antebellum social order.[39] In abusing black women, not only did white men reassert their authority over the individual victims, they took power and masculinity from black men. In essence, white men used black women's bodies indirectly as implements to degrade black men. As Gerda Lerner has asserted, "Men in patriarchal societies who cannot protect the sexual purity of their wives, sisters, and children are truly impotent and dishonored."[40] Explicit and even implicit sexual forms of violence further served white aims of subjugation and control by inducing silence in the victims through their humiliation. Besides the very real possibility of violent retribution for reporting any crimes against them, black victims of sexualized violence faced the additional humiliation of having to describe acts considered by most as "unspeakable."[41] Thus, it is likely that there were many more sexual crimes perpetrated against black women by whites than were actually reported to the Freedmen's Bureau or to local officials. Although sexualized violence was just one weapon in the arsenal used by many white Texans, it played a significant role in the terrorization of the larger black community during Reconstruction.

Although there were few means of protection available to them, black Texas women cannot be viewed as simply passive victims of racial violence. Many lost their lives protecting themselves and their family members from violence or suffered additional abuse in retaliation for reporting crimes perpetrated against them. Some stayed in Texas after the war just long enough to reconstitute their families and then moved on to other states. But the majority, it seems, believed they would receive at least a modicum of justice when they reported their assailants to the Bureau, and many did. The Freedmen's Bureau, however, was limited in many ways in its ability to protect black women from violence, and its demise in Texas resulted from those internal limitations coupled with constant white hostility.

In just over four years, the number of violent offenses reported to the Bureau by freedwomen was so great and the brutality so vicious, it is difficult to imagine what the transition to freedom would have been like for them without the presence of the Freedmen's Bureau. One historian's general assessment of the Bureau adequately describes its failure to make significant changes for African Americans in Texas: it was "a well-intentioned experiment" but exerted "only a temporary and limited influence on the fundamental patterns of postwar Southern crime and punishment."[42] It was up to African American women themselves to defend their families and their communities from violent whites during Reconstruction and, in the process, claim the citizenship they deserved as free people.

NOTES

1. Rebecca A. Kosary, "To Degrade and Control: White Violence and the Maintenance of Racial and Gender Boundaries in Reconstruction Texas, 1865–1868" (Ph.D. dissertation, Texas A&M University, 2006); Kidada E. Williams, *They Left Great Marks on Me: African American Testimonies of Racial Violence from Emancipation to World War I* (New York: New York University Press, 2012), 7.

2. Victoria Bynum, *Unruly Women: The Politics of Social and Sexual Control in the Old South* (Chapel Hill: University of North Carolina Press, 1992); Catherine Clinton, "Bloody Terrain: Freedwomen, Sexuality, and Violence during Reconstruction," in *Half Sisters of History: Southern Women and the American Past*, ed. Catherine Clinton (Durham, N.Car.: Duke University Press, 1994); Laura F. Edwards, *Gendered Strife and Confusion: The Political Culture of Reconstruction* (Chicago: University of Illinois Press, 1997); Drew Gilpin Faust, "'Trying to Do a Man's Business': Slavery, Violence, and Gender in the American Civil War," *Gender and History* 4 (1992): 197–214; Paula Giddings, *When and Where I Enter: The Impact of Black Women on Race and Sex in America* (New York: Bantam Books, 1984); Jacquelyn Dowd Hall, "The Mind That Burns in Each Body: Women, Rape, and Racial Violence," *Southern Exposure* 12 (1984): 61–71; Darlene Clark Hine and Kathleen Thompson, *A Shining Thread of Hope: The History of Black Women in America* (New York: Broadway Books, 1998); Martha Hodes, *White Women, Black Men: Illicit Sex in the Nineteenth-Century South* (New Haven, Conn.: Yale University Press, 1997); Jacqueline Jones, *Labor of Love, Labor of Sorrow: Black Women, Work and the Family from Slavery to the Present* (New York: Vintage Books, 1985); Rebecca A. Kosary, "To Punish and Humiliate the Entire Community: White Violence Perpetrated against African-American Women in Texas, 1865–1868," in *Still the Arena of Civil War: Violence and Turmoil in Reconstruction Texas, 1865—1874*, ed. Kenneth Wayne Howell (Denton: University of North Texas Press, 2012); Hannah Rosen, "The Gender of Reconstruction: Rape, Race and Citizenship in the Post-Emancipation South" (Ph.D. dissertation, University of Chicago, 1999); Dorothy Sterling, ed., *We Are Your Sisters: Black Women in the Nineteenth Century* (New York: W. W. Norton, 1984); Williams, *They Left Great Marks*.

3. Catherine Clinton, "Reconstructing Freedwomen," in *Divided Houses: Gender and the Civil War*, ed. Catherine Clinton and Nina Silber (New York: Oxford University Press, 1992); Kimberle Crenshaw, "Mapping the Margins: Intersectionality,

Identity Politics, and Violence against Women of Color," *Stanford Law Review* 43 (1991): 1241–99. Sean Michael Kelly examines the problems black women encountered in attempting to assert autonomy within their own homes in "Plantation Frontiers: Race, Ethnicity, and Family along the Brazos River of Texas, 1821–1886 (Ph.D. dissertation, University of Texas, 2000), 309, 322, 327–28.

4. Clinton, "Reconstructing Freedwomen," 310, 312, 318–319. See also Gerda Lerner, ed., *Black Women in White America: A Documentary History* (New York: Random House, 1992), 153.

5. Although women could not vote, both black and white women in some instances could sue and be sued in the state of Texas after the Civil War. This was hardly the rule, however; women were generally excluded from the judicial system based on their gender, and black women faced additional restrictions based on race—particularly in the early years of Reconstruction. Hall, "Mind That Burns," 62; Lerner, *Black Women in White America*, 149.

6. "Records of Criminal Offenses Committed in the State of Texas," Assistant Commissioner, Texas, Vols. 11–13, Bureau of Refugees, Freedmen, and Abandoned Lands, Record Group 105, roll 32, National Archives [hereafter BRFAL, with individual cased cited as "CO no." followed by incident numbers]. Texas Freedmen's Bureau agents recorded a total of 1,681 incidents of violence against blacks, with 281 perpetrated against black women and twenty-five against children. The "Report of Outrages," however, does not specifically categorize either gender or age—for either perpetrators or victims. The statistics used here with regard to violence against black women thus represent only those incidents where the gender of the victim can be accurately determined. This is an especially difficult task, since many entries omit victims' names and any explanation or circumstances surrounding the incident. These omissions, together with the fact that obviously not every case of abuse of black women made its way to the Bureau offices, suggests that the number of black women victims is probably higher. Further, of the 281 incidents of violence perpetrated against black women, the majority (92 percent) were perpetrated by individuals; of the twenty-one incidents perpetrated by groups of two or more, a third were crimes of a sexual nature. It is also difficult to determine the context for the crimes. See, for example, CO no. 406. The offense is listed simply as "homicide," so the context of the crime is not immediately apparent. The circumstances, however, explain that the victim was shot and killed "because she would not commit adultery with him," making this a crime of a sexual nature. This is just one example out of many in the records where the context is only apparent after a review of the circumstances. Many of the letters written by local Bureau agents to headquarters contain more descriptive language and have, therefore, been additionally useful in determining the context surrounding some of the violent incidents. All tabulations in this chapter are by the author and based on the aforementioned "Records of Criminal Offenses Committed in the State of Texas."

7. Civil "action" includes arresting, filing charges against, trying, and assessing fines. Bureau "action" includes the same, although agents also frequently turned perpetrators over immediately to civil authorities, since they had limited jurisdiction in many cases. It is possible that some of these cases were prosecuted after

agents filed reports. With the widespread practice of jury nullification, however, it is doubtful that any significant number would have resulted in convictions. For limitations and constraints on the Freedmen's Bureau generally, see James Oakes, "A Failure of Vision: The Collapse of the Freedmen's Bureau Courts," *Civil War History* 25 (1979): 66–76.

8. CO nos. 308, 107, 838, 1653. The best source for numerous examples of civil authorities actively and outwardly participating in racial violence throughout the former Confederacy is the thirteen-volume *Klan Report*, although the report is extremely limited on Texas. See U.S. Congress, Join Select Committee on the Condition of Affairs in the Late Insurrectionary States, *Report of the Joint Select Committee to Inquire into the Condition of Affairs in the Late Insurrectionary States*, 13 vols. (Washington, D.C.: Government Printing Office, 1872).

9. Frequently, the whipping of black women and men amounted to a form of sexualized violence wherein women were whipped on their "bare parts" or otherwise "shamefully" beaten. In addition, it was quite common for victims to be partially or even totally stripped of their clothing prior to whippings.

10. CO nos. 474, 476, 141, 319.

11. CO nos. 1721, 108, 109, 14, 163. White women participated in other forms of brutality against black women and children. See, for example, CO nos. 1639, 372, 1846, 743. As stated previously, it is difficult to determine the gender of perpetrators because there is not a specific category in the records.

12. William H. Sinclair (inspector) to J. T. Kirkman Acting Assistant Adjutant General, February 26, 1867, box 21, BRFAL. One woman was convicted of helping her husband escape from jail with a pick axe. See also *List of Freedmen and Women Confined in the Texas Penitentiary, Nov. 6, 1866*, Penitentiary Papers, Texas State Library, Austin, Texas.

13. CO nos. 1975, 901, 366.

14. Giddings, *When and Where I Enter*, 47–48, 62; Elizabeth Fox-Genovese, *Within the Plantation Household: Black and White Women of the Old South* (Chapel Hill: University of North Carolina Press, 1988), 49–50, 64–65, 202–203, 290.

15. Angela Y. Davis, *Women, Race and Class* (New York: Random House, 1981), 9–10; Fox-Genovese, *Within the Plantation Household*, 322; Deborah Gray White, *Ar'n't I a Woman? Female Slaves in the Plantation South* (New York: W. W. Norton, 1985), 98–99. Fox-Genovese and White posit that slave women often used pregnancy, real or feigned, as a negotiating tool to get better treatment and lighten the workload; Davis describes slave owners' complete disregard for slave women even in the later months of pregnancy. See also Thelma Jennings, "'Us Colored Women Had to Go through a Plenty': Sexual Exploitation of African-American Slave Women," *Journal of Women's History* 1 (1991), 54.

16. Davis, *Women, Race and Class*, 10; CO no. 204; Jennings, "'Us Colored Women Had to Go through a Plenty,'" 56–57.

17. For a particularly brutal incident, see Sinclair to Kirkman, July 2, 1867, BRFAL; CO no. 1133. This type of brutality, aimed specifically at black women as carriers of their race, seems to have extended well past the Reconstruction period and into the twentieth century, as seen in the experience of Mary Turner. She

"vowed to find those responsible" and "have them punished in the courts" after her husband was lynched in Georgia in 1918. Taken by a mob and hung upside down by her ankles, Mary was doused with gasoline and set on fire, and her eight-month pregnant belly was cut open with a knife used to slaughter pigs—all while she was alive. The baby fell to the ground and cried briefly, before a man crushed the baby's skull under his heel. The mob then fired "hundreds of bullets" into Mary's upside down, dangling, mutilated body. James Allen, ed., *Without Sanctuary: Lynching Photography in America* (Santa Fe, N. Mex.: Twin Palms, 2000), 14.

18. See Clinton, "Bloody Terrain," 142. See also Wilma King, *Stolen Childhood: Slave Youth in Nineteenth-Century America* (Bloomington: Indiana University Press, 1995).

19. A. H. Mayer to Henry A. Ellis, November 24, 1866, vol. 120, Liberty Sub-district, Records of the Subordinate Field offices for the State of Texas, BRFAL. On the Texas Black Code, see Barry A. Crouch, "'All the Vile Passions': The Texas Black Code of 1866," *Southwestern Historical Quarterly* 97 (1993): 13–34; H. P. N. Gammel, *The Laws of Texas, 1822–1897,* 10 vols. (Austin: Gammel, 1898). On legalization of marriage, see Barry A. Crouch, "'Chords of Love,'" 262. See Barry A. Crouch and Larry Madaras, "Reconstructing Black Families: Perspectives from the Texas Freedmen's Bureau Records," *Prologue* 18 (1986): 109–122, for a discussion of black children who were "actually" orphans in Texas during the period.

20. See John T. Raper to Gregory, November 29, 1865, unlisted letters 1865–1866, BRFAL; also O. H. P. Garret to A. J. Hamilton, December 11, 1865, Governor's Papers [Hamilton], Texas State Library, Austin; Gammel, *Laws of Texas,* 5:979–81; "Laws in Relation to Freedmen," *Senate Executive Document,* 39th Cong., 2nd sess., No. 6 (Serial 1276), 225–226. John Dix to Richardson, May 31, 1868, Operations Reports, BRFAL. For an examination of Bureau agent John Dix and the Reconstruction process in Nueces County, see Randolph Campbell, *Grass-Roots Reconstruction in Texas* (Baton Rouge: Louisiana State University Press, 1997), 197–219.

21. Leon Litwack, *Been in the Storm So Long: The Aftermath of Slavery* (New York: Alfred A. Knopf, 1979), 238. See also Sean Michael Kelley, "Plantation Frontiers," 322, 327–328. Kelley describes black men asserting their "patriarchal urge" over their dependents, which not only caused problems between black families and white landowners but frequently caused strife within families as black women attempted to assert their own autonomy.

22. CO nos. 584, 1624, 2140; see also nos. 706, 712, 1255, 1361, 2104.

23. See, for example, CO no. 584—listed as an abuse perpetrated against a woman. The circumstances reveal that the woman and her children were all beaten, yet the children are not listed separately, and it is unknown how may children she had.

24. Karen Anderson, *Teaching Gender in U.S. History* (Washington, D.C.: American Historical Association, 1997), 29. This topic is thoroughly discussed in Nell Irvin Painter's "Soul Murder and Slavery: Toward a Full Cost Accounting," in *U.S. History as Women's History: New Feminist Essays,* ed. Linda Kerber, Alice Kessler-Harris, and Kathryn Kish Sklar (Chapel Hill: University of North Carolina Press, 1995).

25. CO nos. 369, 497. It must be noted that neither of these offenses is recorded in Bureau records as incidents of rape or attempted rape against specific children. They are listed as acts of physical assault committed against the mothers. Thus, to say that the number of children injured during the period is twenty-five is inaccurate, for it does not take these (and many others like them) into account. More important, the rapes are almost indiscernible in the description of circumstances surrounding the incidents. At times the terms of "raped" or "ravished" seem to be almost an afterthought.

26. Lisa Cardyn has examined sexualized violence perpetrated by the Ku Klux Klan during the later years of Reconstruction in this context. See Cardyn, "Sexualized Racism/Gendered Violence: Trauma and the Body Politic in the Reconstruction South" (Ph.D. dissertation, Yale University, 2003), 7. For works on rape in warfare, especially in recent conflicts, see Beverly Allen, *Rape Warfare: The Hidden Genocide in Bosnia-Herzegovina and Croatia* (Minneapolis: University of Minnesota Press, 1996); Libby Tata Arcel, "Deliberate Sexual Torture of Women in War: The Case of Bosnia-Herzegovina," in *International Handbook of Human Response to Trauma,* ed. Arieh Y. Shalev, Rachel Yehuda, and Alexander C. McFarlane (New York: Plenum, 2000); Andrew Bell-Fialkoff, "A Brief History of Ethnic Cleansing," *Foreign Affairs* 72 (1993): 110–21; Patrick J. Bracken and Celia Petty, eds., *Rethinking the Trauma of War* (London: Free Association Books, 1998); Siobhan K. Fisher, "Occupation of the Womb: Forced Impregnation as Genocide," *Duke Law Journal* (October 1996): 91–133; Roy Gutman, *A Witness to Genocide: The 1993 Pulitzer Prize-Winning Dispatches on the "Ethnic Cleansing" of Bosnia* (New York: Macmillan, 1993); Catharine MacKinnon, "Rape, Genocide, and Women's Human Rights," *Harvard Women's Law Journal* 17 (1994): 5–16; Ruth Siefert, "The Second Front: The Logic of Sexual Violence in Wars," *Women's Studies International Forum* 19 (1996): 35–43; Meredeth Turshen, "The Political Economy of Rape: An Analysis of Systematic Rape and Sexual Abuse of Women during Armed Conflict in Africa," in *Victims, Perpetrators or Actors? Gender, Armed Conflict, and Political Violence,* ed. Caroline O. N. Moser and Fiona C. Clark (London: Zed Books, 2001).

27. Gerda Lerner, ed., *Black Women in White America: A Documentary History* (New York: Vintage Books, 1992), 172. See also MacKinnon, "Rape, Genocide, and Women's Human Rights," 5–16; Seifert, "Second Front," 35–43.

28. Kimberle Crenshaw, "Mapping the Margins"; Karen A Getman, "Sexual Control in the Slaveholding South: The Implementation and Maintenance of a Racial Caste System," *Harvard Women's Law Journal* 7 (1984): 115–52; Jennifer Wriggins, "Rape, Racism, and the Law," *Harvard Women's Law Journal* 6 (1983): 103–41; Lerner, *Black Women in White America,* 72.

29. Many historians have posited that black women were, in fact, more vulnerable to rape and other forms of sexual abuse after emancipation. According to Laura Edwards, "Emancipation heightened the vulnerability of African-American women to violence at the hands of white men, who used rape and other ritualized forms of sexual abuse to limit black women's freedom and to reinscribe antebellum racial hierarchies." Edwards, *Gendered Strife and Confusion,* 199. See also

Hazel V. Carby, *Reconstructing Womanhood: The Emergence of the Afro-American Woman Novelist* (New York: Oxford University Press, 1987), 39; Clinton, "Bloody Terrain," 331; Davis, *Women, Race and Class,* 175–76; Hall, "Mind That Burns," 63; James Smallwood, "Black Freedwomen after Emancipation: The Texas Experience," *Prologue* 27 (1995): 313; Allen Trelease, *White Terror: The Ku Klux Klan Conspiracy and Southern Reconstruction* (Baton Rouge: Louisiana State University Press, 1995), 232, 341; Wriggins, "Rape, Racism," 119.

   30. John D'Emilio and Estelle B. Freedman, *Intimate Matters: A History of Sexuality in America,* 2nd ed. (Chicago: University of Chicago Press, 1997), 107.

   31. The Bureau's "Record of Criminal Offenses" does not list black men as perpetrators of rape or attempted rape on black women—although one incident describes the "constant ravishing of a favorite black man" (CO no. 497). This is a surprising oversight in the Bureau's violence compilation, inasmuch as some black women did report such crimes to agents who then alerted civil authorities in many cases. See, for example, L. H. Warren (Agent, Houston) to Mayor De Daligethy, June 13, 1867, Vol. 102, p. 27; Warren to Judge B. P. Fuller, June 27, 1867, Vol. 102, 57–58, BRFAL. Unfortunately, there is no record of charges being filed in these specific cases. Jacquelyn Dowd Hall speaks to the prevalence of black-on-black rape and its near inevitability during the period: "In a society that defines manhood in terms of power and possessions, black men are denied the resources to fulfill their expected roles. . . . inevitably, they turn to domination of women, the one means of asserting traditional manhood within their control." Hall, "Mind That Burns," 70.

   32. CO nos. 2073, 2074, 2075, 2077.

   33. Gammel, *Laws of Texas,* 5:161.

   34. Lerner, *Black Women in White America,* 164; CO no. 1893; see Gammel, *Laws of Texas,* 5:161; D'Emilio and Freedman, *Intimate Matters,* 104–108.

   35. Of the 281 incidents of violence against black women recorded in the Bureau records, 2.5 percent (7) are noted specifically as rape or attempted rape in the "Offense Nature" or crime column. In that same number of cases, 2.5 percent (7), rape is not noted specifically, but instead "assault and battery" or some other generic description is noted in the crime column, with rape or "shameful treatment" described in the circumstances surrounding the attack.

   36. CO nos. 308, 1587.

   37. Cardyn, "Sexualized Racism/Gendered Violence," 62. "Bucking" was a common form of punishment used during the antebellum and Reconstruction periods. For firsthand accounts see, for example, Henry Bibb, *The Life and Adventures of Henry Bibb: An American Slave* (1849; reprint with an introduction by Charles J. Heglar, Madison: University of Wisconsin Press, 2001), 103–105; Louis Hughes, *Thirty Years a Slave: From Bondage to Freedom: The Institution of Slavery as Seen on the Plantation in the Home of the Planter* (1897; reprint with a foreword by William L. Andrews, Montgomery, Ala.: New South Books, 2002), 42; and George P. Rawick, *The American Slave: A Composite Autobiography* (Westport, Conn.: Greenwood Press, 1972), 61–62, 142–43, 202.

   38. See, for example, Byron Porter to J. T. Kirkman, March 4, 1867, Bastrop, Texas, BRFAL.

39. D'Emilio and Freedman, *Intimate Matters,* 104. See also Judith Lewis Herman, "Crime and Memory," in *Trauma and Self,* ed. Charles B. Strozier and Michael Flynn (Lanham, Md.: Rowman and Littlefield, 1996), 13.

40. Gerda Lerner, "Women and Slavery," *Slavery and Abolition* 4 (December 1983), 176.

41. Historically, rapes are rarely reported and conviction rates are, even today, appallingly low. See, for example, Susan Estrich, *Real Rape* (Cambridge, Mass.: Harvard University Press, 1987), 16–20; Gary D. LaFree, *Rape and Criminal Justice: The Social Construction of Sexual Assault* (Belmont, Calif.: Wadsworth, 1989), 53–112; Diana E. H. Russell, *Sexual Exploitation: Rape, Child Sexual Abuse and Workplace Harassment* (Los Angeles: Sage, 1984), 284. Although there is some variation in specific language used to describe matters of sex according to race and class during the nineteenth century, it should not be assumed that former slaves would be less humiliated in describing such abuse. In addition, Freedmen's Bureau agents were clearly reluctant to use sexually descriptive language in their reports. On race and sexual attitudes, see D'Emilio and Freedman, *Intimate Matters,* 85–108. On the different traumas suffered by victims of sexual and nonsexual assaults, see David P. Valentiner, "Coping Strategies and Posttraumatic Stress Disorder in Female Victims of Sexual and Nonsexual Assault," *Journal of Abnormal Psychology* 105 (1996): 456. For black women's experience specifically, see also Charlotte Pierce-Baker, *Surviving the Silence: Black Women's Stories of Rape* (New York: W. W. Norton, 1998).

42. Edward Ayers, *Vengeance and Justice: Crime and Punishment in the Nineteenth-Century American South* (New York: Oxford University Press, 1984), 155.

9

"Three Cheers to Freedom and Equal Rights to All"

JUNETEENTH AND THE MEANING OF CITIZENSHIP

Elizabeth Hayes Turner

I n July 1865 an item appeared in the Clarksville *Standard* that began with a question: "What will become of the negro race then?" The writer launched into his own answers, calling on the divine and using all the logic of a Southern slaveholder:

> This, indeed, is a serious question, and one which Mr. Chas. Sumner, and his followers had done well to consider six years ago. . . . By this sudden abolition of slavery, they have paved the way to the critical extermination of the black race in America. . . . At all events, the two races, both free cannot live together. The negro can never become a citizen at the South. . . . The negro can never compete with the white race, either in intellectual, or in the agricultural field of labor. . . . the freed negro must be restrained, and kept in tutelage, which varies . . . little from his previous status of legalized slavery. . . . The negro's freedom cannot be entrusted to his own keeping . . . and his nominal freedom must be . . . controlled. . . . God has so ordained it, and man cannot alter the decree of God.[1]

For all the bluster that supporters of slavery put forth, for all the calls for gradual abolition, for all the violence used against slaves when leaving their masters, and the brutality perpetrated against freedmen during Reconstruction, emancipation prevailed, and black Texans have memorialized this event annually in every sizable city and in remote

counties ever since. Whatever joy may have accompanied the declaration of freedom in Texas on June 19, 1865, the harsh tone of white Texans, printed nearly a month after emancipation's arrival, foreshadowed
a history of resistance to the rulings of Congress, the U.S. president, and
the rise of a liberated people. That some whites deterred the progress
of constitutional rights did not, however, erase the memory of emancipation, stem the increasing demands for political and legal equality,
or dim economic aspirations. These goals were iterated year after year
in annual freedom day celebrations. Despite the strained race relations
and profound struggle for legal equality that followed the war, the yearly
celebration of freedom's arrival in Texas suffused the event with historical memory as well as an eye to the future. Texas emancipation celebrations, named "Juneteenth" in the 1890s, supported and encouraged
former slaves in the creation of a usable past and in the determination to
seek an equitable future. As black minister Alexander Crummell of San
Antonio reasoned, "Historical consciousness was critical to any struggle
for equality."[2]

Historians and sociologists have called such liberation events sites of
memory, or *lieux de mémoire*. From the writings of Maurice Halbswach
and Pierre Nora, concepts of collective memory, historical consciousness, and the power of memory to shape political agendas have influenced social historians to see such occasions as more than celebrations
of the past but as meaningful encounters with the future as well. Such
was the case for African Texans when they embarked on their journey from freedom toward civil rights. Juneteenth celebrations served
to build African American collective memory and counteract prevail-
ing white devotion to the Lost Cause. They reinforced a commitment
to constitutional principles of citizenship, equal protection under the
laws, and voting rights. With that, in the years after a costly Civil War,
emancipation celebrations held a subversive underpinning that spoke
to the aspirations of a people determined to earn the right of equality.[3]

The awakening of freedom in Texas began as a dreaded federal intervention by whites and as a long-awaited Union liberation by slaves.
Military force set into motion by the Civil War resulted in a host of
unanticipated events in Texas—all of which serve as backdrop to the
creation of freedom memories. These included the introduction of
occupying Union troops, many of them black; the announcement of

emancipation; a ragged abolition process as some whites violently re-sisted the end of slavery; the introduction of Congressional (or Radical) Reconstruction in 1867 furthering black aspirations; and the organizing and politicization of annual jubilee celebrations. Texas was the last state in the Confederacy to liberate its slaves, but its Juneteenth celebrations have remained an annual affair and are now recognized as a state holi-day or state holiday observance day in forty-three states in the nation.

Unbeknownst to most black Texans in 1862, Congress had already ordered the emancipation of slaves in Washington, D.C. Over the objec-tions of an overwhelming majority of slaveholders, on April 16, 1862, President Abraham Lincoln signed legislation that ended slavery in the nation's capital. It was the first time the federal government had acted to free slaves en masse in a single city outside of wartime military com-mand. Only several hundred miles to the west, slaves still toiled in states loyal to the Union. To the south, in Virginia, the Confederate Congress had authorized the use of slave labor in support of military operations. The legislation enacted by the U.S. Congress and signed by President Lincoln to free the Federal District's bondspeople raised flags of hope for all enslaved people in the two embattled nations. For the first time, Congress had proven that it had the power and the will to end slavery even without the use of force![4]

Five months later, September 1862, Lincoln took the next step toward liberation when he delivered a preliminary proclamation that offered to compensate Confederate owners for their slaves' eventual freedom if the state returned to the Union by January 1863. No rebel states took up the offer, so on January 1, 1863, the Emancipation Proclamation went into effect. This powerful executive order theoretically emancipated slaves in those states still in rebellion while leaving in bondage enslaved folk in states loyal to the Union, such as Kentucky and Delaware. As a war-time exigency, it served a purpose—to inform slaves that to earn their freedom they must escape from their masters and no longer serve the Confederate cause. The passage to freedom would prove dangerous, and men, women, and children lost their lives trying to escape. Just how many slaves fled to the Union troops advancing in the South the presi-dent could not guess, but when hordes escaped across Confederate lines to the Yankees, the military scrambled to provide food, housing, and paid work.[5]

While the president and his generals debated what to do with their newly won "contrabands," the "First Freed" in Washington reordered their lives. No sooner had Congress acted than African Americans in the District moved to create a host of schools where early education meant opportunities for traditional learning and skilled work for former slaves. A year later they celebrated freedom in the ornate Fifteenth Street Presbyterian Church, "in which blessings were invoked on the members of Congress who passed the decree abolishing slavery, and the President for the measures he had taken to liberate the slaves of the country."[6] Such jubilees held in churches enjoined former slaves to remember the sacred roots of their liberation history.

If the United States capital claimed its "First Freed' on April 16, 1862, as an outcome of the bloody Civil War, Galveston at the fringes of the Confederacy held that honor for Texas. Founded in 1839 with 1,000 residents and 250 structures, Galveston by 1860 had become the most important commercial city in the state. Considered the entrepôt of Texas, it was the only deepwater port between New Orleans and Tampico, Mexico. Because it was the principal port of entry for the state, citizens of Texas demanded an excellent wharf, and in 1854 Galveston businessmen developed the Galveston Wharf Company. Transporting goods overland to and from other parts of the state depended on the Galveston, Houston and Henderson Railroad, which completed its first leg to Houston in 1860. Still it continued to carry goods during the war, sending the booty brought by blockade runners north into the interior.[7] During the war, the city of 7,000 in 1860 shrank to 2,500 by 1864 when a yellow fever epidemic decimated the populace still further. The estimated slave population on the island in the 1850s was 1,500, but by 1862 the number had dropped to 1,240 according to tax records. Because owners took their bondspeople into the interior, it is difficult to say just how many remained on the island when Union troops arrived in June 1865.[8]

On June 2, 1865, nearly two months after the Civil War ended at Appomattox Court House in Virginia, Galveston became the site of the surrender by Gen. Edmund Kirby Smith, who commanded the Confederate Trans-Mississippi Department.[9] Standing witness to the surrender was Union Brig. Gen. Edmund J. Davis, who would become Texas governor during Reconstruction, and Gen. John Bankhead Magruder, who, along with Kirby Smith, made it clear to Davis that they feared the retribution of an occupying Union army, especially as Texas was falling into chaos.[10] Kirby Smith, one of the last Confederate generals to lay down his arms, had hoped to continue the fighting in order to gain better peace terms, but his soldiers would not sacrifice their lives to what surely seemed a lost cause, and his army melted away looting and pillaging as they left the ranks.

Civil War scholars estimate that as many as 90,000 Texans may have served as soldiers for the Confederacy, and possibly as many as 19,000 gave their lives for the Southern cause.[11] Still, 38,000 Confederate soldiers in the Trans-Mississippi Department journeyed home, some of them ransacking along the way. Meanwhile, on June 11, 1865, Austin succumbed to thieves who stole the state treasury in the dark of night and presumably escaped to Mexico. More dangerous looting came when soldiers and civilians attacked a Confederate armory in Tyler. They stole guns and ammunition, invaded a warehouse, and broke into a pharmaceutical laboratory. Marauders seized cotton and other valuables from businesses and factories in San Antonio, Huntsville, and Gilmer. Others simply invaded homes seeking to steal what they could and frightening unprotected women and children.[12]

Fearing arrest for treason, Kirby Smith fled to Mexico along with many of his soldiers, seeking escape before Union forces entered Texas. The delayed surrender and the notion that President Jefferson Davis had tried to make his way west to continue the fighting spelled trouble for Confederate Texans. Such actions raised fears among Union commanders Philip H. Sheridan and Ulysses S. Grant that Texas rebels, especially those stealing Confederate arms, horses, and supplies, were trying to brew another revolt, perhaps with the help of the French Imperial Army that had enthroned Archduke Ferdinand Maximilian Joseph as emperor of Mexico in June 1864.[13]

These apprehensions led to the decision to bring an occupying army to Texas ready to quell all rebellions and outrages, secure the border against Mexican armies, protect emancipated slaves, reorder race relations among the state's inhabitants, and reestablish civil government under Union supervision. As a result of actions taken by soldiers from the Trans-Mississippi Department, on June 5 Capt. Benjamin Sands of the U.S. Navy came ashore to hoist the Stars and Stripes over the Galveston customhouse. The audience of Texans, still grieving over the loss of the war, stood silent as the captain greeted them. Texas came under occupation by Union troops just at a point when other Southern states saw the removal of Yankee soldiers. The treachery in Texas resulted in its military occupation; indeed, civil government and the emancipation of slaves required a Union presence.[14]

White Texans feared the impending occupation by Union troops, especially black soldiers, and the Houston *Tri-Weekly Telegraph* published intelligence from New Orleans that "some considerable numbers of troops will be sent" and "some nigger troops will be sent to Texas."[15] General Sheridan, commander of the Military Division of the Southwest, thought it best to send a force immediately to Texas, and army troops began to arrive in Galveston as early as June 16. The 114th Ohio, Thirteenth Army Corps, came directly from Mobile, and four more transports arrived on June 18.[16]

General Sheridan had a hand in deciding who would command the occupying three-corps "Army of Observation" in Texas. On June 10, 1865, he commissioned Maj. Gen. Gordon Granger to become Union commander of the Department of Texas. The *New York Times* described Granger as "one of the most distinguished division commanders ever known. Brevetted no less than six times for 'gallant and meritorious conduct' and once for 'distinguished gallantry and good conduct,' he was in every respect a great and distinguished officer." Born in New York in 1822, Granger graduated from the U.S. Military Academy at West Point in 1845 and was in the same class as Robert E. Lee. He entered the U.S. Army as a second lieutenant just in time (1847) to see service in the Mexican War.[17] His rise in the army proved meteoric even for wartime; he was promoted to major general and given command of the Army of Kentucky. By 1865 he had command of the XIII Corps, which would be divided into three segments and sent to Texas. Just before he left New Orleans in June 1865, the *New Orleans Times* sent Granger off with this promotional aimed at white Texans: "The people of Galveston may well be congratulated that so gallant, efficient and courteous an officer as Major Gen. Gordon Granger is to establish his headquarters in their city."[18]

General Granger arrived in Galveston on Wednesday, June 19, 1865, by steamer from New Orleans, accompanied by "two transports of colored troops," a significant first for the people of Galveston.[19] Legend has it that on the day of his arrival Granger strode to the antebellum home known as Ashton Villa near the intersection of Broadway and Bath Avenue (currently 25th Street) and from the balcony he read General Orders No. 3, announcing the end of slavery in the Lone Star State. The order came in the form of a proclamation from the "Executive of the United States," meaning that the legality of the abolishment of slavery in Texas was based on the January 1, 1863, Emancipation Proclamation, subsuming General Orders No. 3 under the president's order. It read: "The people of Texas are informed that in accordance with a proclamation from the Executive of the United States all slaves are free. This involves an absolute equality of personal rights and rights of property, between former masters and slaves, and the connection heretofore existing between them, become that between employer and hired labor." Included in the directive was this notice: "The freedmen are advised to remain at their present homes and work for wages. They are informed that they will not be allowed to collect at military posts, and that they will not be supported in idleness either there or elsewhere."[20] Whereas the bondspeople of Washington, D.C., were freed by Congress with the president's signature, freedom came to Texas by presidential proclamation to be later enshrined in the U.S. Constitution as the Thirteenth Amendment.

The day after Granger's entrance to Galveston, three more steamers arrived from Mobile filled with officers and troops. The *Clinton* brought with it Granger's staff and the Thirty-Fourth Iowa Regiment, 800 strong; next came the *Rice*, with the Eighty-Third Ohio Regiment, 600 strong; and finally the *Exact* with part of the Illinois Ninety-Fourth Regiment, 250 strong. From New Orleans came the *Shooting Star* with provisions, ice, and salt. Somewhere between 1,650 and 1,800 Union soldiers advanced into the port of Galveston. Sheridan's orders, as outlined by his superior, Gen. Ulysses Grant, and with a troop presence of approximately 51,000, were to secure coastal areas, including Galveston, Matagorda Bay, and Corpus Christi, and to occupy the Rio Grande east of Piedras Negras, an unimaginably difficult task; some might say a mission impossible, yet one that would prove to have tremendous consequences for the freedpeople of Texas.[21]

Almost as soon as the Northern forces arrived in Galveston, Granger's staff began posting in the local newspapers a series of general orders, the most famous of which is General Orders No. 3. Every issue of the Galveston newspapers as well as newspapers across the state circulated these orders for approximately two weeks so news could spread quickly concerning emancipation, the occupation of Galveston Island, and the army's determination to parole Confederate soldiers. Less known are the orders that established Union army control over the city of Galveston and then over the large and sparsely inhabited state. It is apparent that the army command meant to establish an authoritative presence because Galveston was soon to become an armed camp with Union soldiers arriving and Confederate troops paroling.[22]

Although Texas was the last state in the Confederacy to emancipate its slaves, it was not the last state or territory to do so. Delaware held a handful of slaves, and Kentucky, where over 10,000 slaves still labored, refused to emancipate its slaves even at the end of the war. The only route to freedom for male slaves in those states was to join the Union army while their loved ones remained behind and reaped a whirlwind of resentment from whites. Kentucky slaveholders put up a bitter defense over property rights until December 1865, when the states ratified the Thirteenth Amendment, ending slavery in the United States.[23] The last remaining holdout for slavery was in the Indian Territory, where the Cherokee, Choctaw, Chickasaw, Creek, and Seminole nations had brought their slaves in the 1830s. By war's end, 8,000 slaves, 14 percent of the population in these tribal lands, remained in bondage. Finally, in 1866 the United States concluded treaties with each of the five Indian nations ensuring freedom for their slaves and extending to the freedpeople citizenship rights in the nation.[24]

In Texas the news of freedom traveled slowly through the state, with some slaves still held in bondage months or even years after June 1865.[25] Often, the most direct method for hearing the news was from slave owners, but others learned of freedom from Yankee troops that began moving west from Galveston the day after their arrival. The Thirty-Fourth Iowa Regiment, commanded by Col. George W. Clark, along with the 114th Ohio, under the command of Col. John H. Kelly, moved into Houston on June 20. An air of foreboding sounded in the local newspapers as they reported that the "the forces of the United States have taken formal possession of the State." The Houston city council promised cooperation with the occupying forces but warned that the city might be overwhelmed with "the sudden change in the relations of our negro population" and advised the city to prepare itself by enforcing the vagrancy laws against "large classes of idle persons." On June 18 another of Granger's divisions, the Eighth Illinois Infantry, entered East Texas from Louisiana heading toward Marshall; and then on June 28 more forces, including two black regiments, entered Tyler. A third division of Granger's troops landed to the south, like the others entering the state from the Gulf of Mexico.[26]

The successful emancipation of slaves in Texas depended in great part on the presence of Union troops, but only approximately half of the troops were sent to the areas of greatest slave concentration. That is explained by a drama of international concern that took Union troops to South Texas and unfolded as soldiers descended along the Rio Grande. At the close of the Civil War, the United States, in order to uphold the Monroe Doctrine, demanded that French troops withdraw from the continent. Napoleon III had sent a French army to Mexico to prop up the faltering Archduke of Austria and emperor of Mexico, Ferdinand Maximilian Joseph. His ascendancy to the throne had been achieved by collusion between France and wealthy Mexicans hoping to thwart the revolutionary forces of Benito Juárez. At the same time that the United States sought to rid the Western Hemisphere of European interlopers, Confederate governors, generals, and soldiers were fleeing across the border to settle in Mexico under Maximilian's liberal immigration policies. About 2,500 Confederates, including Kirby Smith and Magruder, fled to Mexico, where Maximilian offered them colonization rights and 640-acre plots of land for settlement. General Magruder, who had been assigned commander over Texas in 1861, held administrative posts under Emperor Maximilian.[27]

If necessary, Union troops were prepared to hold the Texas border against any invasion promoted by the Mexican conflict, but General Sheridan was equally concerned over the lost materiel stolen from Confederate warehouses and its use in a possible invasion against Union-held Texas. Sheridan pushed to secure the border, and by July nearly half of the soldiers sent to Texas were headed to the Rio Grande. Fewer than four hundred slaves lived between the Nueces River and the Rio Grande;

thus, the threat of invasion from Mexico by ex-Confederates and Imperial forces—not the emancipation of slaves—was by far the most important reason for the presence of Union troops in South Texas.

This emergency had a deleterious effect on the safe passage of many slaves from bondage to freedom in other parts of the state.[28] Indeed, Sheridan received word from officers in Texas that they heard "'frequent complaints . . . of the barbarities practiced towards . . . freedmen,' but could do nothing about them for want of troops."[29] Unable to make much headway as troops headed west along the Rio Grande, reinforcements were added from the XXV (Colored) Corps of Virginia with 20,000 black soldiers massed along Texas's southeastern shore from Corpus Christi to the mouth of the Rio Grande.[30] The *Dallas Herald* may have exaggerated when it reported that "forty thousand U.S. troops were on the Rio Grande, 6,000 only of whom were white." It took two years for the Mexican threat to be resolved, and it did not completely end until the French army withdrew in March 1867 and Mexican forces under Juárez finally captured Maximilian. They executed him by firing squad on June 19, 1867, a date that seethes with irony.[31]

The introduction of black soldiers to Texas presented a formidable challenge to white residents, fearful as they were of armed blacks. Indeed on June 20, two regiments, comprising at least 1,500 federal troops, moved to Houston, and as they were preparing their quarters in the courthouse square a black member of the regiment was murdered by a white civilian, who fled the scene. The argument seemed to stem from the perennial issue of rights to public space, for the knifing took place on the sidewalk, after an intense altercation.[32] For freedpeople, on the other hand, the presence of black soldiers often inspired courage, instilling in them pride of patriotism and loyalty to the Union. An occupying army filled with black soldiers entering Texas, many from states loyal to the Union, presented to the newly emancipated a glimpse of what freedom could bring. Serving in the military, they believed, would bring better claims to citizenship, equality, and economic opportunity. In other Southern states, when black soldiers arrived as fighting or occupation units freedpeople responded with a newly acquired sense of patriotism and loyalty to the nation that had liberated them. Free blacks from the North, catalyzed by the strike at slavery, modeled citizenship responsibilities as well as rights.[33] In cities such as Galveston, Houston,

San Antonio, Marshall, and Tyler, the presence of black troops no doubt inspired African Americans to realize the advantages of freedom and citizenship.

Had Texas been in the line of fighting during the Civil War, more black Texans might have served in the Union army and keenly felt victory with the death of slavery. As it was, few from Texas were able to escape to Union lines during the Civil War. From an African American population of 36,000 eligible men, only forty-seven black Texans served the Union cause.[34] Yet five years later, the hope of joining the U.S. Army was realized when they were recruited to serve in the Ninth and Tenth U.S. Cavalry as well as the Twenty-Fourth and Twenty-Fifth Infantry. These enlistments encouraged patriotism, and "Buffalo Soldiers" themselves gained training, education, and a stable income.[35]

Although fewer in number than troops assigned to South Texas, federal armies began moving through northeast to central Texas. Under the command of Maj. Gen. Wesley Merritt, six cavalry regiments traveled from Shreveport through Marshall to Austin and finally to San Antonio. About 5,500 men left Shreveport on July 9 to make the 600-mile trek to San Antonio. They arrived around August 9 or 10, men and beasts sweating in the July-August heat, their columns at least several miles long.[36]

As Merritt's troops moved to the interior of Texas, young Felix Haywood found himself in the path of the liberating forces.[37] Haywood's narrative captured what has become the most often quoted and iconic description of emancipation in Texas. Living in Bexar County, Haywood had survived slavery into his early twenties and worked as a ranch hand for his owner, William Gudlow. At age ninety-two, his humor and sense of irony teased out these freedom memories:

> The end of the war, it come jus' like that like you snap your fingers.
> . . . Hallelujah broke out. "Abe Lincoln freed the nigger with the
> gun and the trigger; and I ain't goin' to get whipped any more.
> I got my ticket, Leavin' the thicket. And I'm a-headin' for the
> Golden Shore!" Soldiers, all of a sudden, was everywhere comin'
> in bunches, crossin' and walkin' and ridin'. Everyone was a-singin'.
> We was all walkin' on golden clouds. Hallelujah! "Union forever,
> Hurrah, boys, hurrah! Although I may be poor, I'll never be a slave

Shoutin' the battle cry of freedom." Everybody went wild. We all felt like heroes and nobody had made us that way but ourselves. We was free. Just like that, we was free. . . . Nobody took our homes away, but right off colored folks started on the move. They seemed to want to get closer to freedom, so they'd know what it was like [as if] it was a place or a city.[38]

Most often the joyous immediate celebrations of freedom came with the presence of Union soldiers. Henry Baker, working in the field on a small plantation in Washington County, recalled that he and his parents witnessed what was probably Gen. George A. Custer's cavalry traveling east in late October. Still working as a slave, Baker saw "bout 200 or 300 soldiers cumin' down de road. We'ns run to de marster house. Some of we'ns waz under de house whin de soldiers gits der. One soldier man says dat we'ns free an' could go whur we'ns pleased. Der was lot of rejoicin' an' singin', we'ns so happy dat we'ns didn't know whut to do. Der waz a general breakin' up, de niggers didn't know whur dey waz goin', dey jus' went."[39] When federal troops reached Garfield just east of Austin, young Rosina Hoard saw them coming. "I remembah seein' de "blue bellies" a goin' over de fields. Dey was de Yankee soldiers. Den all ob de slaves got to sayin', We is free we is now free. De "blue bellies" done told us dat we is free! I know dat de slaves was glad to be free, 'cause I know how dey could stay or dey could leave."[40] Slaves still held in bondage long after June 19 courageously took leave of their masters to strike off on their own in the presence of armed troops.

The relative absence of Union troops in portions of northeast and central Texas had equally important effects on the emancipation process. Many slaves, particularly in remote areas or in the counties south of Houston where the greatest number of slaves lived, never saw a Union soldier or learned of freedom until their masters or Freedmen Bureau agents announced it. Their emancipation stories were often less joyous; they acted more resigned to remaining with their former owners and working on shares. No Union presence meant little protection, and if they tried to leave they feared violence. In those cases, freedpeople chose to remain with their former masters, their fortunes dependent on the goodwill of the whites surrounding them. From June to the end of the year, many freedpeople across the state found themselves giving birth to freedom without the aid of a military midwife. The resulting dangers cannot be overemphasized for areas where resistance to emancipation still lingered. Bushwhackers and desperadoes roamed the country and murdered with impunity those trying to flee from slavery. As Rebecca Czuchry stresses in her essay in this volume, freedwomen were particularly vulnerable to brutalization. One of the worst areas was Corners Country, comprising Grayson, Fannin, Hunt, and Collin Counties. There, some two hundred blacks and white Unionists were murdered by unreconstructed rebels whose resentments over the outcome of the war left a path of revenge that lasted until the mid-1870s.[41] In Bosque County, northwest of Waco, four freedmen were sold after July 1865, and slave owners threatened to kill any slave expecting to flee. Others were held "nearly naked" and beaten. Complaints came to Texas military officials by concerned Unionists, who saw in the former Confederates' actions a treasonous disloyalty.[42]

White attitudes exacerbated blacks' insecurity. Some white Texans argued that there should be gradual emancipation and that the Emancipation Proclamation was "but a military order which has now spent its force since the war is over." Holding on to such notions would impede the progress of the state toward reunification, warned Union provisional governor A. J. Hamilton. Referring to President Andrew Johnson's proclamation of May 29, 1865, all those taking an oath of amnesty were required to "support, protect, and defend the Constitution of the United States and the Union of the States thereunder; and . . . abide by . . . all laws and proclamations which have been made . . . with reference to the emancipation of slaves."[43] If white Texans had any doubts as to the intentions of the occupying army and its resolve to uphold federal law and the Emancipation Proclamation, Governor Hamilton made it clear in a multipage address to the people of Texas that notions of gradual emancipation were delusional. "If the rebellion is conquered[,] slavery is dead—one is as much a fact as the other. I could not . . . satisfy those who are not willing to believe it, that slavery was never a good, and emancipation not an evil."[44]

Although the official declarations promising freedom for former slaves were possibly well intended, military protection for every slave in the entire state was impossible given the Union army's limited presence. Depredations were indeed made against freedpeople in northeast

Texas, but other factors impeded full freedom for former slaves even where federal troops remained. General Granger's General Orders No. 3 instructed them to stay where they were and work for wages. More foreboding, however, was a circular from the office of the provost marshal general disseminated June 28, which announced that "no persons formerly slaves will be permitted to travel on the public thoroughfares without passes or permits from their employers."[45] In Houston the threat of imprisonment for enjoying their freedom—what Houston mayor William Anders called vagrancy—began to curtail the movement of freedpeople.[46] Freedom's promise in the days after June 19 diminished as General Granger and Colonel Laughlin, provost marshal general, declared that "negroes will not be allowed to wander as vagrants through the country; they are advised to stay . . . and work for wages; if they do not they will be made to work for the Government without wages."[47] As a result of these directives favoring the control of freedpeople, threatening reenslavement, and catering to former Confederates, General Sheridan removed Granger from his command over Texas on July 19, and he was replaced by Bvt. Maj. Gen. Horatio G. Wright.[48] Still, the prospect of 250,000 freedpeople fleeing farms, plantations, or urban households without resources to support themselves presented a specter of chaos that even occupying armies could not control.

■   ■   ■

Given the difficulties that many African Americans experienced in the aftermath of the war, it is a wonder that they decided emancipation was worth celebrating, but one year later that is exactly what they did, believing that freedom, even with limitations, was a far better state than slavery. Probably as many as 25 percent, or 62,000 slaves, left their owners, and a good percentage of them ended up living in cities.[49] As the first anniversary of emancipation in Texas approached, these freedpeople were the most likely to hold celebrations in honor of their emancipation, and patterns for honoring their freedom day emerged with festivities that included a parade, speeches, and a barbecue feast, a delicacy that slaves relished. In fact, freedpeople put much energy into the preparation of food precisely because slave rations on plantations and in urban households often had been meager, made even more so by the wartime blockade. Although whites complained bitterly about the lack of provisions, slaves suffered the worst privations when wheat and coffee were hard to come by and rations decreased. Sarah Ashley, a young woman in San Jacinto County at the time, remembered that "the Negroes . . . never got enough to eat, so they kept stealing. . . . They gib 'em a peck of meal to last a week and two or three pounds of bacon in chunk, [but] we never seed no flour and sugar, just corn meal, meat and taters."[50] Quite often slaves noted the meals provided by Union soldiers on their perilous journey from slavery to freedom. Will Hamilton remembered that "de cullud folks has lots of trouble after de war. . . . sojers with blue coats comes dere and camps front of Massa Buford's place and pertects de cullud folks. I goes over to dey camp every day and dey gives me lots of good eats."[51]

Displays of plenty at jubilee celebrations put freedpeople in a position of control over what they could consume. Slaveholders generally forbade the consumption of alcohol, fearing drunken dangerous behavior from male slaves and loss of work time from families. These rules made the forbidden drink even more inviting after emancipation, for no master controlled the choice of beer or distilled spirits on days of celebration. Over time the festivities became much more elaborate, with men barbecuing beef in great underground pits throughout the night and women making side dishes, pies, and cakes to create a "great feast" followed by entertainment and relaxation.[52] Dressing in finery to celebrate freedom contrasted even more sharply with slavery, when slaves had almost no choice of garments, when small children sometimes went without clothing, and when men and women were made to wear only rough work clothes. Freedom celebrations offered an incentive to refute all the limitations surrounding the body that slavery had once imposed.

The state's first emancipation celebrations came under the purview of Union troops still occupying Texas cities, and their presence made the events possible without fear of reprisals. Quite often the program included Union army officers, agents of the Freedmen's Bureau, and white Republicans, who as invited guest speakers held honored roles at the podium. For many it proved a moment of solidarity between black and white Republicans. Whereas many former slaves in the Deep South first encountered one another politically in contraband camps or at Union League meetings, Texas slaves also found their cultural and political meeting ground in emancipation celebrations.[53] Moreover, some had long-established kinship ties that strengthened their sense of place and community; they chose to express their freedom memories—and their political aspirations—among their friends and loved ones.

Although little is known about the first emancipation celebrations in Texas, on June 19, 1866, Gen. Philip Sheridan came through Galveston and perhaps witnessed that city's first commemoration. The *Galveston News* was silent on the subject, but Sheridan's presence there could have provided no more elegant expression of the nature of Union efforts to free the slaves in Texas.[54] In San Antonio freedpeople observed their festivities with a parade, followed by a barbecue and a dance.

> The recent pic-nic which was held by the freedmen, last Saturday, the anniversary of the emancipation proclamation at the San Pedro Springs, was quite a grand affair. . . . Several hundred blacks were present on the occasion, besides a number of officers and soldiers of the army, and a few other citizens as spectators. A good deal of dancing was done by the freedmen, and a good deal of "lager" was drunk by the whole gathering. Some speeches were made by an officer of the [Freedmen's] Bureau and by some negroes.[55]

It is certain that Houston also enjoyed freedom festivities with announcements of a "grand barbecue." The *New York Times* reported that on Tuesday, June 19, 1866, "the freedmen celebration of emancipation at Houston passed off quietly." Yet in 1866 there were still depredations upon former bondspeople in parts of Texas where no Union troops encamped. The Houston *Tri-Weekly Telegraph* hinted at the threat of violence on that celebratory day, the white editors earnestly trusting "that nothing will be done by the inconsiderate or ill-disposed to interrupt or mar the merry-making of the freedmen." Still, imagining emancipation as an act perpetrated upon hapless slaves—against their will—the *Telegraph* editors declared that whites should recall slaves' loyalty:

> Throughout the war, up to the last hour, the negroes were faithful and dutiful to their masters. That they are now freedmen is not their act, and whatever may be thought of emancipation, it is none of their doing. . . . The freedmen believe their emancipation a great good—it is natural they should wish to celebrate it. Let them

enjoy its celebration unmolested. We believe . . . that we, their old masters, are still their best friends; . . . let us prove it on this and on all occasions. Generosity and kindness to inferiors is a Southern virtue.[56]

Paternalistic Houstonians believed that slaves had been faithful, yet they saw freedpeople as inferiors who had shown no agency in their own emancipation. These assumptions ignore the history of those who left plantations as soon as the news of freedom reached them, sustaining themselves by their own wits, fleeing to cities, and risking their lives in the process. The notion that whites deserved to be considered their best friends suggests a venality that no friendly words on the page could disguise. In reality, freedpeople were not yet full-fledged citizens in a nation that gave them their so-called freedom. Whites hoped to keep it that way.[57]

Emancipation celebrations contradicted many of the charges brought forward by the editors of the Houston *Tri-Weekly*. Since most Southern whites did not attend these events but observed them from afar, their reports reflected none of the passionate political language that uplifted, inspired, and collectively energized black revelers. That the politicization of Emancipation Day celebrations went unreported by whites reveals an element of drama as freedpeople expressed collectively in public space what they dared not say face to face to their white employers. Emancipation Day gatherings, commonly thought simply to mark the occasion of their escape from bondage, culminated in a form of political subversion, the purpose of which was to gain access to legal and constitutional equality.

The rhetoric of celebration and dissent that accompanied emancipation festivities evolved with the advent of Congressional Reconstruction and ratification of the Reconstruction amendments.[58] As concepts of freedom and its celebration turned into questions regarding rights of citizenship, the annual celebrations reflected a political tone not reported in the earliest gatherings. Questions of equality and participation in politics became the next tier of inquiry, and emancipation celebrations reflected these concerns.

This is not to say that Emancipation Day festivities were without expressions of joy, laughter, and camaraderie. Accompanied by good and abundant food, musical and visual entertainment, as well as religious observances, these were extraordinarily open celebratory moments when freedpeople were able to demonstrate a profound respect for the changes that liberty had brought. The celebrations encouraged festive parties, but they changed over time from simple expressions of joy to complex political and social events. As they became more elaborate, organizers of Emancipation Day parades often commanded prime public space on the main streets of cities, and the celebrants' presence announced claim to the use of these downtown thoroughfares. It was later, in parks or recreational areas outside of the main parade routes, that programs unfolded and brought to the listeners demonstrations of loyalty to the Union, to the Great Emancipator, and to the Republican Party.

In the fifth year after war's end, the freedpeople of Houston celebrated the official day of freedom with all the pomp and ceremony that the occasion could command. Unlike previous years when travel for rural folk proved difficult and conditions more hazardous, a great swell of people descended upon the Bayou City. By 1870 the African American population of Harris County had reached 6,500 of a total of 17,375 (37 percent), and huge numbers, although uncounted, took to the streets.[59] In the intervening five years, the participants had devised a pattern of observance that included religious worship and a long parade with bands, horsemen, and marchers from various organizations. The parade inevitably ended in a public park or a shady grove where tables were set for the main day feast. The *Houston Evening Telegraph* announced the arrival of celebrants for the Emancipation Day festivities with a toast to the document that provided their freedom:

> Today being the anniversary of the Proclamation of the emancipation of the colored people of Texas, at an early hour the subjects of that famous and historical document began to arrive from the surrounding country, the streets to be filled with the sable horsemen and the sidewalks of Main and other streets with colored women and girls, neatly attired in their holiday costumes. About 9, some strains from the Galveston colored band, which came up on the last night's train, announced the presence of those musicians and the near commencement of the day's exercises.

Later that day a "detachment of about twenty in firemen's dress, with drum and colors and a Marshal, who marched at the head with a drawn sword; came up Commerce street into Main, and proceeded to the colored Methodist church."[60]

The importance of a parade down Houston's most heavily traveled commercial streets should not be underestimated. The firemen with their flags, the marshal bearing his sword, the horsemen astride their mounts, the bystanders in their finery, and the Galveston band with its exultant music—all announced a new presence, an undeniable entourage of freedpeople who commanded the arteries of downtown Houston. Claiming public space in this manner was important for both blacks and whites to acknowledge. The visible demonstrations solidified African American identity and announced to the city that this day should be set aside for the memory of freedom, for a lieu de memoire, to inspire and to encourage those whose lives had seen the ravages of slavery and endured the hardships of freedom. It demanded that public space be shared, and this contrasted dramatically with the "requirement" that blacks step aside for whites on public sidewalks lest the "interloper" lose his life, as had occurred in 1865 in the presence of Union troops.[61] For whites the importance of yielding city streets to black demonstrators pressed them to reorient their thinking and to concede that Main Street, previously "owned" by whites, was now public space available to all residents. White newspaper editors already realized that sharing the right to open public demonstrations was a portent of the future, and readers would need to adapt. In time, emancipation celebrations were not just tolerated by whites but praised and accepted as an annual tradition.[62]

Publically displayed freedom festivals also inspired and educated the citizenry. At the end of the Civil War only 10 percent of freedpeople were literate, a result of their enslavement and denial of education. For a population that could not read newspapers or books, observing the parade, hearing the bands, listening to the oratory, and participating in the public demonstration included them in an affirmation of African American history and memory. For this first generation of freedpeople, such public celebrations imparted knowledge of their past, supported a collective memory of struggle and triumph, and presented a cogent plan for the future—including their rights to full citizenship. At the same time, the presence of former slaves added a dimension of authenticity, for these were the very people for whom emancipation became a life-changing event. At these occasions, literate blacks, some of whom may have been educated outside the South, assumed the roles of race leaders in cities such as Houston and Galveston, raising their own expectations of political and social prominence and lifting the hopes of a younger generation for their own emergence into public life.[63]

The festivities in Houston in 1870 continued on to the Methodist church, to solemnize the events of the day. Church services often preceded the parade in emancipation celebrations, but that year prayer came after the parade and before the speech making. After worship, the paraders marched to the grounds of the Gregory Institute in downtown Houston. Union general Edgar M. Gregory, the first assistant commissioner of the Texas Freedmen's Bureau, had donated the land to freedpeople, and the institute became a public school in 1876.[64] There the program commenced with a reading of the Emancipation Proclamation, the most important symbolic representation of this commemorative ritual. No Juneteenth celebration henceforth would be complete without a reading of President Lincoln's proclamation.

The next year, 1871, news of celebrations in Galveston came from one of the earliest black newspapers in Texas. Founded in 1871 by Richard Nelson, the *Representative* not only described the festivities but also reprinted Nelson's speech, allowing freedpeople, whites, and historians to recall the events from an African American point of view. Nelson, born in Florida in 1842 and educated in Georgia, lived as a free black before the war. In 1866 he settled in Galveston as a commission merchant, a county justice of the peace, and editor of the *Representative*, which he founded on Republican principles, "without regard to color, race, or previous condition of servitude."[65]

Nelson called the event Freedom Day and reported "a line of men proudly marching along under banners that expressed their love to each other, to the Union, and to the sacred cause of liberty." He exclaimed, "They are proud of their Freedom Day: they are proud of their liberty, as they continue their procession through the streets of their city." The celebrants marched to McKinney's Grove at the edge of town, where the ceremonies began. In an ironic twist on the meaning of equality, Nelson reported that women were not allowed to march in the parade but could cheer the men on as bystanders. Nelson wrote, "The ladies

SPEECH OF THE HON. RICHARD NELSON,

ON THE

ANNIVERSARY CELEBRATION OF EMANCIPATION.
JUNE 19, 1871.

FELLOW CITIZENS:

I feel the weight of the honor confered upon me by the kind partiality of my friends, in selecting me to speak to you on the anniversary of the birth-day of our freedom, and while I feel sensibly indeed, that my feeble abilities are over-taxed I shall not shrink from the task, well knowing, that the same kindred spirit which animates my heart on this occasion, thrills with extacy each throbbing heart within the sound of my voice, and that the same partiality which called me here will protect me from too severe a criticism, in this new field of labor and of love.

Had I been called upon to plow the field, to plant, to toil, to labor under the direction of some master, such would have been an old familiar calling. But to be called upon to speak to you of that bright boon, so brilliantly foreshadowed in the DECLARATION OF INDEPENDENCE, "that all men are created with the equal right to life, to liberty and the pursuit of happiness, and that such rights are unalianable;" I am filled with wonder and amazement that my race was so long denied the boon so boldly proclaimed as belonging to all creation alike. Ninety-five years ago American Independence was declared, and five years ago that sweet sound reached our ears in the Proclamation, we this day celebrate as one of Emancipation from Slavery.

Memory itself must forever punish us if we can forget that blessed boon so dearly bought, yet so freely given. It is not saying too much when we as a race, declare our never-ceasing gratitude to that noble Union Army that plucked us as brands from the burning and made us free. All hail the Proclamation of Emancipation.

My fellow freemen, why do we linger round the sacred thought that life is only worth itself when possessed in freedom? Because it is the birthright of every sacred element of mankind. Without freedom man is not man, he is but a thing, an animal, a slave.

But in this land now we are realizing the full inspiration that animated the fathers when they penned the Declaration of Independence near one hundred years ago.

Let us this day renew our love of that spirit which came hovering over our heads in the words of our Declaration of Freedom from the head and heart of that God-given inspiration, of that martyred, now Sainted President Abraham Lincoln, who ushered in this, to us, millenium of a perfect freedom in the Proclamation that severed the fetters which bound our manhood to the iron wheel of despotism. Let us revere the name of Abraham Lincoln, and teach our children to honor his memory, as the white man's father taught his children to revere the name of the beloved Washington. He is to us, what Washington is to our white brethren, He gave to them liberty and freedom, and Abraham Lincoln gave to us the same. Let us not forget either to honor always that noble soldiery who went forth with life in hand and death in the van to win our freedom. I never see a Union Soldier that I do not want to grasp him by the hand, and say I thank you from an honest heart. But I am too tedious, I will close with a call for three cheers for freedom and equal rights to all, and I say all honor to the Proclamation Day. May we live many years to celebrate the Anniversaries as they come and go each one lending a brighter ray to freedom's cause. Remembering, that on this day throughout this now land of perfect liberity, near four Millions of our race are this hour holding a jubilee and a thanksgiving as a rich tribute and a boon to FREEDOM'S CAUSE.

Richard Nelson, founder of the *Representative*, gave the Emancipation Day speech in Galveston on June 19, 1871. Courtesy of The Portal to Texas History, University of North Texas.

were somewhat displeased because they could not express their love of liberty by marching also, but when they attain to the blessings of female suffrage, this matter will be decided."[66] Although Nelson may have expressed the male sentiment of the day toward women's rights, a revolution was in the making, for at the turn of the century the Galveston emancipation program would be organized entirely by the Women's Nineteenth of June Committee while the men tended to the barbecue and planned games and fishing expeditions.[67]

Details of the 1871 Galveston program, which included a parade, are slim, but Nelson's emphasis was on the speeches. An entirely partisan affair, the program was composed of one white and four black Republicans in addition to many community leaders. The dignitaries were well known for their political prospects during Congressional Reconstruction. From the audience's point of view, these black Republicans had reached unimaginable heights as the state's elected leaders. This was true despite the rivalries and competition among them. Frank J. Webb, editor of the Galveston *Republican* and an ardent party member, read the Emancipation Proclamation. Johnson Reed, who was elected to the district clerkship over two white Democratic candidates in 1869 and served as president of the state Union League in 1871, gave a noteworthy speech "describing the blessings of freedom." Texas state senator George Ruby of Galveston held forth the longest, "noting the progress of the race, and advising no relaxation in that path which they had chosen, but rather [to] renew endeavors to acquire the culture only derivable from education and self-respect." Judge Chauncey Brewer Sabin, a Republican of German descent, who served as an associate justice of the Texas supreme court in 1870 and won a seat in the Texas house in 1873, addressed the crowd with the mantra "get land; get land."[68] Finally, Nelson took the stand and, calling himself orator of the day, gave tribute to the Union soldiers and to his idol, Abraham Lincoln: "It is not saying too much when we as a race, declare our never-ceasing gratitude to that noble Union Army that plucked us as brands from the burning and made us free." Nelson intoned, "I never see a Union soldier that I do not want to grasp him by the hand, and say I thank you from an honest heart. . . . three cheers to freedom and equal rights to all." To Lincoln he gave his highest praise:

All hail the Proclamation of Emancipation. . . . Let us this day renew our love of that spirit which came hovering over our heads in the words of our Declaration of Freedom from the head and heart of that God-given inspiration, of that martyred, now Sainted Abraham Lincoln, who ushered in this, to us, millennium of a perfect freedom in the Proclamation that severed the fetters which bound our manhood to the iron wheel of despotism. Let us revere the name of Abraham Lincoln, and teach our children to honor his memory.[69]

Emancipation Day celebrations provided a stage not only for revering the past but also for drawing critical attention to the leaders' political struggles. Reconstruction politics could not be avoided in the oratory of emancipation; ten African Americans were elected in February 1868 to the Texas Constitutional Convention of 1869, an historic first for the Lone Star State. The constitutional convention, organized as it was under the legal auspices of Congressional Reconstruction, gave the newly constituted Republican Party 87 percent of the seats (78 of 90), and, although this might have given Republicans a great advantage, the party delegates split into three factions, with black delegates among those who sought equality for African Texans.[70] Although Texas created a fairly conservative constitution, it added important gains for African Americans—voting and office holding, legitimizing children born to slave parents, and recognizing women's property rights. Their deliberations in the convention presaged a victory for thirteen black representatives (two senators and eleven representatives) who won seats in the Twelfth Texas Legislature and aided in the eventual ratification of the Fourteenth and Fifteenth Amendments. These constituted certain victories gained by black representatives in cooperation with white Republicans. These and other political issues dominated Emancipation Day celebrations as they heralded the work of black representatives in state office.[71]

By the 1890s, Juneteenth celebrations had become staging grounds for Populist Party politicking, and the speechmaking at one Dallas Emancipation Day festival resonated with the rhetoric of a political rally. Black Populist Melvin Wade "denounced the city council, Gov. Culberson and

President McKinley, and the entire office-holding tribe, as a band of blood-suckers." The Populist newspaper *Southern Mercury* reported that "Melvin . . . worked a few good licks for this party yesterday and fired hot shot into the Democrats and Republicans." Repudiating the Republicans for putting shackles of industrial slavery "so tightly [on blacks] that the iron had eaten into the flesh," he urged his listeners to abandon the party of Lincoln for the party of the future. As the Republican Party retreated from the South, so the political environment for African Americans changed, but emancipation celebrations still marked the site of political rallies alongside the barbecued meat, parades, and rallies.[72]

White Southern newspaper editors, when they reported on Emancipation Day celebrations, did not often see the politicization of freedom's festivities, possibly because they noted the event's trappings while ignoring their substance. Sometimes whites proclaimed freedom a positive advancement for former bondspeople, but news accounts reveal little understanding of the aspirations of African Texans during and after Congressional Reconstruction. The *Galveston News* predicted the worst outcome for freedpeople in 1867. Its editors wrote, "There is every reason . . . to believe that the emancipation of black people on the soil where they had been held as slaves means nothing less than their gradual extermination. The opinion held in the South that slavery was a blessing to the negro, is evidently correct."[73]

It would be nearly thirty years before the *News* editors—and whites throughout the state—admitted that they had been wrong. By 1893 the *Galveston News* had changed its tune: "It was a generally conceived opinion throughout the South at the time the slaves were freed that under emancipation their numbers would decrease, and that as a race they would not work, unless they were compelled to. The first idea has been proven erroneous by the statistics of the census bureau, and the second proposition has also been shown to be fallacious." In fact, the population of African Texans had grown by 307,000 in thirty years, and although the economic struggle had been difficult freedom had been celebrated every year.[74] The dire predictions of demise quoted in July 1865, the admonitions that "the freed negro must be restrained" and "the negro's freedom cannot be entrusted to his own keeping," proved the theoretical fallacies of a slaveholding class.[75]

Remnants of this limited comprehension of the human need for freedom would continue through the Jim Crow era, but emancipation celebrations—Juneteenth by the turn of the century—served to refute the notion that slavery was preferable to freedom or that politics was for whites only. Juneteenth provided a countermemory to Southern reverence for the Lost Cause and became an annual reminder that "Southern civilization" touted by a white ruling class had been propped up by the institution of enslavement no longer practiced in most parts of the world. Juneteenth observances reminded both blacks and whites of the incomparable benefits that accrued to both races as a result of emancipation. The Civil War and its outcome led to the rise of a republican free wage labor system; imperfect as it was, it nonetheless refuted slavery and granted African Americans access to land ownership. The effect of African American claims to rights brought about three constitutional amendments that ended slavery, defined citizenship, and extended the vote. These national changes brought home to Texans the struggles for equality at the local level that challenged all citizens, but in postwar Texas African Americans were at last able to exert their political will and express their designs in annual emancipation festivities.

The history of emancipation in Texas began well before June 19 with voices from the Deep South and the District of Columbia. The path to freedom was tied inextricably to the occupation of Texas by Union troops and Freedmen's Bureau officers from June 1865 through the 1870s. The staggering number of freedpeople running from slave owners, some dying in the process, record a collective will to reach liberty's shore. In 1865 perhaps white Texans had simply refused to see the future of the state as a land without bondage because they had lived with it for some forty years. Freedpeople, on the other hand, grasped freedom and held on to it as their loadstone, inexorably drawn to its promise of human advancement, its responsibilities, and its hope for happiness. Remembering the trials of slavery and then emancipation by those who had lived it gave the earliest celebrations a vital core of living memory. These occasions soon incorporated African Americans' political aspirations and dreams of the future. Celebrations of freedom, half commemorative half political, provide a window into the ideologies of African Texans before the turn of the century. These sites of memory, renewed annually, spoke of their designs to engage in community organizing, establish civil rights, achieve economic independence, and carry out a day of rejoicing over the fruits of freedom.

NOTES

1. Clarksville *Standard*, July 15, 1865.

2. W. Fitzhugh Brundage, *The Southern Past: A Clash of Race and Memory* (Cambridge, Mass.: Harvard University Press, 2005), 57.

3. Maurice Halbwachs, *Les cadres sociaux de la mémoire* (Paris: Presses universitaires de France, 1925); Halbwachs, *La mémoire collective* (Paris: Presses universitaires de France, 1950); Halbwachs, *The Collective Memory*, trans. by Francis J. Ditter, Jr., and Vida Yazdi Ditter (New York: Harper and Row, 1980), 78; Halbwachs, *On Collective Memory* (Chicago: University of Chicago Press, 1992); Pierre Nora, *Realms of Memory: Rethinking the French Past,* 3 vols. (New York: Columbia University Press, 1996–98); Nora, "Between Memory and History: Les Lieux de Mémoire," *Representations* 26 (Spring 1989), 12. See also David W. Blight, *Race and Reunion: The Civil War in American Memory* (Cambridge, Mass.: Harvard University Press, 2001), 2.

4. *New York Times,* April 15, 1862; Kate Masur, *An Example for All the Land: Emancipation and the Struggle over Equality in Washington, D.C.* (Chapel Hill: University of North Carolina Press, 2010), 22–25; Robert S. Pohl and John R. Wennersten, eds., *Abraham Lincoln and the End of Slavery in the District of Columbia* (Washington, D.C.: Eastern Branch Press, 2009), foreword, 53–66; Robert Harrison, *Washington during Civil War and Reconstruction: Race and Radicalism* (Cambridge: Cambridge University Press, 2011), 110–17.

5. Steven Hahn, *A Nation under Our Feet: Black Political Struggles in the Rural South from Slavery to the Great Migration* (Cambridge, Mass.: Harvard University Press, 2003), 70–73; Allen C. Guelzo, *Lincoln's Emancipation Proclamation: The End of Slavery in America* (New York: Simon and Schuster, 2004), 212–18; Louis Gerteis, *From Contraband to Freedom: Federal Policy toward Southern Blacks* (Westport, Conn: Greenwood Press, 1973), 11–14. See also David W. Blight, *Beyond the Battlefield: Race, Memory, and the American Civil War* (Amherst: University of Massachusetts Press, 2002), 80.

6. *Washington Star,* April 17, 1863; Pohl and Wennersten, *End of Slavery,* foreword, 85–86; Elizabeth Clark-Lewis, ed., *First Freed: Washington D.C. in the Emancipation Era* (Washington D.C.: Howard University Press, 2002), xii–xiii; Masur, *Example,* 25–27.

7. Elizabeth Hayes Turner, *Women, Culture, and Community: Religion and Reform in Galveston, 1880–1920* (New York: Oxford University Press, 1997), 19–23.

8. Ruby Garner, "Galveston during the Civil War" (M.A. thesis, University of Texas at Austin, 1927), 99–103, 131–34; Charles W. Hayes, *Galveston: History of the Island and City* (Austin: Jenkins Garrett Press, 1974 [1879]), 621–28; *Galveston Daily News,* March 1 and March 10, April 30, May 5, 1865; John Edwards, "Social and

Cultural Activities of Texans during the Civil War and Reconstruction, 1861–73"
(M.A. thesis, Texas Tech University, 1985), 241–42; Randolph B. Campbell, *An Empire for Slavery: The Peculiar Institution in Texas* (Baton Rouge: Louisiana State University Press, 1989), 233, 243.

9. General Kirby Smith surrendered at Galveston all the troops under his command, but an official surrender organized by proxy had taken place earlier in New Orleans. Kirby Smith sent Gen. Simon Buckner to negotiate the surrender to Gen. Edward R. S. Canby in New Orleans on May 26, 1865. Kirby Smith signed the surrender papers in Galveston on June 2 and then fled to Mexico for fear of being prosecuted for treason. In November he returned to Virginia, where he took the Union loyalty oath. Carl H. Moneyhon, *Texas after the Civil War: The Struggle of Reconstruction* (College Station: Texas A&M University Press, 2004), 6; William L. Richter, *The Army in Texas during Reconstruction, 1865–1870* (College Station: Texas A&M University Press, 1987), 13.

10. James Smallwood, *Time of Hope, Time of Despair: Black Texans during Reconstruction* (Port Washington, N.Y.: Kennikat Press, 1981), 25; Edward T. Cotham, *Battle on the Bay: The Civil War Struggle for Galveston* (Austin: University of Texas Press, 1998), 182.

11. Moneyhon, *Texas after the Civil War*, 8; Kenneth W. Howell, "The Prolonged War: Texans Struggle to Win the Civil War during Reconstruction," in *Texans and War: New Interpretations of the State's Military History*, ed. Alexander Mendoza and Charles David Grear (College Station: Texas A&M University Press, 2012), 198–99.

12. Cotham, *Battle on the Bay*, 180–82; James M. Smallwood, Barry A. Crouch, and Larry Peacock, *Murder and Mayhem: The War of Reconstruction in Texas* (College Station: Texas A&M University Press, 2003), 10; Richter, *Army in Texas*, 12; Ernest Wallace, *Texas in Turmoil, 1849–1875* (Austin: Steck-Vaughn, 1965), 145–46; Nancy Cohen-Lack, "A Struggle for Sovereignty: National Consolidation, Emancipation, and Free Labor in Texas, 1865," *Journal of Southern History* 58 (February 1992), 62.

13. Moneyhon, *Texas after the Civil War*, 6; Richter, *Army in Texas*, 12–13; Wallace, *Texas in Turmoil*, 142; Cohen-Lack, "Struggle for Sovereignty," 58, 62. Jefferson Davis was captured on May 10, 1865, in Irwinville, Georgia, foiling plans by Confederate officers to establish a rebel government in Mexico with Davis at the helm. Wallace, *Texas in Turmoil*, 142–45.

14. Cotham, *Battle on the Bay*, 183; Richter, *Army in Texas*, 15; Cohen-Lack, "Struggle for Sovereignty," 59.

15. Houston *Tri-Weekly Telegraph*, June 14, 1865. Gen. Jack Hamilton had been appointed military governor of Texas by June 1865; Richter, *Army in Texas*, 14.

16. Houston *Tri-Weekly Telegraph*, June 19, 1865; *Dallas Herald*, July 1, 1865.

17. Richter, *Army in Texas*, 14; *New York Times*, January 12, 1876. Ezra J. Warner, *Generals in Blue: The Lives of the Union Commanders* (Baton Rouge: Louisiana State University Press, 1964), 181; Clint Granger, *Falcon 6* (Bloomington, Idaho: Xlibris, 2010), 785–87.

18. *New Orleans Times,* June 18, 1865, reprinted in Galveston's *Flake's Daily Bulletin,* June 23, 1865. W. M. Polk, "Memoranda on the Civil War," *Century Illustrated Magazine* 33 (April 1887), 962–64.

19. *Dallas Herald,* July 1, 1865.

20. *Galveston Daily News,* June 21, 1865; *Flake's Daily Bulletin,* June 29, 1865.

21. Galveston's *Flake's Tri-Weekly Bulletin,* June 20, 1865; Wallace, *Texas in Turmoil,* 147; Kenneth W. Howell, "The Prolonged War: Texans Struggle to Win the Civil War during Reconstruction," in Mendoza and Grear, *Texans and War,* 199.

22. Houston *Tri-Weekly Telegraph,* June 26, 1865; Galveston *Civilian and Gazette,* July 8, 1865; *Flake's Daily Bulletin,* June 29, 1865.

23. Ira Berlin, Barbara Fields, Thavolia Glymph, Joseph Reidy, and Leslie S. Rowland, eds., *Freedom: A Documentary History of Emancipation, 1861–1867,* Series I, Vol. 1: *The Destruction of Slavery* (Cambridge: Cambridge University Press, 1985), 53–54.

24. See Daniel F. Littlefield, Jr., *Africans and Creeks: From the Colonial Period to the Civil War* (Westport, Conn.: Greenwood Press, 1979); Littlefield, *The Chickasaw Freedmen: A People without a Country* (Westport, Conn.: Greenwood Press, 1980); Theda Perdue, *Slavery and the Evolution of Cherokee Society, 1540–1866* (Knoxville: University of Tennessee Press, 1979); Murray R. Wickett, *Contested Territory: Whites, Native Americans, and African Americans in Oklahoma, 1865–1907* (Baton Rouge: Louisiana State University Press, 2000); J. Leitch Wright, Jr., *Creeks and Seminoles: The Destruction and Regeneration of the Muscogulge People* (Lincoln: University of Nebraska Press, 1986).

25. Smallwood, *Time of Hope,* 32; Campbell, *Empire for Slavery,* 249.

26. *Dallas Herald,* July 22, 1865, citing *Marshall Republican,* July 7, 1865; Richter, *Army in Texas,* 16–17.

27. Eugene C. Harter, *The Lost Colony of the Confederacy* (Jackson: University of Mississippi Press, 1985), 15–17. Confederate colonists reported in 1866 that they went to Mexico as men "who *could not and would not* live under *the Black Republican government." Galveston News,* June 20 1866.

28. Andrew Rolle, *The Lost Cause: The Confederate Exodus to Mexico* (Norman: University of Oklahoma Press, 1992), 34–37, 44–56; Cotham, *Battle on the Bay,* 187; Richter, *Army in Texas,* 23; *Dallas Herald,* July 15, 1865; Harter, *Lost Colony,* 18; U.S. Census Bureau, *Population of the United States in 1860* (Washington, D.C., 1864), 484–87.

29. "Condition of Affairs in Texas," 39th Cong., 2nd sess., H. Ex. Doc. 61 (serial volume 1292), 4, cited in William A. Dobak, *Freedom by the Sword: The U.S. Colored Troops, 1862–1867* (New York: Skyhorse, 2013), 441.

30. Richter, *Army in Texas,* 17. The XXV (Colored) Corps had fought at the siege of Petersburg from 1864 to 1865 and the Battle of the Crater, July 30, 1864, and became the first Union troops to enter Richmond at the close of the war. The XXV Corps was disbanded in January 1866.

31. *Dallas Herald,* July 15 and July 22, 1865; Richter, *Army in Texas,* 14, 17, 24; Harter, *Lost Colony,* 18.

32. *Dallas Herald,* July 1, 1865.

33. Ira Berlin, Joseph Reidy, and Leslie S. Rowland, eds., *Freedom, A Documentary History of Emancipation, 1861–1867,* Series II: *The Black Military Experience* (Cambridge: Cambridge University Press, 1982), 15; Richter, *Army in Texas,* 26–27.

34. Berlin et al., *Freedom,* 15.

35. Alwyn Barr, *Black Texans: A History of African Americans in Texas, 1528–1995,* 2nd ed. (Norman: University of Oklahoma Press, 1996), 86–87; Barr, "The Influence of War and Military Service on African Texans," in Mendoza and Grear, *Texans and War,* 102–103. See also William A. Dobak and Thomas D. Phillips, *The Black Regulars, 1866–1898* (Norman: University of Oklahoma Press, 2001).

36. *Dallas Herald,* July 22, 1865; Richter, *Army in Texas,* 18–19.

37. Richter, *Army in Texas,* 19.

38. For Felix Haywood, see George P. Rawick, ed., *The American Slave: A Composite Autobiography, Supplement,* Series 2, Vol. 5: *Texas Narratives,* Part 4 (Westport Conn.: Greenwood Press, 1979), 1689–92.

39. For Henry Baker, see Rawick, *American Slave,* Vol. 2, Part 4, 147; Richter, *Army in Texas,* 19.

40. For Rosina Hoard, see Rawick, *American Slave,* Vol. 5, Part 4, 1735.

41. Smallwood et al., *Murder and Mayhem,* 3; Barry A. Crouch, "A Spirit of Lawlessness: White Violence; Texas Blacks, 1865–1868," *Journal of Social History* 18 (Winter 1984), 218–21.

42. Cohen-Lack, "Struggle for Sovereignty," 70.

43. *Bellville Countryman,* August 2, 1865; Andrew Johnson, Amnesty Proclamation of May 29, 1865, *New York Times,* May 30, 1865.

44. "Proclamation by A. J. Hamilton, Provisional Governor, to the People of Texas," *Bellville Countryman,* August 2, 1865; Huntsville *Item,* August 4, 1865.

45. *Dallas Herald,* July 15, 1865.

46. Houston *Tri-Weekly Telegraph,* June 26, 1865.

47. *Dallas Herald,* July 22, 1865.

48. Richter, *Army in Texas,* 20–21; William L. Richter, *Overreached on All Sides: The Freedmen's Bureau Administrators in Texas, 1865–1868* (College Station: Texas A&M University Press, 1991), 8–10.

49. Campbell, *Empire for Slavery,* 250.

50. For Sarah Ashley, see Rawick, *American Slave,* Vol. 2, Part 1, 89.

51. For William Hamilton, see Rawick, *American Slave,* Vol. 5, Part 4, 1640.

52. Thad Sitton and James H. Conrad, *Freedom Colonies: Independent Black Texans in the Time of Jim Crow* (Austin: University of Texas Press, 2005), 104; Michelle Mears, *And Grace Will Lead Me Home: African American Freedmen Communities of Austin, Texas, 1865–1928* (Lubbock: Texas Tech University, 2009), 134.

53. Hahn, *Nation under Our Feet,* 73.

54. *New York Times,* June 21, 1866; *Galveston News,* June 20, 1866.

55. Austin *Southern Intelligencer,* June 21, 1866, citing San Antonio *Herald,* June 12, 1866; Judith Berg Sobré, *San Antonio on Parade: Six Historic Festivals* (College Station: Texas A&M University Press, 2003), 56.

56. *New York Times,* June 21, 1866; *Tri-Weekly Telegraph,* June 20, 1866.

57. Lawrence D. Rice, *The Negro in Texas: 1874–1900* (Baton Rouge: Louisiana State University Press, 1971), 141; Barr, *Black Texans,* 41. Soon enough, former slaveholders gradually lost their paternalistic attitudes, and between 1865 and 1867 the legislature replaced paternalism with Black Codes as well as segregated railway cars and schools. Churches were segregated voluntarily at the end of the war.

58. Thirteenth Amendment (slavery's end), December 6, 1865; Fourteenth Amendment (citizenship and due process), July 9, 1868; and Fifteenth Amendment (voting rights for black men), February 3, 1870.

59. The total population of Harris County in 1860 was 9,070, the slave population 2,053 (23 percent).

60. Houston *Evening Telegraph,* June 21, 1870.

61. Kathleen Ann Clark, *Defining Moments: African American Commemorative and Political Culture in the South, 1863–1913* (Chapel Hill: University of North Carolina Press, 2005), 30. For freedom festivals in northern cities, see Shane White, "'It Was a Proud Day': African Americans, Festivals, and Parades in the North, 1741–1834," *Journal of American History* 81 (June 1994): 13–50.

62. Mitch Kachun, *Festivals of Freedom: Memory and Meaning in African American Emancipation Celebrations, 1808–1915* (Amherst: University of Massachusetts Press), 6–7; Clark, *Defining Moments,* 30–31.

63. Kachun, *Festivals of Freedom,* 6–7.

64. Richter, *Overreached on All Sides,* 7. "The building was a plain four-room brick structure on Jefferson Avenue between Smith and Louisiana streets. The Texas legislature incorporated the Gregory Institute in August 1870. Richard Allen, representative from Houston, probably played a major role in the passage of the incorporation act and was one of the first commissioners for the private school." Merline Pitre, "Gregory Institute," *Handbook of Texas Online,* Texas State Historical Association, www.tshaonline.org/handbook/online/articles/kcg07.

65. Galveston *Representative,* June 26, 1871. In 1873, Nelson founded the Galveston *Spectator,* which continued until 1885. Merline Pitre, *Through Many Dangers, Toils, and Snares: The Black Leadership of Texas* (Austin: Eakin Press, 1985), 93–94; J. Mason Brewer, *Negro Legislators of Texas and Their Descendants: A History of the Negro in Texas Politics from Reconstruction to Disfranchisement* (Dallas: Mathis, 1935), 51.

66. Galveston *Representative,* June 26, 1871.

67. In 1904, Laura Austin read the Emancipation Proclamation, and another young woman, dressed as Lady Liberty, gave a speech alongside the male dignitaries. Galveston *City Times,* June 10, June 11, and June 17, 1904. Turner, *Women, Culture, and Community,* 250–51.

68. Paul M. Lucko, "Webb, Frank J.," *Handbook of Texas Online,* Texas State Historical Association, www.tshaonline.org/handbook/online/articles/fwekv; Pitre, *Through Many Dangers,* 100, 168–73; Smallwood, *Time of Hope,* 153; Lucko, "Reed, Johnson," *Handbook of Texas Online,* Texas State Historical Association, www.tshaonline.org/handbook/online/articles/frezs; Rice, *Negro in Texas,* 34–36, 104;

Merline Pitre, "Ruby, George Thompson," *Handbook of Texas Online*, Texas State Historical Association, www.tshaonline.org/handbook/online/articles/fru02; Randolph B. Campbell, "Sabine, Chauncey Brewer," *Handbook of Texas Online*, Texas State Historical Association, www.tshaonline.org/handbook/online/articles/fsa02.

69. Galveston *Representative*, June 26, 1871.

70. Randolph B. Campbell, *Gone to Texas: A History of the Lone Star State* (New York: Oxford University Press, 2003), 278–82.

71. Ann Patton Malone, "Matt Gaines: Reconstruction Politician," in *Black Leaders: Texans for their Times,* ed. Alwyn Barr and Robert A. Calvert (Austin: Texas State Historical Association, 1981), 65–66, 70–71.

72. Dallas *Southern Mercury*, June 24, 1897.

73. *Galveston News,* June 21, 1867.

74. *Galveston Daily News,* June 20, 1893. The Texas African American population in 1860 was 183,000, and by 1890 it was 490,000.

75. Clarksville *Standard*, July 15, 1865.

10

Edmund J. Davis—Unlikely Radical

Carl H. Moneyhon

In 1860, Judge Edmund J. Davis broke with the mainstream of his Democratic associates and became an opponent of secession and an open advocate of Texas remaining in the Union. A year later he moved even further away from the political mainstream as an anti-Confederate and in 1862 left the state to join the Union army. Commanding a regiment of Union cavalry from Texas and rising to the rank of brigadier general, Davis insistently urged the government of Abraham Lincoln to undertake an invasion of his home state. On his return to Texas after the war, the judge aggressively opposed placing local government back in the hands of former Confederates and in the process joined the Republican Party and embraced the radical stance of accepting black suffrage. Looking at Davis earlier in his career and prior to the secession crisis, an observer hardly could have predicted the course that he took. This essay examines Davis's move from pro-slavery Democratic politician to Radical Republican and offers an explanation for his unpredictable path.

E. J. Davis was, of course, not the only Texan to adopt an anti-Confederate position during the Civil War era. Historians have spent a considerable amount of time exploring what usually is referred to as Texas Unionism. In his 1984 study *Texas Divided,* James Marten hypothesized that Unionism emerged from ideological differences. He found Unionists emerging from the Jacksonian minority within the Democratic Party, a minority associated with Gov. Sam Houston, and the remnants of the antebellum Whig party. He further recognized that ethnic minorities, particularly Germans and Hispanics, reinforced this coalition. On the other hand, Dale Baum's *The Shattering of Texas Unionism,* published in 1998, pinned anti-secession votes to economic and cultural forces. Baum found that those possessing the border state culture and economic outlook of the state's northern tier of counties (more akin to those of Kentucky and Tennessee than the Deep South), German Lutherans, and members of the Disciples of Christ, a group traditionally hostile to political action, were more likely to be anti-Confederate than others. Others have located anti-Confederate sentiment in regional interests and even class membership. Perhaps the most all-encompassing definition was provided by Walter Buenger in his "Texas and the Riddle of Secession" when he attributed its sources to "cultural bias, ideology, party allegiance, the leadership of forceful personalities, and self-interest."[1] An examination of E. J. Davis shows, however, that even these generalizations fail to explain his actions. For Davis many of these factors played a role in his history, but in the end his unique personal experiences became even more important in determining his choices.

E. J. Davis should not have opposed the war. He should not have become one of the state's principal advocates of black suffrage afterward. His heritage, rooted in the culture of the Deep South, argued against such a course. He was the son of William Godwin Davis, a native of Virginia, and Mary Ann Channer Davis, an English immigrant who had settled in Charleston, South Carolina. William married Mary Ann in 1812, after he had moved to that town, where he opened a blacksmith shop and operated a cartage company that carried cotton from the backcountry to the Charleston market. Five years after their marriage they moved to St. Augustine, Florida, where William pursued a variety of land speculation schemes on Key Largo and Key Biscayne. E. J. Davis was born in St. Augustine on October 2, 1827. At an early age he considered a military career and even applied for an appointment to West Point. E.J. failed to secure admission to the military academy and instead followed his family to Galveston sometime in the 1840s. William did not have notable success in Galveston, but the family did have enough to own several slaves, probably household servants. E.J. thus came from a family Southern in its origins, one that was tied at least in a small way to the institution of slavery. Davis's family unquestionably was Southern to its roots.[2]

E.J.'s father had been involved in politics in Florida, and E.J. also became interested early in his life. As his career progressed he identified himself with the Democratic Party and initially embraced its views on

Edmund J. Davis and wife Lizzie in New Orleans.
Courtesy of David and Harriet Condon Collection.

the controversial question of slavery. He associated with the Democrats even though his first campaign saw him supporting Zachary Taylor, the Whig candidate, in the 1848 presidential race. In the border country, however, support for Taylor was not unusual, for the former general was seen as a hero of the Mexican-American War and partly responsible for settling the question of the border between Texas and Mexico. No matter the ambiguity of his stand in 1848, by 1853 Davis definitely associated himself with the Democratic Party. That year he ran for the position of district attorney in the Twelfth Judicial District as a Democrat. He subsequently ran successfully as a Democrat for the position of district judge in 1855 and 1857.

The 1855 campaign was of particular significance relative to Davis's thinking regarding the growing Southern concern about the future of slavery. Northerners had responded to the Kansas-Nebraska Act of 1854, which potentially opened territory north of the Missouri Compromise line with demands that slavery be kept out of the nation's territories and forced Southerners onto the defensive. In 1855, Texas Democrats, in what was called the "bomb shell" convention, announced a party platform for the first time and demanded that any candidate running as a Democrat subscribe to it. In response to Northern pressure to restrict the spread of slavery, the convention's platform demanded the opening of all federal territories to slavery and insisted that the federal government recognize the right of slave owners to carry their peculiar property into any state of the Union. The platform contended further that opposition to these rights by Northerners undermined the compact under which Texas had entered the Union, and it threatened to consider the Union broken unless Northerners recognized these rights. Implicit in the platform was the idea that, if the North broke the national contract, then Southerners had the right to secede from the Union. As a Democrat, Davis had to stand on the party's platform.[3]

In the subsequent campaign Davis did not just passively subscribe to the position laid out in the state Democratic platform. He openly supported it. At the county convention in Corpus Christi several months after the "bomb shell" meeting, Davis served on the Committee of Address. The committee's resolutions endorsed the platform of the state convention and went even further than the state platform, opposing any congressional interference with slavery, not only in the territories but also within the existing states. Predicting that slavery would continue to exist and expand, the committee suggested that in the future the national government might even need to acquire more territory for the institution's preservation and protection. As in the state platform, the Corpus Christi address concluded that any attack upon slavery was an assault on the contractual basis of the Union, an assault that would break up the nation. Davis helped write the address, then signed it.[4]

Davis's party loyalty continued during the 1857 campaign season. The Democratic convention at Waco on May 4 went even further in tying candidates to the party's platform. The delegates required that all individuals running as Democrats make an open pledge of their support for it. The platform, largely a repeat of that of 1855 with elaboration made by a meeting in Austin in 1856, reemphasized the party's position that it was the right of citizens of the various states to carry their property, slaves, with impunity throughout the Union. Again the delegates threatened secession if the North persisted in its efforts at restricting or even abolishing slavery. Running as a Democrat meant accepting this position. Although Davis, elected to go to Waco, was unable to attend, his run for office that autumn showed that he still accepted the party's basic position on states' rights.[5]

Davis's ideas about the rights of Southern slaveholders persisted, but after 1857 his thinking about secession changed. While many Democrats began agitating for immediate secession at this time, Davis adopted the position that secession should be only a last resort for the South. He never explicitly stated the reasons for this shift in his point of view, but his son Britton later related his own belief that his father was influenced by Forbes Britton, his new father-in-law. If so, the shift in thought indicates further the importance of peculiar individual experiences in shaping a person's course through time.[6]

Davis probably had known Britton as a prominent private citizen and politician for some time. Britton was an important businessman and politician in southern Texas. He had settled in Corpus Christi after his military service in the Mexican-American War. He became successful financially, involving himself in numerous business activities and purchasing a ranch. He also speculated in land and promoted a variety of internal improvement projects, including a railroad out of Corpus Christi. In 1857 he ran successfully for the state senate, then again in 1859, and in that body he became a leader of efforts to secure protection of the frontier from Native American and Mexican raiders. As chairman of the Committee on the Militia, he worked for an expansion of the federal military presence on the border and also promoted plans to raise state forces to be used for the same ends. In his second term he introduced a successful bill that authorized Gov. Hardin R. Runnels to place a thousand men on a line from the Rio Grande to the Red River, although Runnels left the decision to Sam Houston, who had defeated him in the 1859 elections. In both his private and political life Britton became associated with the regional interests of Corpus Christi and the country between the Nueces and the Rio Grande.[7]

Forbes Britton, E. J. Davis's father-in-law. Courtesy of David and Harriet Condon Collection.

Davis's political interests made him a natural ally of Britton. In 1853,
Davis had supported the gubernatorial candidacy of Elisha M. Pease
after the candidate promised to support a transcontinental railroad
that would move through the border country and advanced a program
to expel Indians from the area. The next year Davis had served on a
committee in Laredo that called for the federal government to send
mounted troops to the Rio Grande. Davis's connection with Britton became more personal in the winter of 1857 when he filled in for the judge
of the Fourteenth District, encompassing Corpus Christi and Nueces
County. He met Britton's daughter Anne Elizabeth at parties while in
Corpus Christi that Christmas. After a relatively short courtship, E.J.
and Lizzie were married on April 6, 1858. The marriage tied Davis to a
man whose political interests closely paralleled his own. That Britton,
whose own ideas about how the South should react to Northern threats
against slavery were changing, might influence Davis on that question
could be expected.[8]

Neither Davis nor Britton explained what produced their increasing
alienation from the secessionist wing of the Democratic Party after 1857,

but in part it may have been produced by their belief that the party's leaders had failed to secure the safety of the border. In that case, regional concerns prompted their shifting viewpoint, and the activities of Juan Cortina along the border in 1859, which Davis helped to suppress, must have made such apprehensions even more relevant. Their apparent support, in 1859, of the gubernatorial candidacy of Sam Houston rather than the regular Democratic candidate, Hardin Runnels, pointed to their changing thoughts. Support for Houston would have made sense because widespread dissatisfaction existed at this point with the governor's frontier policy. Houston, on the other hand, running as an independent, harshly criticized Runnels's policies and promised more effective action. Indeed, after his election Houston actually implemented Britton's plan to put a thousand Texas Rangers along the frontier and also sent Britton to Washington, D.C., to lobby the national government to increase the size of its military force on the border.[9]

For men with regional interests like Davis and Britton, Houston's campaign advanced other issues of concern. Houston's attacks on the Runnels administration did not just involve criticism of his actual frontier policy. He also focused on the Democratic leadership's agitation of the slavery issue and their threats of secession. Houston's concerns were not just ideological or constitutional but also practical. He considered secession to be a threat to the well-being of Texas and particularly of the frontier. He would state the character of this threat more explicitly a year later in a reply he wrote to the governor of South Carolina, who had asked him to support the assembling of delegates from the slaveholding states to prepare for possible secession. In the wake of the John Brown Raid on Harper's Ferry, Gov. William H. Gist had pointed to the continuing "assaults upon the institution of slavery, and upon the rights and equality of the Southern States," as reason for action. In his reply, Houston included a passage of particular significance to the frontier. "Texas is a border State," he wrote. "Indians ravage a portion of her frontier. Mexico renders insecure her entire Western boundary. Her slaves are liable to escape and no fugitive slave law is pledged for their recovery." As in the case of other border states, secession offered no solution to these problems. "Let dissolution come," he wrote, "and the terrible consequences will fall upon all those [border states] first, and with a double force." Houston's warnings surely had resonance with both Davis and

Britton. When Houston sent his 1860 letter to Governor Gist, Britton introduced a resolution into the state senate endorsing his sentiments.[10]

Davis had no public pronouncements on his stance during the 1859 election, but his father-in-law had already openly embraced Houston's position by that time. In the summer, before the election season had fully begun, a Vermont newspaper published an editorial that encouraged Britton to run for Congress. He obviously had become known nationally and was, in the editor's words, a "*sensible* man" who would stand for the Union against the disunionizing efforts of Northern abolitionists and Southern pro-secession fire-eaters. Britton indicated that he did not intend to run, but he also criticized the "blind zealots and reckless demagogues" who took advantage of imaginary lines to divide the nation. He concluded that men such as these should never be allowed to break down the ties that held the nation together. Davis's later actions indicated that he had come to see the situation in much the same way as his father-in-law.[11]

Opposition to secession did not, however, mean that either Davis's or Britton's Unionism was unqualified. Their attitude toward secession had changed, but they remained supportive of the rights of slave owners. This was apparent in the crisis that developed after the election of the Republican Party's candidate, Abraham Lincoln, in the presidential election in the autumn of 1860. For many Texans, Republican success meant that they faced a full-scale assault upon slavery. The editor of the Corsicana *Navarro Express* stated this feeling immediately after news of the results when he wrote, "The North has gone overwhelmingly for *Negro Equality* and *Southern Vassalage!* Southern men will you *Submit* to this *Degradation?*" A mass meeting in Fort Worth answered the editor's question when it resolved, "We are unwilling to submit to the administration of Abraham Lincoln, and that we will not submit." Pressure for a convention to consider secession forced men like Davis and Britton to define their position on the question of national unity more clearly.[12]

Forbes Britton explained the limits of Unionism for himself and men like him; certainly his son-in-law's subsequent actions indicated that he still aligned himself with Britton. In a letter to the *Texas State Gazette* written in mid-December 1860, Britton advised delaying action and waiting to see the intentions of the Lincoln government. For him, the election of Lincoln provided no cause for precipitous action by the slave states, and he believed leaders might still find some sort of compromise. He advised, "The time for crimination and recrimination has passed. We want no harsh assertions against either section—assertions so common among the hand racked politicians with whom our country has been recently so . . . cursed." On the other hand, he assured his readers that he was "opposed to the last extreme to this Government being administered on the principles of preventing slavery where it does not exist and abolishing it where it does." In addition, he believed that the states of the South should stand together to assure that the victorious party adhere to the Constitution. If this did not happen he would "advocate the severance of all ties that bound me to such a Union by secession, dissolution, revolution or any other means by which it may be designated." In short, Britton believed secession might be necessary, but Texans should wait for a real threat before acting.[13]

Texas's Democratic leadership was unwilling to wait for some sort of overt action against slavery by the Lincoln government. They encouraged public meetings across the state, and these demanded the calling of a convention to determine the state's relationship to the Union. On December 3, 1860, a small group of state leaders called for an election on January 8, 1861, to elect delegates to attend a convention in Austin on January 21. At this time Davis began to make his own thoughts on the crisis clear. At a public meeting in Brownsville on December 27, 1860, he announced that he would run for the convention as a candidate from Cameron County. Although in later years his political opponents would allege that his candidacy proved that he had supported secession, he unquestionably did not. Although, like his father-in-law, he may have adopted a wait-and-see attitude, he was not an immediate secessionist. In the campaign he ran against two out-and-out secessionists and, in correspondence with his brother, E.J. maintained his strong opposition to breaking up the country. His brother Waters remembered that "in becoming a candidate he did so hoping that he might be able to prevent the secession of Texas, and thereby save our State from the misfortune it brought on us."[14]

Davis did not go to Austin. His pro-secession opponents overwhelmed him in the balloting on January 8. Even had he been elected, he could have done little to block the rush to disunion. Secessionists dominated the convention, and on the second day of the meeting, with only eight of the 174 delegates opposed, the majority agreed to an ordinance of secession to be submitted to the people on February 23. There was no need to wait to see what the newly elected Republican president would do, according to the delegates. That party had already used the federal government to "strike down the interests and prosperity of the people of Texas and her sister slave-holding States." The Republicans had embraced the doctrine of the equality of races and attacked the "beneficent and patriarchal system of African slavery," an attack that violated the "experience of mankind" and "Divine Law." They could see little reason to await further proof of Lincoln's or the Republican Party's intentions of interfering with slavery and the rights of Southerners.[15]

Davis apparently did not campaign against passage of the ordinance in the election that followed. It may have been apparent that little chance existed to stop its passage. The convention not only had drafted the ordinance and sent it to the people for a vote, it also made moves to take the state out of the Union before the election. Delegates created a Committee of Public Safety and charged it with forcing the surrender of U.S. troops in the state and assuming control of federal property. On February 16, 1861, state troops under Col. Ben McCulloch besieged the San Antonio headquarters of U.S. forces in Texas. Negotiations with the pro-Southern army commander, Gen. David E. Twiggs, produced the surrender of all federal troops and the state takeover of forts, weapons, munitions, and supplies belonging to the federal government. The convention, for all practical purposes, had declared war on the U.S. government a full week before the secession election. Only the failure of General Twiggs to resist prevented the outbreak of armed conflict. Voters could hardly have reversed the direction state leaders had taken.[16]

Davis could do little to stop Texas voters from approving secession, but he remained convinced that it was a mistake. He and his wife arrived in San Antonio in mid-February, the same time that McCulloch forced the surrender of federal troops. He had temporarily traded judicial districts with Judge Thomas J. Devine and was holding court in the city. The couple boarded at a hotel on the city's main plaza, where he discussed the situation with numerous Southern officers in the U.S. Army who were staying at the hotel while on the way to the coast to leave Texas. He spent several evenings with Col. Robert E. Lee of the Second U.S. Cavalry, who had been on his way back to Washington but then been detained when McCulloch arrived. Davis not only demonstrated his belief that secession would be detrimental to Texas but also indicated that he believed no legal basis existed for secession and showed decidedly nationalist feelings in his arguments. Stating his own Southern background and the participation of his ancestors in the nation's wars, he appealed to Lee to "stand by the Union." In discussions with Edmund Kirby Smith, Davis also appealed to nationalist sentiment, reminding Smith of his family's long service to the nation and urging him to "stand to the old Flag." Neither man followed Davis's advice.[17]

In the February 23 vote, support for the secession ordinance passed easily, 46,154 to 14,747. Initially Davis appeared to accept the will of the people. This willingness soon gave way, however, as the convention proceeded to enact measures that the judge's legal mind considered wrong. These actions forced further changes in Davis's thoughts about events and his own role in them. The convention had adjourned on February 4, but before leaving Austin it had sent delegates to Montgomery, Alabama. There, on February 9, representatives from South Carolina, Georgia, Alabama, Mississippi, and Louisiana formed the Confederate government. After the popular vote, the Texas convention reassembled and on March 5 voted to join this new Confederacy. When Governor Houston complained that the convention had exceeded its authority in this action, the convention responded on March 14 by requiring all public officials to take an oath of allegiance to the new government. Houston refused and on March 18 the convention removed him from office. As district judge, Davis faced the same dilemma as the governor: accept the state's entry into the Confederacy or leave office.[18]

For Davis, a skilled and successful attorney, the convention's decision to join the Confederacy raised the same serious questions concerning the legality of the newly created government that had been raised by Houston. As a result, he stepped down from office. In an address to voters in his judicial district published on April 3, Davis explained his decision. In the past, he wrote, changing a constitution or amending it had been done either in a convention elected for that purpose or by a direct vote of the people. Now, a convention elected to consider the state's relationship with the Union had assumed powers beyond its charge. The convention had not been elected to create a new government. Nonetheless, without a vote of the people, it had acted as a constitutional convention, altered the state constitution, enacted legislation when the regularly elected legislature still existed, raised an army, disposed of public property, and created new offices. Finally, the convention annexed the state to the Confederacy. Some had said that the election implicitly gave the convention these powers, but Davis denied the legitimacy of such an argument. The public could not possibly have even implicitly given consent to joining the Confederacy since at the time of the election the Confederacy did not even exist. The convention, he contended, had created an unconstitutional government. In a statement reflecting a very conservative constitutional view, Davis wrote, "For my part, I have been taught to believe that the spirit of our institutions limited the authority of all public servants, to that plainly expressed in the appointments. To me it is a new dogma that authority, under any circumstances, is to be *implied* and I know of no distinction in this respect favorable to the authority of a Convention." As a result, he declared, "I cannot swear to support a Constitution or a Government to the establishment of which, my consent, as one of the people, has not been asked."[19]

With this statement Davis withdrew from public life and returned to his family. Some Unionists would pursue a different course. James W. Throckmorton, one of the men who voted against secession in the state convention, determined after the vote for secession, "the die is cast; the step has been taken, and regardless of consequences I expect and intend to share the fortunes of my friends and neighbors." When war came he intended to be with his countrymen. Davis, on the other hand, simply could not accept what the convention had done. He returned home to Lizzie, who was pregnant with their second child, and assumed responsibility for the affairs of his father-in-law, who had died. He remained critical of the state government as well. On May 1 he delivered his last public address in Corpus Christi, detailing further the reasons for his opposition to the newly created government. In that address he assured his listeners that he accepted the will of the people in carrying out secession. The convention had been called to consider this measure, the people had ratified their decision. On the other hand, repeating the same reasoning that he had given when explaining his resignation, he concluded that all other actions of the convention had been unwarranted, an illegal assumption of power not given to the delegates. He encouraged his listeners to insist that each action be examined, then legitimized or negated by the legislature or a new convention authorized to do so. This time he also went beyond his April 3 address to criticize the Confederate government, which he believed could never represent or properly defend Texas. Accepting secession, he could not recognize the Confederacy.[20]

Davis may have been content to remain peaceably at home, raising criticism of the Confederate government, but that possibility was coming to an end as he delivered his May 1 address. Events forced him once again along a new course. The Confederacy's need for soldiers most directly created his problem, although the increasing suppression of Unionist sentiment may also have played a role. In April 1861, Gov. Edward Clark, who had assumed the office after the removal of Houston, called for the first volunteers to meet requests of the Confederate government. After the first rush to the colors, volunteering slowed down and Confederate enrolling officers found it more difficult to secure men. To ensure that the state could comply with Confederate drafts, on November 15 the newly elected governor, Francis R. Lubbock, called on the legislature to revise the state militia laws. It complied with new legislation that made all males between the ages of eighteen and thirty-five liable to military service. More important, the legislature gave the governor the power to draft men from the militia into Confederate service if requisitions made by the Confederate government were not filled. For E. J. Davis the new militia laws forced another decision. If called up, would he serve or not?[21]

Davis's problems increased when Confederate officials began to suppress all anti-Confederate sentiment. By March 1862, Col. Henry E. McCulloch, who commanded forces in South Texas, warned superiors that many men were crossing the Rio Grande to avoid military service and intended opposing Confederate authorities. The situation had developed to the point that he feared the authorities would have to crush these escapees, "even if it has to be done without due course of law." Considering these men lawless, McCulloch suggested that a declaration of martial law was necessary to restore Confederate authority and uphold the militia laws. In April, Gen. Hamilton P. Bee, who replaced McCulloch, came to the same conclusion and proclaimed martial law in the area from San Antonio to the Rio Grande. Bee's proclamation does not survive, but it probably looked like Gen. Paul Octave Hébert's extension of martial law through the entire state later that May. In addition to requiring the registration of all eligible men of military age, Hébert ordered the removal of all disloyal people from the state. Davis would have been liable to either conscription or arrest under these regulations, and he indicated that he could not remain at peace in Texas holding the position he did. A decision had to be made, Lizzie later recalled, when the family received word that militant secessionists intended to force him into the service. Would he fight for a government that he believed had no constitutional authority or not? Could he cease his criticism? His answer was no.[22]

Given Davis's view of the legitimacy of the state's place in the Confederacy, his decision was not surprising. Still liable for military service at the age of thirty-five, he determined to leave the state rather than fight or be persecuted by Confederate officials. On May 3, 1862, he left quickly for the Mexican border. In his haste, he had to leave behind Lizzie and sons Britton and Waters, the latter only two months old. He was joined by John L. Haynes, a merchant from the border town of Rio Grande City who had been a successful merchant and businessman. Elected to the state legislature in 1857 and again in 1859, Haynes had embraced much the same position as Davis in the sectional crisis and had actively opposed secession in the election. Like Houston and Davis, he resigned in spring 1861 rather than take an oath of allegiance to the Confederacy. William Alexander, an Austin attorney who had been active in pro-Union politics in 1860 and 1861, joined the two in their flight to the border.[23]

The conditions under which Davis left the state help to account for his subsequent action. Some Texans fled to spend the war years in relative peace in Mexico or the North. William Alexander, for example, spent the war studying Spanish and Mexican law. Davis, however, decided to have an active role in removing what he considered a usurping government from Texas and spent much of the war promoting an invasion of the state. He left Mexico shortly after he arrived and sailed to New Orleans, where other Texas refugees initially gathered. In July he traveled to Washington, D.C., where he took advantage of the connection he had made with Gen. Samuel P. Heintzelman during the Cortina War to begin his push for a return to Texas. In early August he finally met with President Lincoln, to whom he argued that many Texans remained loyal and wanted to return to their proper place in the Union. He believed that if the federal government would provide 3,000 rifles for a force of loyalists they could quickly recapture the state. His plan consisted of an occupation of the Rio Grande border first, then a march northward into the San Antonio area. The president sent Davis to discuss the plan with the secretary of war, but in the end they provided no assurances that they would mount the desired invasion. They did authorize Davis to recruit a regiment of cavalry among the state's loyalist refugees. Unable to accomplish his desired goal, Davis returned to New Orleans, where he began recruiting the First Texas Cavalry, U.S.[24]

Davis never gave up on the idea that Texas could be returned to the Union, and from 1862 to 1865 he continued to pursue that goal. In January 1863 he and the two companies of the First Texas Cavalry that had been equipped headed for Galveston to provide a garrison after its capture by Union forces the previous October. The day before his ship arrived, however, Confederates recaptured the town and Davis narrowly avoided capture. Frustrated in this first effort, he returned to Mexico to recruit more men and forward them to New Orleans. That summer of 1863, he returned to Washington and again pressed unsuccessfully for an invasion, only to return to Texas to find that Gen. Nathaniel Banks had already planned an attack on Sabine Pass. Once again, Davis and his regiment joined an invasion only be turned around when Banks's naval force failed to overcome the area's defenses. Then, in October of that year, he accompanied another expedition that occupied Brownsville, only to be frustrated in his plans for a return to the San Antonio area by a drought-induced lack of forage and an inability to find suitable horses. After the Brownsville invasion stalled he received orders to return to Louisiana, where he received command of a cavalry brigade that successfully protected the retreating Union army after its Red River campaign. Through the rest of the war his command spent most of its time suppressing small Confederate units in that state. Davis ended the war as a brigadier general.[25]

Davis's overall military experience, with its frustrations and ultimate involvement in brutal fighting in the bayou country of Louisiana, may have hardened his feelings toward the Confederacy and its supporters, but other events more directly connected with his own life may have played an even greater role in determining his feelings toward personal and political friends who had gone with the Confederacy. The treatment of his wife during the war provided one source of anger. In August 1862, Lizzie tried to join her husband in New Orleans and appealed to Gen. Hamilton P. Bee, Confederate commander in charge of the area from San Antonio to the border, for a pass to leave the state. Bee had been one of Davis's political friends. A member of the Texas house from Laredo and Speaker of the house in the Seventh Legislature, he had attended the Davis wedding. Bee gave her the document and Lizzie and her two young boys traveled to Brownsville to cross into Mexico. There they met Col. Philip Luckett, another political associate of Davis and his best man at the wedding, but now in charge of forces along the border. Luckett informed her that he had received word from Bee that she was not to be allowed to cross the Rio Grande. Instead, she was to be returned to Corpus Christi. Lizzie later recalled the exchange with Luckett. When she complained that in her condition, having given birth to Waters only five months before, the return might kill her, the man who had been a friend replied "it makes no *difference* whether *you are killed one way or another;* and if you attempt to cross the River, you will be *shot* and your body will float down the river, and be like so many deserters, you will never be heard of again!"[26]

Accompanied by a Confederate officer, Lizzie and the boys returned to Corpus Christi, where she was informed that rumors indicated E. J. intended to lead an invasion force into the state. General Bee told her that if that happened she would be moved deeper into the interior of the state and, further, she should be prepared to have her throat cut. Lizzie remembered that she had replied, "Come and cut it." The friendship that Davis had held with both Luckett and Bee ended, never to be restored. Although Davis never addressed the treatment of his wife, Lizzie's account of the incident indicates that it hardened the feelings of both toward these men and other Confederate leaders. In the end, Lizzie and the boys did rejoin E. J. when they traveled to Brownsville once again, secretly boarded the ferry, and crossed the Rio Grande undetected on Christmas Eve 1862.

Another event that toughened Davis's attitudes toward Confederates occurred on March 15, 1863. After the unsuccessful Galveston venture, Davis had returned to Matamoros and busied himself organizing his cavalry regiment. He faced a hostile opposition across the border. Reflecting attitudes among Confederates, a newspaper correspondent in

Brownsville wrote, "Judge Davis has come to a bad place for his health, for if he should fall into the hands of any of our soldiers, they would hang him to the first tree." Tension was worsened by the fact that Confederate soldiers and Davis's recruits were located directly across the Rio Grande within hailing distance of each other. They daily exchanged insults, and the situation caused General Bee to worry that his men might attack Davis's camp. On March 15 they did just that, crossing the river into Mexican territory and assaulting the men of the First Texas Cavalry.[27]

The raiders killed several of the refugees in the camp before they found Davis in a nearby house with his wife and children. They clearly intended to hang Davis, but for whatever reason they carried him off along with Capt. William W. Montgomery and several other refugees. Before they left they assured Lizzie Davis that they would do nothing before delivering the men to General Bee. Instead, when the attackers were across the river, they separated into two parties. One group took Davis and the other took Captain Montgomery. Exactly why the events that followed took place is not known; the men who took Montgomery lynched him, but those who took Davis just hid him from Confederate authorities. The episode created serious tension on the border, with Mexican officials threatening either to attack the Confederate positions across the Rio Grande or to cut off the border to the critical cotton trade. In response, Bee ultimately made his men turn Davis over and returned him to Mexican officials. Texans looked at Davis and his men, however, as "notorious traitors and renegades," and the editor of the *San Antonio Herald* argued that in the future "any Texan would be justified in shooting [Davis] down like a dog, should he be found voluntarily upon our soil."[28]

His seizure and the murder of Montgomery produced considerable anger in Davis. Hamilton Bee later recalled that in the wake of the affair Davis had written him an irate letter. He blamed Bee, as commander of Confederate troops on the Rio Grande, for what had taken place. Davis told his former associate that he considered him a war criminal and informed him that if ever captured he would not be treated as a prisoner of war but would be tried for the attack on the Texas refugees and the death of Montgomery. Davis charged the general with what he considered to be war crimes. The hostility of the Union refugees toward men like Bee also was expressed in the inscription placed on Montgomery's gravestone. When Union forces took Brownsville, they immediately began looking for Montgomery's body. After finding it, they buried him in Brownsville with a military ceremony held on the public square. On the headstone they inscribed his name followed by a condemnation of the Confederate officers who had allowed the murder to occur. He had been killed "by the traitors H P Bee, Lucket, Chilton, Bowin, Dick Taylor and the miserable wretches under him." Davis, and indeed probably most Texas refugees, had moved from seeing the Confederate leaders of Texas as just presiding over an illegal government to being traitors to the Union.[29]

At the war's end Davis and probably many of the men who served under him had become strident anti-Confederates. Events had transformed his Unionism into a militant hostility to those who had taken the state out of the Union. A quartermaster who accompanied Davis on several expeditions in Louisiana in the autumn of 1864 recognized this feeling. The men, he believed, were a "hard set of soldiers." More critical in terms of influencing how these men would respond to the postwar world, he found that they were "men who are not afraid of the Confederates, but hate them." In June 1865, when sent to Galveston with documents for the surrender of Confederate forces in Texas, Davis met with his childhood friend, Gen. E. Kirby Smith, and Gen. John B. Magruder, the Confederate commander. He assured them no one intended to punish them with any "severe measures," but he did not suggest that there would be no punishment of some sort. Davis did not believe by this time that former Confederates could ever be trusted with control over state or local governments.[30]

Davis mustered out of the volunteer army in September 1865 and returned to Corpus Christi. Whether he planned to remain in Texas at this time is uncertain, for he actively sought a commission in the regular U.S. Army. The downsizing of the military in the wake of the war, however, ensured that he did not get the desired appointment, and instead he reestablished his law practice and also turned to settling the affairs of Lizzie's family. Forbes Britton had died in February 1861, leaving his family to take care of his large ranching concerns. With a spread of over 2,000 acres, 1,000 head of cross-bred Durham cattle, forty horses, and 3,000 sheep that Britton apparently had acquired from George W. Kendall, the estate required close supervision. As late as January 1866, Davis operated the ranch and proposed that his brother-in-law partner with him in running it. Davis had considered selling it but thought that the two of them might be able to make it profitable. The two never reached a satisfactory agreement, and Davis put it on the market as the agent of his mother-in-law the following summer. In the end, however, events pushed Davis back into politics.[31]

Given the concerns with the actual loyalty of former Confederates, these events forced him to embrace new measures to prevent them returning to power. Early in the postwar period Davis concluded that the policy of Reconstruction, initiated by President Andrew Johnson, was producing that very thing. The president laid out the general terms of his plan for restoring the Southern states to their normal place in the Union on May 29 with his amnesty proclamation and the terms he laid out for the readmission of North Carolina to the Union. The first proclamation conferred an amnesty on all who had participated in the rebellion who would swear an oath of loyalty to the Union. The restoration of political rights came with the oath. He did provide for some exceptions—including high-ranking members of the Confederate army, elected Confederate officials, and wealthy Southerners who had owned more than $20,000 in property in 1860—but even in the latter cases a presidential pardon could bring about a restoration of these rights. A liberal granting of these pardons allowed such Texans as John H. Reagan, who had served as postmaster general of the Confederacy, quickly to regain the potential for political action. As to restoration of the state, the president asked only that the politically eligible citizens call a constitutional convention and write a new constitution that assured a "republican form of government." These provisions became the basis for Presidential Reconstruction in Texas.[32]

Given Davis's point of view, he publicly opposed the president's program. In fact, Gen. E. R. S. Canby believed that the president's realization of Davis's position had led him personally to block his receiving a commission in the regular army. Consequently, Davis's concerns that the president's program would restore Confederates to power prompted his reentry into politics. In January 1866 he ran successfully for a place in the constitutional convention called under the president's Reconstruction program. For the most part in the convention, Davis supported the proposals of provisional governor Andrew J. Hamilton. Hamilton had laid out the program that he believed necessary to secure the state's restoration to its full privileges in the Union in his message to the delegates at the beginning of the convention. He had insisted that the delegates take action that showed the North that Texans recognized the result of the war, conceded what he called the "spirit and principles," and accepted the "actual changes" that had taken place. Such concessions required that the convention repudiate the principle of secession, denying it as a right and then doing nothing to legitimize it. In addition, he believed that the delegates had to recognize emancipation and also guarantee basic civil rights to blacks. At this point, it meant ensuring that African Americans had the right to equal treatment before the law, particularly in the courts, and to own property. Hamilton had not yet concluded that blacks should receive any political rights, although he did believe that they should not be excluded from voting because of their race. Rather than a racial restriction on voting, he suggested that some sort of property or educational test might accomplish much the same end without an unquestionable, and unacceptable to many in the North, racial exclusion.[33]

Davis backed Hamilton's general plan of Reconstruction, but he also embraced an even more radical position than Hamilton's when he favored granting blacks political as well as civil rights. On February 14, 1866, he introduced a resolution that called for an extension of the franchise to all adult male blacks as of July 4, 1866. Whether Davis actually intended unrestricted suffrage is unclear, for Unionists later remembered that none of their party actually supported unrestricted suffrage. On the other hand, he went beyond Governor Hamilton in positively supporting voting rights for blacks. Unlike the governor, he showed no reluctance to take this step. Davis offered no explanation of his stand on the franchise. Possibly his experience with African American troops during the war had convinced them of their right to exercise the vote. On the other hand, an observation by Benjamin C. Truman, the correspondent sent to Texas to observe the convention by the *New York Times,* may point to a more important cause. Reflecting the reaction of Unionists to their wartime experiences, the persecutions they had experienced, and their distrust of former Confederates, Truman concluded that the men who supported black suffrage "prefer that even negroes rather than secessionists should rule the country." Davis unquestionably had no trust in the former Confederates. The same day that he had introduced his resolution calling for the black franchise, he also voted to table a resolution expressing the convention's "gratification" for the opportunity to resume normal relations with the federal government. Davis wanted consideration delayed until it could be determined how many members were "really gratified" at this opportunity.[34]

The course of the convention, the subsequent election, and the action of the Twelfth Legislature proved the final step in turning the reluctant Unionist of 1861 to the Radical Republican of 1867. The new constitution not only failed to provide political rights to the freedmen, it seriously restricted their civil rights. Though allowing blacks to own property, it excluded them from juries and allowed them to testify in court cases only if they were an injured party. The constitution barred interracial marriage and prohibited blacks from sharing in the public school fund. In the 1866 election conservatives carried the day, electing such candidates as Willis L. Robards, a former Confederate officer running for state comptroller who campaigned promising "that this should be the white man's government." The subsequent state legislature showed that men like Robards were in power, when despite warnings that similar laws passed in other Southern states had raised concerns in the North it implemented apprenticeship, vagrancies, and labor laws that clearly discriminated against blacks and imposed controls on their labor.[35]

The actions of the constitutional convention, the election, and the subsequent legislature were the last straw for Davis. He wrote former governor and fellow Unionist Elisha M. Pease after the election that the results "ought to satisfy every loyal man North and South that the Secession party is just as well defined and just as intensely malignant against the Union and Unionists as in the palmist days of the Confederacy." In the same letter he briefly courted the idea of creating a separate state out of western Texas, even if having to stage a revolution. It was a step he believed had to be taken "unless we are prepared, quietly to let the rebels again cement their power over us."[36]

For Davis the return of former Confederates to power was totally unacceptable. In two letters written to Pease in November and December 1866, he provided the clearest indication of the hostility that now drove him. Texans had to recognize the war's result; they could not continue to ignore its consequences. Davis insisted that this meant they must certainly recognize the freedom of their former slaves, but it also required that they compensate those they had harmed during the war. Specifically he meant that the property that had been confiscated during the war should be returned. He even wanted the arrest of Confederate officials guilty of crimes against the state's loyal population. At this point he believed Congress must now intervene in the process and new state governments must be created. In addition, for Davis clearly the time had come for unrestricted black suffrage. As a result, he joined provisional governor Hamilton, E. M. Pease, and others in the North in appealing for congressional intervention and, in the words of a convention of Southern loyalists at Philadelphia, insisting that the national government "confer on every citizen in the States we represent the American birthright of impartial suffrage and equality before the law."[37]

From 1866 forward, Edmund J. Davis worked as best he could to achieve the goals that he set forth in Philadelphia. The work of Davis and men like him played a role in congressional intervention in the Reconstruction process in the spring of 1867, an intervention that required each former Confederate state to begin again—write new constitutions and elect new governments. This time, however, they must include adult black men as voters. Under the plan, Davis returned to Austin, where he presided over a new constitutional convention. Subsequently, with the support of black voters, he was elected governor of the state in 1869. As governor and then leader of the state's Republican Party, Davis worked to change Texas and particularly to protect the former slaves in both their political and civil rights until his death in 1883.[38]

E. J. Davis's course from the sectional crisis until his death underscores the complexity of anti-Confederate sentiment in Texas. No single factor led him along the path that took him from states' rights Democrat and pro-slavery Southerner to conditional Unionist, strident anti-Confederate and nationalist, and on to advocacy of black suffrage and civil rights. Prediction in the 1850s of where he would stand in the 1860s would have been impossible. Sectional interests, family, ideology, wartime experiences, and reactions to Confederate intransigence after the war drove him along the path he took. For historians, Davis's life serves as a reminder that, although general patterns may explain behavior, in the end the unique experiences of the individual may be even more important in producing these actions. No easy explanation can account for the emergence of one of the more radical men of Texas history.

NOTES

1. Walter Buenger, "Texas and the Riddle of Secession," in *Lone Star Blue and Gray: Essays on Texas in the Civil War,* ed. Ralph A. Wooster (Austin: Texas State Historical Association, 1995), 9. See also Buenger, *Secession and the Union in Texas* (Austin: University of Texas Press, 1984); James Marten, *Texas Divided: Loyalty and Dissent in the Lone Star State, 1856–1874* (Lexington: University Press of Kentucky, 1984), 22, 31; Dale Baum, *The Shattering of Texas Unionism: Politics in the Lone Star State during the Civil War Era* (Baton Rouge: Louisiana State University Press, 1998), 53–57; Claude Elliott, "Union Sentiment in Texas, 1861–1865," *Southwestern Historical Quarterly* 50 (April 1947): 449–77; Richard McCaslin, "Wheat Growers in the Cotton Confederacy: The Suppression of Dissent in Collin County, Texas, during the Civil War," *Southwestern Historical Quarterly* 96 (April 1993): 526–39; David Paul Smith, "Conscription and Conflict on the Texas Frontier, 1863–1865," *Civil War History* 36 (September 1990): 250–61; Walter D. Kamphoefner, "New Perspectives on Texas Germans and the Confederacy," in *The Fate of Texas: The Civil War and the Lone Star State,* ed. Charles D. Grear (Fayetteville: University of Arkansas Press, 2008), 105–21. For an assessment of forces motivating individual Unionists, see John L. Waller, *Colossal Hamilton of Texas: A Biography of Andrew Jackson Hamilton, Militant Unionist and Reconstruction Governor* (El Paso: Texas Western Press, 1968); Kenneth Wayne Howell, *Texas Confederate, Reconstruction Governor: James Webb Throckmorton* (College Station: Texas A&M University Press, 2008); Howell, "'When the Rabble Hiss, Well May Patriots Tremble': James Webb Throckmorton and the Secession Movement in Texas, 1854–1861," *Southwestern Historical Quarterly* 109 (April 2006): 465–94; Dale A. Somers, "James P. Newcomb: The Making of a Radical," *Southwestern Historical Quarterly* 72 (April 1969): 449–69; Randolph B. Campbell, "George W. Whitmore: East Texas Unionist," *East Texas Historical Journal* 28 (Spring 1990): 17–28.

2. U.S. Bureau of the Census, Slave Schedules, 1860, Galveston and Nueces Counties, microfilm, National Archives, Washington, D.C. For Davis's early life and career, see Carl H. Moneyhon, *Edmund J. Davis: Civil War General, Republican Leader, Reconstruction Governor* (Fort Worth: TCU Press, 2010), chaps. 1–2.

3. *Galveston News,* June 23, 1855.

4. Austin *Texas State Gazette,* September 8, 1855.

5. Ernest William Winkler, ed., *Platforms of Political Parties in Texas, University of Texas Bulletin* 53 (Austin: University of Texas, 1916), 64–68, 71–74; Llerena Friend, *Sam Houston: The Great Designer* (Austin: University of Texas Press, 1954), 248; Anna Irene Sanbo, "Beginnings of the Secession Movement in Texas," *Southwestern Historical Quarterly* 18 (July 1914), 57, 59.

6. Britton Davis to Editors, *Reader's Digest,* October 24, 1939.

7. "Forbes Britton," *Handbook of Texas* (Austin: Texas State Historical Association, 1996), 1:744; Patsy McDonald Spaw, ed., *The Texas Senate,* Vol. 1: *Republic to Civil War, 1836–1861* (College Station: Texas A&M University Press, 1990), 285, 287, 305.

8. Corpus Christi *Nueces Valley,* November 21, December 5, 1857; Austin *Texas State Gazette,* March 12, 1860; Annie Moore Schwien, *When Corpus Christi Was Young* (Corpus Christi, Tex.: La Retama Public Library, n.d.), 4; E. J. Davis to E. M. Pease, June 2, 1853, Graham-Pease-Niles Collection, Center for Austin History, Austin Public Library [hereafter G-P-N Collection]; E. J. Davis to E. M. Pease, March 13, 1854, Governor's Papers, Texas State Library and Archives Commission [hereafter TSLAC].

9. Buenger, *Secession and the Union in Texas,* 36; Randolph B. Campbell, *Gone to Texas: A History of the Lone Star State* (New York: Oxford University Press), 2003, 338; Spaw, *Texas Senate,* 285, 287, 305, 315; Forbes Britton to Sam Houston, March 3, 1860, Governor's Papers, TSLAC; E. J. Davis to Waters Davis, November 16, 1859, *Triweekly Dallas Herald,* November 30, 1850.

10. Austin *Southern Intelligencer,* January 25, 1860; Spaw, *Texas State Senate,* 317.

11. Forbes Britton to Editor, January 7, 1859, *Daily Times* [place and date of publication unknown], clipping in Lizzie Davis Civil War Scrapbook, David and Harriet Condon Collection, Middleburg, Virginia.

12. Corsicana *Navarro Express,* November 16, 1860; "December 8 Fort Worth Meeting," *Dallas Herald,* December 19, 1860.

13. Austin *Texas State Gazette,* January 12, 1861.

14. *Dallas Herald,* December 12, 1860; Austin *Tri-Weekly Texas State Gazette,* January 12, 1861; Water S. Davis to Editor, *Galveston Daily News,* October 14, 1873; see also *Galveston Daily News,* October 14, 1873, for charge that Davis had been a secessionist.

15. Ernest W. Winkler, ed., *Journal of the Secession Convention of Texas* (Austin: Austin Printing, 1912), 47–49.

16. Linda S. Hudson, "The Knights of the Golden Circle in Texas, 1858–1861: An Analysis of the First (Military) Degree Knights," in *The Seventh Star of the Confederacy: Texas during the Civil War,* ed. Kenneth W. Howell (Denton: University of North Texas Press, 2009), 56–57.

17. Unpublished biography of E. J. Davis, James P. Newcomb Papers, Dolph Briscoe Center for American History [hereafter Brisco Center] (first quote); E. J. Davis to Wm. P. Doran, August 7, 1876, E. J. Davis Letters, Rosenberg Library, Galveston (second quote); Britton Davis to *Reader's Digest,* October 24, 1939.

18. Randolph B. Campbell, *Gone to Texas: A History of the Lone Star State* (New York: Oxford University Press, 2003), 244–45.

19. "To the Citizens and Voters of the 12th District, April 3, 1861," circular in David and Harriet Condon Collection, Middleburg, Virginia.

20. Claude Elliott, *Leathercoat: The Life History of a Texas Patriot* (San Antonio, Tex.: Standard Printing, 1938), 59; Corpus Christi *Daily Ranchero,* May 11, 1861.

21. Kenneth E. Hendrickson, Jr., "The Confederate Governors of Texas," in Howell, *Seventh Star,* 231, 234.

22. H. E. McCulloch to S. B. Davis, March 3, 25, 1862, in *The War of the Rebellion: A Compilation of the Official Records of the Union and Confederate Armies,* 128 vols. (Washington, D.C. Government Printing Office, 1880–1902) [hereafter *OR*], Series I, Vol. 9, 704–705; P. O. Hébert to S. Cooper, October 11, 1862, *OR,* Series I, Vol. 53, 454–55; General Order No. 1, December 30, 1861, *San Antonio Herald,* January 25, 1862; Letter of Anne E. Davis, September 14, 1871, *San Antonio Express,* October 7, 1871.

23. Haynesfamily.com, www.haynesfamily.com/John1821; Alwyn Barr, "Haynes, John Leal," *Handbook of Texas Online,* Texas State Historical Association, www.tshaonline/handbook/online/articles/fhabk.

24. Edmund J. Davis to Samuel P. Heintzelman, August 8, 1862, Samuel P. Heintzelman Papers, Library of Congress; Abraham Lincoln to E. M. Stanton, August 4, 1862, in Roy F. Basler, ed., *Collected Works of Abraham Lincoln* (Rutgers, N.J.: Rutgers University Press, 1953), 5:357; *New York Tribune,* October 8, 1862.

25. Moneyhon, *Edmund J. Davis,* chap. 3.

26. Lizzie Davis to Dear Friend, September 14, 1871, newspaper clipping in David and Harriet Condon Collection, Middleburg, Virginia.

27. *San Antonio Herald,* March 28, 1863; H. P. Bee to A. G. Dickinson, March 15, 1863, *OR,* Series I, Vol. 15, 1017.

28. *San Antonio Herald,* March 17 (first quote), 28, April 4, 11 (second quote), 1863; H. P. Bee to A. G. Dickinson, March 15, 1863, *OR,* Series 1, Vol. 15, 1016–17.

29. Milo Kearny, ed., "The Fall of Brownsville, 1863, by John Warren Hunger," in *More Studies in Brownsville History* (Brownsville, Tex.: American University at Brownsville, 1989), 221; Nannie M. Tilley, ed., *Federals on the Frontier: The Diary of Benjamin F. McIntyre, 1862–1864* (Austin: University of Texas Press, 1963), 278 (quote); H. P. Bee to A. J. Hamilton, November 6, 1865, Hamilton Papers, Governors Papers, TSLAC.

30. Letter of Patterson to George, Morganza, Louisiana, February 1865, copy in author's possession; E. J. Davis to J. Schuyler Crosby, April 29, 1865, General's Papers, Record Group 94, National Archives, Washington, D.C.; E. J. Davis to William P. Doran, August 3, 7, 26, 1876, E. J. Davis Letters, Rosenberg Library, Galveston, Tex.; E. J. Davis to E. M. Pease, November 24, 1866, P-G-N Papers.

31. E. J. Davis to E. M. Pease, November 24, 1866, P-G-N Papers; E. J. Davis to Charles Worthington, January 27, 1867, J. B. Wells Papers, Brisco Center; Galveston *Flake's Bulletin,* August 15, 1866.

32. James D. Richardson, ed., *A Compilation of the Messages and Papers of the Presidents 1789–1897* (Washington, D.C.: Government Printing Office, 1909), 6:310–14; E. J. Davis to E. M. Pease, November 24, 1866, P-G-N Papers.

33. *Journal of the Constitutional Convention, Assembled at Austin, February 7, 1866. Adjourned April 2, 1866* (Austin: Printed at the Southern Intelligencer Office, 1866), 16–27; E. J. Davis to E. M. Pease, November 24, 1866, P-G-N Papers.

34. *Journal of the Constitutional Convention, 1866,* 29 (second and third quotes), 38; *New York Times,* March 11, 1866. That Davis may actually have desired an educational qualification on the suffrage may be seen in C. Caldwell to Editor, *Galveston Daily News,* April 1, 1867; Letter from Houston, *New York Times,* March 25, 1866; *New York Times,* March 11, 1866 (first quote).

35. W. L. Robards to Editor, *Galveston Daily News,* April 21, 1866; "Robards, Willis L.," *Handbook of Texas Online,* Texas State Historical Association, www .tshaonline.org/handbook/online/articles/fro04; Larry Madaras, ed., *The Dance of Freedom: Texas African Americans during Reconstruction* (Austin: University of Texas Press, 2007), 134–47.

36. E. J. Davis to E. M. Pease, July 14, 1866, P-G-N Papers.

37. E. J. Davis to E. M. Pease, November 24, December 21, 1866, P-G-N Papers; *Philadelphia Inquirer,* September 8, 1866 (quote).

38. See, for example, Moneyhon, *Edmund J. Davis,* chaps. 4–12.

Selected Bibliography

Abernethy, Francis E., ed. *Tales from the Big Thicket.* Denton: University of North Texas Press, 1967.

Allen, Beverly. *Rape Warfare: The Hidden Genocide in Bosnia-Herzegovina and Croatia.* Minneapolis: University of Minnesota Press, 1996.

Allen, James, and Leon Litwack. *Without Sanctuary: Lynching Photography in America.* Santa Fe, N.Mex.: Twin Palms, 2000.

Alonzo, Armando C. *Tejano Legacy: Rancheros and Settlers in South Texas, 1734–1900.* Albuquerque: University of New Mexico Press, 1998.

Anderson, Gary Clayton. *The Conquest of Texas: Ethnic Cleansing in the Promised Land.* Norman: University of Oklahoma Press, 2005.

Anderson, John Q., ed. *Brokenburn: The Journal of Kate Stone, 1861–1868.* Baton Rouge: Louisiana State University Press, 1995.

Anderson, Karen. *Teaching Gender in U.S. History.* Washington, D.C.: American Historical Association, 1997.

Arndt, Karl J. R., and May E. Olson. *German-American Newspapers and Periodicals, 1732–1955.* Munich, 1965.

Ayers, Edward L. *Vengeance and Justice: Crime and Punishment in the Nineteenth-Century American South.* New York: Oxford University Press, 1984.

Baker, Robin E., and Dale Baum, "The Texas Voter and the Crisis of the Union, 1859–1862." *Journal of Southern History* 53 (1987): 395–420.

Barr, Alwyn. *Black Texans: A History of African Americans in Texas, 1528–1995,* 2nd ed. Norman: University of Oklahoma Press, 1996.

———. "The Influence of War and Military Service on African Texans." In *Texans and War: New Interpretations of the State's Military History,* edited by Alexander Mendoza and Charles David Grear, 97–112. College Station: Texas A&M University Press, 2012.

———. "Records of the Confederate Military Commission in San Antonio, July 2–October 10 1862." *Southwestern Historical Quarterly* 73 (1969): 246–68.

Baud, Michael, and Willem Van Schendel. "Toward a Comparative History of Borderlands." *Journal of World History* 8 (1997): 211–42.

Baum, Dale. *The Shattering of Texas Unionism: Politics in the Lone Star State during the Civil War Era.* Baton Rouge: Louisiana State University Press, 1998.

———. "Slaves Taken to Texas for Safekeeping during the Civil War." In *The Fate of Texas: The Civil War and the Lone Star State,* edited by Charles D. Grear, 83–103. Fayetteville: University of Arkansas Press, 2008.

Baumgartner, Alice L. "Teodoro Zamora's Commission." *New York Times,* January 6, 2014.

Bell-Fialkoff, Andrew. "A Brief History of Ethnic Cleansing." *Foreign Affairs* 72 (1993): 110–121.

Berlin, Ira, Barbara Fields, Thavolia Glymph, Joseph Reidy, and Leslie S. Rowland, eds. *Freedom: A Documentary History of Emancipation, 1861–1867,* Series I, Vol. 1: *The Destruction of Slavery.* Cambridge: Cambridge University Press, 1985.

Berlin, Ira, Joseph Reidy, and Leslie S. Rowland, eds. *Freedom, A Documentary History of Emancipation, 1861–1867,* Series II: *The Black Military Experience.* Cambridge: Cambridge University Press, 1982.

Biesele, Rudolph Leopold. *The History of the German Settlements in Texas, 1831–1861.* Austin: Press of Von Boeckmann-Jones, 1930.

Blight, David W. *Beyond the Battlefield: Race, Memory, and the American Civil War.* Amherst: University of Massachusetts Press, 2002.

———. *Race and Reunion: The Civil War in American Memory.* Cambridge, Mass.: Harvard University Press, 2001.

Bodnar, John E. *Remaking America: Public Memory, Commemoration, and Patriotism in the Twentieth Century.* Princeton: Princeton University Press, 1992.

Bracken, Patrick J., and Celia Petty, eds. *Rethinking the Trauma of War.* London: Free Association Books, 1998.

Brewer, J. Mason. *Negro Legislators of Texas and Their Descendants: A History of the Negro in Texas Politics from Reconstruction to Disfranchisement.* Dallas, Tex.: Mathis, 1935.

Brown, Norman D. *Hood, Bonnet, and Little Brown Jug: Texas Politics, 1921–1928.* College Station: Texas A&M University Press, 1984.

Brundage, W. Fitzhugh. *The Southern Past: A Clash of Race and Memory.* Cambridge, Mass.: Harvard University Press, 2005.

Buckingham, Peter H. "The Socialist Party of Texas." In *The Texas Left: The Radical Roots of Lone Star Liberalism,* edited by David Cullen and Kyle Wilkison, 74–91. College Station: Texas A&M University Press, 2010.

Buenger, Walter L. "Flight from Modernity: The Economic History of Texas since 1845." In *Texas through Time,* edited by Walter L. Buenger and Robert A. Calvert, 310–41. College Station: Texas A&M University Press, 1991.

———. "Memory and the 1920s Ku Klux Klan in Texas." In *Lone Star Pasts: History and Memory in Texas,* edited by Gregg Cantrell and Elizabeth Hayes Turner, 119–42. College Station: Texas A&M University Press, 2007.

———. "Secession and the Texas German Community: Editor Lindheimer vs. Editor Flake." *Southwestern Historical Quarterly* 82 (1979): 379–402.

———. *Secession and the Union in Texas.* Austin: University of Texas Press, 1984.

———. "Texas and the Riddle of Secession." In *Lone Star Blue and Gray: Essays on Texas in the Civil War,* edited by Ralph A. Wooster, 1–28. Austin: Texas State Historical Association, 1995.

———. "Texas and the South." *Southwestern Historical Quarterly* 103 (2000): 309–24.

Burnett, Edmund Louis. *Civil War Letters of Louis Lehmann: With Alexander Terrell's and James B. Likens' Texas Cavalry Regiments, 1863–1864*. Hillsboro, Tex.: Hill College Press, 2011.

Burnham, Walter Dean. *Presidential Ballots, 1836–1892*. Baltimore, Md.: Arno Press, 1955.

Bynum, Victoria E. *The Free State of Jones: Mississippi's Longest Civil War*. Chapel Hill: University of North Carolina Press, 2001.

———. *The Long Shadow of the Civil War: Southern Dissent and Its Legacies*. Chapel Hill: University of North Carolina Press, 2010.

———. *Unruly Women: The Politics of Social and Sexual Control in the Old South*. Chapel Hill: University of North Carolina Press, 1992.

Calvert, Robert A., and Arnoldo De León. *The History of Texas*. Arlington Heights, Ill.: Harlan Davidson, 1990.

Campbell, Randolph B. *An Empire for Slavery: The Peculiar Institution in Texas, 1821–1865*. Baton Rouge: Louisiana State University Press, 1989.

———. "George W. Whitmore: East Texas Unionist." *East Texas Historical Journal* 28 (Spring 1990): 17–28.

———. *Gone to Texas: A History of the Lone Star State*. New York: Oxford University Press, 2003.

———. *Grass-Roots Reconstruction in Texas, 1865–1880*. Baton Rouge: Louisiana State University Press, 1997.

———. "History and Collective Memory in Texas: The Entangled Stories of the Lone Star State." In *Lone Star Pasts: History and Memory in Texas*, edited by Gregg Cantrell and Elizabeth Hayes Turner, 270–80. College Station: Texas A&M University Press, 2007.

Cantrell, Gregg. "The Bones of Stephen F. Austin: History and Memory in Progressive-Era Texas." In *Lone Star Pasts: History and Memory in Texas*, edited by Gregg Cantrell and Elizabeth Hayes Turner, 39–74. College Station: Texas A&M University Press, 2007.

Cantrell, Gregg, and Elizabeth Hayes Turner, eds. *Lone Star Pasts: Memory and History in Texas*. College Station: Texas A&M University Press, 2007.

Carby, Hazel V. *Reconstructing Womanhood: The Emergence of the Afro-American Woman Novelist*. New York: Oxford University Press, 1987.

Cardyn, Lisa. "Sexualized Racism/Gendered Violence: Trauma and the Body Politic in the Reconstruction South." Ph.D. dissertation, Yale University, 2003.

Carrigan, William. "Slavery on the Frontier: The Peculiar Institution in Central Texas." *Slavery and Abolition* 20 (1999): 63–86.

Carroll, Mark M. *Homesteads Ungovernable: Families, Sex, Race, and the Law in Frontier Texas, 1823–1860*. Austin: University of Texas Press, 2001.

Cashion, Ty. "What's the Matter with Texas: The Great Enigma of the Lone Star State in the American West." *Montana: The Magazine of Western History* 55 (2005): 2–15.

Chatfield, W. H. *The Twin Cities (Brownsville, Texas; Matamoros, Mexico) of the Border and the Country of the Lower Rio Grande*. 1893; repr., Brownsville, Tex.: Brownsville Historical Association, 1991.

Cheeseman, Bruce S., ed. *Maria von Blücher's Corpus Christi: Letters from the South Texas Frontier, 1849–1879.* College Station: Texas A&M University Press, 2002.

Clark, Kathleen Ann. *Defining Moments: African American Commemorative and Political Culture in the South, 1863–1913.* Chapel Hill: University of North Carolina Press, 2005.

Clinton, Catherine, and Nina Silber, eds. *Divided Houses: Gender and the Civil War.* New York: Oxford University Press, 1992.

Cohen-Lack, Nancy. "A Struggle for Sovereignty: National Consolidation, Emancipation, and Free Labor in Texas, 1865." *Journal of Southern History* 58 (February 1992): 57–98.

Collins, Carr P., Jr. *Royal Ancestors of Magna Charta Barons: The Collins Genealogy.* Dallas: n.p., 1959.

Collins, Vinson Allen. "Settling the Old Poplar Place." In *Tales from the Big Thicket,* edited by Francis E. Abernethy, 58–68. Denton: University of North Texas Press, 1967.

———. *A Story of My Parents: Warren Jacob Collins and Tolitha Eboline Collins.* Livingston, Tex.: n.p., 1962.

Confino, Alon. "Collective Memory and Cultural History: Problems of Method." *American Historical Review* 102 (1997): 1386–1403.

Cook, Robert. "(Un)furl That Banner: The Response of White Southerners to the Civil War Centennial of 1961–1965." *Journal of Southern History* 68 (2002): 879–912.

Cotham, Edward T. *Battle on the Bay: The Civil War Struggle for Galveston.* Austin: University of Texas Press, 1998.

Crane, Susan A. "Writing the Individual Back into Collective Memory." *American Historical Review* 102 (1997): 1372–85.

Crawford, Audrey. "A Women's Tour of Early Houston." Summer Seminar for Public School History Teachers at the University of Houston, June 10, 2002.

Crenshaw, Kimberle. "Mapping the Margins: Intersectionality, Identity Politics, and Violence against Women of Color." *Stanford Law Review* 43 (1991): 1241–99.

Crouch, Barry A. "'All the Vile Passions': The Texas Black Code of 1866." *Southwestern Historical Quarterly* 97 (1993): 12–34.

———. "A Spirit of Lawlessness: White Violence; Texas Blacks, 1865–1868," *Journal of Social History* 18 (1984): 217–32.

Crouch, Barry A., and Larry Madaras. "Reconstructing Black Families: Perspectives from the Texas Freedmen's Bureau Records." *Prologue* 18 (1986): 109–122.

D'Emilio, John, and Estelle B. Freedman. *Intimate Matters: A History of Sexuality in America.* 2nd ed. Chicago: University of Chicago Press, 1997.

Davis, Angela Y. *Women, Race, and Class.* New York: Random House, 1981.

De la Teja, Jesús F., ed. *A Revolution Remembered: The Memoirs and Selected Correspondence of Juan N. Seguín.* 2nd ed. Austin: Texas State Historical Society, 2002.

De León, Arnoldo. *Mexican Americans in Texas: A Brief History.* Arlington Heights, Ill.: Harlan Davidson, 1993.

———. *They Called Them Greasers*. Albuquerque: University of New Mexico Press, 1982.

Dietrich, Wilfred O. *The Blazing Story of Washington County*. Rev. ed.. Wichita Falls, Tex.: Nortex, 1973 [1950].

Dobak, William A. *Freedom by the Sword: The U.S. Colored Troops, 1862–1867*. New York: Skyhorse, 2013.

Dobak, William A., and Thomas D. Phillips. *The Black Regulars, 1866–1898*. Norman: University of Oklahoma Press, 2001.

Downing de De Juana, Ana Cristina. "Intermarriage in Hidalgo County, 1860–1900." M.A. thesis, University of Texas-Pan American, 1998.

Downs, Gregory P. "Three Faces of Sovereignty: Governing Confederate, Mexican, and Indian Texas in the Civil War Era." In *Civil War Wests: Testing the Limits of the United States*, edited by Adam Arenson and Andrew R. Graybill. Berkeley: University of California Press, 2015.

Drake, W. Magruder. "Two Letters of H. Winbourne Drake, Civil War Refugee in Northwest Louisiana." *Louisiana History* 7 (1966): 71–76.

Edwards, Laura F. *Gendered Strife and Confusion: The Political Culture of Reconstruction*. Urbana: University of Illinois Press, 1997.

Elliott, Claude. *Leathercoat: The Life History of a Texas Patriot*. San Antonio: Standard Printing, 1938.

———. "Union Sentiment in Texas, 1861–1865." *Southwestern Historical Quarterly*, 50 (1947): 449–77.

Estrich, Susan. *Real Rape*. Cambridge, Mass.: Harvard University Press, 1987.

Faust, Drew Gilpin. "'Trying to Do a Man's Business': Slavery, Violence, and Gender in the American Civil War." *Gender and History* 4 (1992): 197–214.

Felmly, Bradford K., and John C. Grady. *Suffering to Silence: 29th Texas Cavalry, C.S.A., Regimental History*. Quanah, Tex.: Nortex Press, 1975.

Fickle, James. "The Louisiana-Texas Lumber War of 1911–1912." *Louisiana History* 16 (1975): 59–85.

Fisher, Siobhan K. "Occupation of the Womb: Forced Impregnation as Genocide." *Duke Law Journal* (1996): 91–133.

Foley, Neil. *The White Scourge: Mexicans, Blacks, and Poor Whites in Texas Cotton Culture*. Berkeley: University of California Press, 1997.

Follett, Richard. *The Sugar Masters: Planters and Slaves in Louisiana's Cane World, 1820–1860*. Baton Rouge: Louisiana State University Press, 2005.

Foster, Gaines M. *Ghosts of the Confederacy: Defeat, the Lost Cause, and the Emergence of the New South, 1865 to 1913*. New York: Oxford University Press, 1987.

Fox-Genovese, Elizabeth. *Within the Plantation Household: Black and White Women of the Old South*. Chapel Hill: University of North Carolina Press, 1988.

Franklin, John Hope, and Loren Schweniger. *Runaway Slaves: Rebels on the Plantation*. Oxford: Oxford University Press, 1999.

Friend, Llerena. *Sam Houston: The Great Designer*. Austin: University of Texas Press, 1954.

Gaston, Paul M. *The New South Creed: A Study in Southern Mythmaking.* New York: Alfred Knopf, 1970.

Gates, Arnold, ed. *The Rough Side of War: The Civil War Journal of Chesley A. Mosman, 1st Lieutenant, Company D, 59th Illinois Volunteer Infantry Regiment.* Garden City, N.Y.: Basin, 1987.

Genovese, Eugene D. "Yeoman Farmers in a Slaveholders' Democracy." *Agricultural History* 49 (1975): 331–42.

Gerteis, Louis. *From Contraband to Freedom: Federal Policy toward Southern Blacks.* Westport, Conn: Greenwood Press 1973.

Getman, Karen A. "Sexual Control in the Slaveholding South: The Implementation and Maintenance of a Racial Caste System." *Harvard Women's Law Journal* 7 (1984): 115–52.

Giddings, Paula. *When and Where I Enter: The Impact of Black Women on Race and Sex in America.* New York: Bantam Books, 1984.

Gilbert, Loy J. "Salt of the Earth: Making Salt at the Neches Saline." *Chronicles of Smith County, Texas* 11 (1972): 1–12.

Glymph, Thavolia. *Out of the House of Bondage: The Transformation of the Plantation Household.* New York: Cambridge University Press, 2008.

Graf, LeRoy P. "The Economic History of the Lower Rio Grande Valley, 1820–1875." Ph.D. dissertation, Harvard University, 1942.

Granger, Clint. *Falcon 6.* Bloomington, Idaho: Xlibris, 2010.

Grear, Charles David. "'All Eyes of Texas Are on Comal County': German Texans' Loyalty during the Civil War and World War I." In *Texans and War: New Interpretations of the State's Military History,* edited by Alexander Mendoza and Charles David Grear, 133–53. College Station: Texas A&M University Press, 2012.

———, ed. *The Fate of Texas: The Civil War and the Lone Star State.* Fayetteville: University of Arkansas Press, 2008.

———. *Why Texans Fought in the Civil War.* College Station: Texas A&M University Press, 2010.

Greeley, Andrew. *Why Can't They Be Like Us? America's White Ethnic Groups.* New York: E. P. Dutton, 1971.

Green, James R. *Grass Roots Socialism: Radical Movements on the Southwest, 1895–1943.* Baton Rouge: Louisiana State University Press, 1978.

Guelzo, Allen C. *Lincoln's Emancipation Proclamation: The End of Slavery in America.* New York: Simon and Schuster, 2004.

Gunter, Pete A. Y. *The Big Thicket: An Ecological Reevaluation.* Denton: University of North Texas Press, 1993.

Gutman, Roy. *A Witness to Genocide: The 1993 Pulitzer Prize–Winning Dispatches on the "Ethnic Cleansing" of Bosnia.* New York: Macmillan, 1993.

Hahn, Steven. *A Nation under Our Feet: Black Political Struggles in the Rural South from Slavery to the Great Migration.* Cambridge, Mass.: Harvard University Press, 2003.

Hahn, Steven, Steven F. Miller, Susan E. O'Donovan, John C. Rodrigue, and Leslie S. Rowland, eds. *Land and Labor, 1865.* Chapel Hill: University of North Carolina Press, 2008.

Halbwachs, Maurice. *Les cadres sociaux de la mémoire.* Paris: Presses universitaires de France, 1925.

———. *La mémoire collective.* Paris: Presses universitaires de France, 1950.

———. *The Collective Memory.* New York: Harper and Row, 1980.

———. *On Collective Memory.* Chicago: University of Chicago Press, 1992.

Hall, Jacquelyn Dowd. "'The Mind That Burns in Each Body': Women, Rape, and Racial Violence." *Southern Exposure* 12 (1984): 61–71.

Harrison, Robert. *Washington during Civil War and Reconstruction: Race and Radicalism.* Cambridge: Cambridge University Press, 2011.

Harter, Eugene C. *The Lost Colony of the Confederacy.* Jackson: University of Mississippi Press, 1985.

Hayes, Charles W. *Galveston: History of the Island and City.* Austin: Jenkins Garrett Press, 1974 [1879].

Hine, Darlene Clark, and Kathleen Thompson. *A Shining Thread of Hope: The History of Black Women in America.* New York: Broadway Books, 1998.

Hinojosa, Gilberto M. *A Borderlands Town in Transition.* College Station: Texas A&M University Press, 1983.

Hodes, Martha. *White Women, Black Men: Illicit Sex in the Nineteenth-Century South.* New Haven, Conn.: Yale University Press, 1997.

House, Aline. *Big Thicket: Its Heritage.* San Antonio, Tex.: Naylor, 1967.

Howell, Kenneth W. "The Prolonged War: Texans Struggle to Win the Civil War during Reconstruction." In *Texans and War: New Interpretations of the State's Military History,* edited by Alexander Mendoza and Charles David Grear, 196–212. College Station: Texas A&M University Press, 2012.

———, ed. *The Seventh Star of the Confederacy: Texas during the Civil War.* Denton: University of North Texas Press, 2010.

———, ed. *Still the Arena of Civil War: Violence and Turmoil in Reconstruction Texas, 1865–1868.* Denton: University of North Texas Press, 2012.

———. *Texas Confederate, Reconstruction Governor: James Webb Throckmorton.* College Station: Texas A&M University Press, 2008.

———. "'When the Rabble Hiss, Well May Patriots Tremble': James Webb Throckmorton and the Secession Movement in Texas, 1854–1861." *Southwestern Historical Quarterly,* 109 (April 2006): 465–94.

Hutton, Patrick. "Recent Scholarship on Memory and History." *History Teacher* 33 (2000): 533–48.

Irby, James A. *Backdoor at Bagdad: The Civil War on the Rio Grande.* El Paso: Texas Western Press, 1977.

Jenkins, Jeffery A., Justin Peck, and Vesla M. Weaver. "Between Reconstructions: Congressional Action on Civil Rights, 1891–1940." *Studies in American Political Development* 24 (2010): 57–89.

Jenkins, John H. *Basic Texas Books.* Austin: Texas State Historical Association, 1988.

Jennings, Thelma. "'Us Colored Women Had to Go through a Plenty': Sexual Exploitation of African American Slave Women." *Journal of Women's History* 1 (1991): 45–74.

Johnson, Joan Marie. *Southern Ladies, New Women: Race, Region, and Clubwomen in South Carolina, 1890–1930.* Gainesville: University Press of Florida, 2004.

Johnson, Walter. *River of Dark Dreams: Slavery and Empire in the Cotton Kingdom.* Cambridge, Mass.: Harvard University Press, 2013.

Johnston, Marguerite. *Houston the Unknown City, 1836–1946.* College Station: Texas A&M University Press, 1991.

Jones, Jacqueline. *Labor of Love, Labor of Sorrow: Black Women, Work and the Family from Slavery to the Present.* New York: Basic Books, 1988.

Jordan, Terry G. "Germans and Blacks in Texas." In *States of Progress: Germans and Blacks in America over 300 Years,* edited by Randall Miller, 89–97. Philadelphia: German Society of Pennsylvania, 1989.

———. *German Seed in Texas Soil: Immigrant Farmers in Nineteenth-Century Texas.* Austin: University of Texas Press, 1966.

———. "The Imprint of the Upper and Lower South on Mid-Nineteenth-Century Texas." *Annals of the Association of American Geographers* 57 (1967): 67–90.

Jung, Moon-Ho. *Coolies and Cane: Race, Labor, and Sugar in the Age of Emancipation.* Baltimore, Md.: Johns Hopkins University Press, 2006.

Kachun, Mitch. *Festivals of Freedom: Memory and Meaning in African American Emancipation Celebrations, 1808–1915.* Amherst: University of Massachusetts Press, 2003.

Kammeier, Heinz-Ulrich. *"Halleluja, jetzt sehen wir Amerika": Auswanderung aus dem Kreis Lübbecke und Umgebung, 1836–1889.* Espelkamp: Verlag Marie L. Leidorf, 1994.

Kamphoefner, Walter D. "Missouri Germans and the Cause of Union and Freedom." *Missouri Historical Review* 106 (2012): 115–36.

———. "New Perspectives on Texas Germans and the Confederacy." In *The Fate of Texas: The Civil War and the Lone Star State,* edited by Charles D. Grear, 105–21. Fayetteville: University of Arkansas Press, 2008.

Kamphoefner, Walter D., and Wolfgang Helbich, eds. *Germans in the Civil War: The Letters They Wrote Home.* Chapel Hill: University of North Carolina Press, 2006.

Kelley, Sean. "'Mexico in His Head': Slavery and the Texas-Mexico Border, 1810–1860." *Journal of Social History* 37 (2004): 709–23.

———. "Plantation Frontiers: Race, Ethnicity, and Family along the Brazos River of Texas, 1821–1886." Ph.D. dissertation, University of Texas, 2000.

Kerber, Linda, Alice Kessler-Harris, and Kathryn Kish Sklar. *U.S. History as Women's History: New Feminist Essays.* Chapel Hill: University of North Carolina Press, 1995.

Kerby, Robert L. *Kirby Smith's Confederacy: The Trans-Mississippi South, 1863–1865.* New York: Columbia University Press, 1972.

Kiel, Frank Wilson. "Treue der Union: Myths, Misrepresentations, and Misinterpretations." *Southwestern Historical Quarterly* 115 (2012): 283–92.

King, Wilma. *Stolen Childhood: Slave Youth in Nineteenth-Century America.* Bloomington: Indiana University Press, 1995.

Knight, Lawrence P. "Becoming a City and Becoming American: San Antonio, Texas, 1848–1861." Ph.D. dissertation, Texas A&M University, 1997.

Kosary, Rebecca A. "To Degrade and Control: White Violence and the Maintenance of Racial and Gender Boundaries in Reconstruction Texas, 1865–1868." Ph.D. dissertation, Texas A&M University, 2006.

Küffner, Cornelia. "Texas-Germans' Attitudes toward Slavery: Biedermeier Sentiments and Class-Consciousness in Austin, Colorado, and Fayette Counties." M.A. thesis, University of Houston, 1994.

LaFree, Gary D. *Rape and Criminal Justice: The Social Construction of Sexual Assault.* Belmont, Calif.: Wadsworth, 1989.

Lathrop, Barnes F. "Disaffection in Confederate Louisiana: The Case of William Hyman." *Journal of Southern History* 24 (1958): 308–18.

———. "The Lafourche District in 1861–1862: A Problem in Local Defense." *Louisiana History* 1 (1960): 99–129.

———. "The Lafourche District in 1862: Invasion." *Louisiana History* 2 (1961): 175–201.

———. "The Lafourche District in 1862: Militia and Partisan Rangers." *Louisiana History* 1 (1960): 230–44.

———. "The Pugh Plantations, 1860–1865: A Study of Life in Lower Louisiana." Ph.D. dissertation, University of Texas, 1945.

Lerner, Gerda, ed. *Black Women in White America: A Documentary History.* New York: Random House, 1992 [1972].

Littlefield, Daniel F., Jr. *Africans and Creeks: From the Colonial Period to the Civil War.* Westport, Conn.: Greenwood Press, 1979.

———. *The Chickasaw Freedmen: A People without a Country.* Westport, Conn.: Greenwood Press, 1980.

Litwack, Leon F. *Been in the Storm So Long: The Aftermath of Slavery.* New York: Alfred A. Knopf, 1979.

Lonn, Ella. *Foreigners in the Confederacy.* Chapel Hill: University of North Carolina Press, 1940.

———. *Salt as a Factor in the Confederacy.* University: University of Alabama Press, 1965.

Lott, Virgil N., and Mercurio Martínez. *The Kingdom of Zapata.* Austin: Eakin Press, 1953.

Loughmiller, Campbell, and Lynn Loughmiller, comps. and eds. *Big Thicket Legacy.* Austin: University of Texas Press, 1977.

Lowe, Lise. *Immigrant Acts: On Asian American Cultural Politics.* Durham: Duke University Press, 1996.

Lowe, Richard G., and Randolph B. Campbell. *Planters and Plain Folk: Agriculture in Antebellum Texas.* Dallas: Southern Methodist University Press, 1987.

MacKinnon, Catharine A. "Rape, Genocide, and Women's Human Rights." *Harvard Women's Law Journal* 17 (1994): 5–16.

Malone, Ann Patton. "Matt Gaines: Reconstruction Politician." In *Black Leaders: Texans for Their Times,* edited by Alwyn Barr and Robert A. Calvert, 49–81. Austin: Texas State Historical Association, 1981.

Marten, James A. *Texas Divided: Loyalty and Dissent in the Lone Star State, 1856–1874.* Lexington: University Press of Kentucky, 1990.

Martin, Charles Young. *The Ancestors and Descendants of General Robert Campbell Martin and His Wife, Mary Winifred Hill Pugh*, edited by Virginia Martin Carmouche. Lake Charles, La.: Anderson Printing, 1965.

Massey, Mary Elizabeth. *Refugee Life in the Confederacy*. Baton Rouge: Louisiana State University Press, 1964.

Masur, Kate. *An Example for All the Land: Emancipation and the Struggle over Equality in Washington, D.C.* Chapel Hill: University of North Carolina Press, 2010.

Matovina, Timothy, and Jesús F. de la Teja, eds. *Recollections of a Tejano Life: Antonio Menchaca in Texas History*. Austin: University of Texas Press, 2013.

McCaslin, Richard B. *At the Heart of Texas: 100 Years of the Texas State Historical Association, 1897–1997.* Austin: Texas State Historical Association, 2007.

———. *Tainted Breeze: The Great Hanging at Gainesville, Texas, October 1862.* Baton Rouge: Louisiana State University Press, 1994.

———. "Voices of Reason: Opposition to Secession in Angelina County, Texas." *Locus* 3 (1991): 180–94.

———. "Wheat Growers in the Cotton Confederacy: The Suppression of Dissent in Collin County, Texas during the Civil War." *Southwestern Historical Quarterly* 96 (1993): 526–39.

McCurry, Stephanie. *Confederate Reckoning: Power and Politics in the Civil War South*. Cambridge, Mass.: Harvard University Press, 2010.

McMichael, Kelly. "'Memories Are Short but Monuments Lengthen Remembrances': The United Daughters of the Confederacy and the Power of Civil War Memory." In *Lone Star Pasts: History and Memory in Texas*, edited by Gregg Cantrell and Elizabeth Hayes Turner, 95–118. College Station: Texas A&M University Press, 2007.

———. *Sacred Memories: The Civil War Monument Movement in Texas*. Denton: Texas State Historical Association, 2009.

McPherson, James. *Battle Cry of Freedom: The Civil War Era*. Oxford: Oxford University Press, 1988.

McWhiney, Grady. "Louisiana Socialists in the Early Twentieth Century: A Study in Rustic Radicalism." *Journal of Southern History* 20 (1954): 137–48.

Mears, Michelle. *And Grace Will Lead Me Home: African American Freedmen Communities of Austin, Texas, 1865–1928*. Lubbock: Texas Tech University, 2009.

Mehrländer, Andrea. *The Germans of Charleston, Richmond, and New Orleans during the Civil War Period, 1850–1870*. Berlin: De Gruyter, 2011.

Meinig, Donald William. *Imperial Texas: An Interpretive Essay in Cultural Geography*. Austin: University of Texas Press, 1969.

Metzenthin-Raunick, Selma. "One Hundred Years *Neu Braunfelser Zeitung*." *American-German Review* 19 (1953): 15–16.

Mills, Cynthia, and Pamela H. Simpson, eds. *Monuments to the Lost Cause: Women, Art, and the Landscapes of Southern Memory*. Knoxville: University of Tennessee Press, 2003.

Moneyhon, Carl H. *Edmund J. Davis: Civil War General, Republican Leader, Reconstruction Governor*. Fort Worth: TCU Press, 2010.

———. *Texas after the Civil War: The Struggle of Reconstruction.* College Station: Texas A&M University Press, 2004.

Morgan, Chad. *Planters' Progress: Modernizing Confederate Georgia.* Gainesville: University Press of Florida, 2005.

Moser, Caroline, and Fiona C. Clark. *Victims, Perpetrators, or Actors? Gender, Armed Conflict, and Political Violence.* London: Zed Books, 2001.

Nichols, James. "The Line of Liberty: Runaway Slaves and Fugitive Peons in the Texas-Mexico Borderlands." *Western Historical Quarterly* 44 (2013): 413–33.

Nicolini, Marcus. *Deutsch in Texas.* Münster: Lit Verlag, 2004.

Nieman, Donald G. "Black Political Power and Criminal Justice: Washington County, Texas, 1868–1884." *Journal of Southern History* 55 (1989): 391–420.

Nora, Pierre. "Between Memory and History: Les Lieux de Mémoire." *Representations* 26 (1989): 7–24.

———. *Realms of Memory: Rethinking the French Past.* 3 vols. New York: Columbia University Press, 1996–98.

Oakes, James. "A Failure of Vision: The Collapse of the Freedmen's Bureau Courts." *Civil War History* 25 (1979): 66–76.

———. *Freedom National: The Destruction of Slavery in the United States, 1861–1865.* New York: W. W. Norton, 2013.

Oates, Stephen. "Texas under the Secessionists." *Southwestern Historical Quarterly* 67 (1963): 167–212.

Olick, Jeffrey K., and Joyce Robbins. "Social Memory Studies: From 'Collective Memory' to the Historical Sociology of Mnemonic Practices." *Annual Review of Sociology* 24 (1998):105–40.

Olmsted, Frederick Law. *Journey through Texas: A Saddletrip on the Southwestern Frontier.* Edited by James Howard. Austin: Von Boeckmann-Jones Press, 1962.

Osterweiss, Rollin G. *The Myth of the Lost Cause, 1865–1900.* Hamden, Conn.: Archon Books,

Perdue, Theda. *Slavery and the Evolution of Cherokee Society, 1540–1866.* Knoxville: University of Tennessee Press, 1979.

Pickering, David, and Judy Fall. *Brush Men and Vigilantes: Civil War Dissent in Texas.* College Station: Texas A&M University Press, 2000.

Pierce-Baker, Charlotte. *Surviving the Silence: Black Women's Stories of Rape.* New York: W. W. Norton, 1998.

Pitre, Merline. *Through Many Dangers, Toils, and Snares: The Black Leadership of Texas.* Austin: Eakin Press, 1985.

Pohl, Robert S., and John R. Wennersten, eds. *Abraham Lincoln and the End of Slavery in the District of Columbia.* Washington, D.C.: Eastern Branch Press, 2009.

Polk, W. M. "Memoranda on the Civil War." *Century Illustrated Magazine* 33 (1887): 962–64.

Preuss, Gene B. "Within Those Walls: The African American School and Community in Lubbock and New Braunfels, Texas." *Sound Historian* (1998): 36–43.

Price, John Milton. "Slavery in Winn Parish." *Louisiana History* 8 (1967): 137–48.

Primm, James Neal. *Lion of the Valley: St. Louis, Missouri, 1764–1980.* 3rd ed. St. Louis: Missouri History Museum Press, 1998.

Rable, George C. "The South and the Politics of Antilynching Legislation, 1920–1940." *Journal of Southern History* 51 (1985): 201–20.

Ramsdell, Charles William. *Reconstruction in Texas.* New York: Columbia University Press, 1910.

———. "Texas from the Fall of the Confederacy to the Beginning of Reconstruction." *Quarterly of the Texas State Historical Association* 11 (1908): 99–219.

Ransleben, Guido Ernst. *A Hundred Years of Comfort in Texas: A Centennial History.* San Antonio, Tex.: Naylor, 1954.

Rawick, George P., ed. *The American Slave: A Composite Autobiography, Supplement,* Series 2: Vols. 2 and 5, *Texas Narratives,* Part 4. Westport, Conn.: Greenwood Press, 1979.

Reynolds, Donald E. *Texas Terror: The Slave Insurrection Panic and the Secession of the Lower South.* Baton Rouge: Louisiana State University Press, 2007.

Rice, Lawrence D. *The Negro in Texas: 1874–1900.* Baton Rouge: Louisiana State University Press, 1971.

Richter, William L. *The Army in Texas during Reconstruction, 1865–1870.* College Station: Texas A&M University Press, 1987.

———. *Overreached on All Sides: The Freedmen's Bureau Administrators in Texas, 1865–1868.* College Station: Texas A&M University Press, 1991.

Robinson, E. E. *The Presidential Vote, 1896–1932.* Stanford, Calif.: Stanford University Press, 1947.

Rolle, Andrew. *The Lost Cause: The Confederate Exodus to Mexico.* Norman: University of Oklahoma Press, 1992.

Rosen, Hannah. "The Gender of Reconstruction: Rape, Race, and Citizenship in the Postemancipation South." Ph.D. dissertation, University of Chicago, 1999.

Rousey, Dennis C. "Aliens in the WASP Nest: Ethnocultural Diversity in the Antebellum Urban South." *Journal of American History* 79 (1992): 152–64.

———. "Friends and Foes of Slavery: Foreigners and Northerners in the Old South." *Journal of Social History* 35 (2001): 373–96.

Sacher, John M. "'A Very Disagreeable Business': Confederate Conscription in Louisiana." *Civil War History* 53 (2007): 141–69.

Sahlins, Peter. *Boundaries: The Making of France and Spain in the Pyrenees.* Berkeley: University of California Press, 1989.

Schaadt, Robert L. *The History of Hardin County Texas.* Kountze, Tex.: Hardin County Historical Commission, 1991.

Schafer, Joseph, ed. and trans. *The Intimate Letters of Carl Schurz, 1841–1869.* Madison: Wisconsin Historical Society, 1928.

Schermerhorn, Calvin. *Money over Mastery, Family over Freedom: Slavery in the Antebellum Upper South.* Baltimore, Md.: Johns Hopkins University Press, 2011.

Schmidt, C. W. *Footprints of Five Generations.* New Ulm, Tex.: n.p., 1930.

Schwartz, Rosalie. *Across the Rio to Freedom: U.S. Negroes in Mexico.* El Paso: University of Texas at El Paso Press, 1974.

Scott, James. *Weapons of the Weak: Everyday Forms of Peasant Resistance.* New Haven, Conn.: Yale University Press, 1986.

Seifert, Ruth. "The Second Front: The Logic of Sexual Violence in Wars." *Women's Studies International Forum* 19 (1996): 35–43.

Shalev, Arieh Y., Rachel Yehuda, and Alexander C. McFarlane, eds. *International Handbook of Human Response to Trauma*. New York: Plenum, 2000.

Simpson, Amos E., and Vincent Cassidy. "The Wartime Administration of Governor Henry W. Allen." *Louisiana History* 5 (1964): 257–69.

Sitton, Thad, and James H. Conrad. *Freedom Colonies: Independent Black Texans in the Time of Jim Crow*. Austin: University of Texas Press, 2005.

Sitton, Thad, and James H. Conrad. *Nameless Towns: Texas Sawmill Communities, 1880–1942*. Austin: University of Texas Press, 1998.

Sitton, Thad, and C. E. Hunt. *Big Thicket People: Larry Jene Fisher's Photographs of the Last Southern Frontier*. Austin: University of Texas Press, 2008.

Smallwood, James. "Black Freedwomen after Emancipation: The Texas Experience." *Prologue* 27 (1995): 303–17.

————. *Time of Hope, Time of Despair: Black Texans during Reconstruction*. Port Washington, N.Y.: Kennikat Press, 1981.

Smallwood, James M., Barry A. Crouch, and Larry Peacock, *Murder and Mayhem: The War of Reconstruction in Texas*. College Station: Texas A&M University Press, 2003.

Smith, David Paul. "Conscription and Conflict on the Texas Frontier, 1863–1865." *Civil War History* 36 (1990): 250–61.

————. *Frontier Defense in the Civil War: Texas Rangers and Rebels*. College Station: Texas A&M University Press, 1992.

————. "The Limits of Dissent and Loyalty in Texas." In *Guerrillas, Unionists, and Violence on the Confederate Home Front*, edited by Daniel E. Sutherland, 133–49. Fayetteville: University of Arkansas Press, 1999.

Sobré, Judith Berg. *San Antonio on Parade: Six Historic Festivals*. College Station: Texas A&M University Press, 2003.

Somers, Dale A. "James P. Newcomb: The Making of a Radical." *Southwestern Historical Quarterly* 72 (2969): 449–69.

Stambaugh, J. Lee, and Lillian J Stambaugh. *A History of Collin County*. Austin: Texas State Historical Association, 1958.

Sterling, Dorothy, ed. *We Are Your Sisters: Black Women in the Nineteenth Century*. New York: W. W. Norton, 1997 [1984].

Sternhell, Yael A. *Routes of War: The World of Movement in the Confederate South*. Cambridge, Mass.: Harvard University Press, 2012.

Stone, Bryan Edward. *The Chosen Folks: Jews on the Frontiers of Texas*. Austin: University of Texas Press, 2010.

Strickland, Jeff. "How the Germans Became White Southerners: German Immigrants and African Americans in Charleston, South Carolina, 1860–1880." *Journal of American Ethnic History* 28 (2008): 52–69.

Taylor, Paul S. *An American Mexican Frontier: Nueces County, Texas*. Chapel Hill: University of North Carolina Press, 1934.

Tevis, Dean. "The Battle at Bad Luck Creek." In *Tales from the Big Thicket*, edited by Francis E. Abernethy, 75–92. Denton: University of North Texas Press, 1967.

Thompson, Jerry D. *Cortina: Defending the Mexican Name in Texas.* College Station: Texas A&M University Press, 2007.

———. *Mexican Texans in the Union Army.* El Paso: Texas Western Press, 1986.

———. *Vaqueros in Blue and Gray.* Austin: Presidial Press, 1977.

———. *Warm Weather and Bad Whiskey: The 1886 Laredo Election Riot.* El Paso: Texas Western Press, 1991.

Thompson, Jerry D., and Lawrence T. Jones III. *Civil War and Revolution on the Rio Grande Frontier: A Narrative and Photographic History.* Austin: Texas State Historical Association, 2004.

Trelease, Allen. *White Terror: The Ku Klux Klan Conspiracy and Southern Reconstruction.* Baton Rouge: Louisiana State University Press, 1995 [1971].

Turner, Elizabeth Hayes. "Juneteenth: Emancipation and Memory." In *Lone Star Pasts: History and Memory in Texas,* edited by Gregg Cantrell and Elizabeth Hayes Turner, 143–75. College Station: Texas A&M University Press, 2007.

———. *Women, Culture, and Community: Religion and Reform in Galveston, 1880–1920.* New York: Oxford University Press, 1997.

Tyler, Ron. "Fugitive Slaves in Mexico." *Journal of Negro History* 57 (1972): 1–12.

Valerio-Jiménez, Omar S. *River of Hope: Identity and Nation in the Rio Grande Borderlands.* Durham, N.Car.: Duke University Press, 2013.

Vielé, Teresa (Griffin). *"Following the Drum": A Glimpse of Frontier Life.* New York: Rudd and Carleton, 1858; reprint, Lincoln: University of Nebraska Press, 1984.

Walker, Donald R. *Penology for Profit: A History of the Texas Prison System, 1867–1912.* College Station: Texas A&M University Press, 1988.

Wallace, Ernest. *Texas in Turmoil, 1849–1875.* Austin: Steck-Vaughn, 1965.

Waller, John L. *Colossal Hamilton of Texas: A Biography of Andrew Jackson Hamilton, Militant Unionist and Reconstruction Governor.* El Paso: Texas Western Press, 1968.

Warner, Ezra J. *Generals in Blue: The Lives of the Union Commanders.* Baton Rouge: Louisiana State University Press, 1964.

West, Elizabeth Howard. "Southern Opposition to the Annexation of Texas." *Southwestern Historical Quarterly* 18 (1918): 74–82.

Wheeler, Kenneth W. *To Wear a City's Crown: The Beginnings of Urban Growth in Texas, 1836–1865.* Cambridge, Mass.: Harvard University Press, 1968.

White, Deborah Gray. *Ar'n't I a Woman? Female Slaves in the Plantation South.* New York: W. W. Norton, 1985.

White, Shane. "'It Was a Proud Day': African Americans, Festivals, and Parades in the North, 1741–1834." *Journal of American History* 81 (June 1994): 13–50.

Wickett, Murray R. *Contested Territory: Whites, Native Americans, and African Americans in Oklahoma, 1865–1907.* Baton Rouge: Louisiana State University Press, 2000.

Williams, Kidada E. *They Left Great Marks on Me: African American Testimonies of Racial Violence from Emancipation to World War I.* New York: New York University Press, 2012.

Willis, Harold W. *A Short History of Hardin County, Texas.* Kountze, Tex.: Hardin County Historical Commission, 1998.

Wilson, William H. *The City Beautiful Movement*. Baltimore, Md.: Johns Hopkins University Press, 1989.

Winters, John D. *The Civil War in Louisiana*. Baton Rouge: Louisiana State University Press, 1963.

Wooster, Ralph, ed. *Lone Star Blue and Gray: Essays on Texas in the Civil War*. Austin: Texas State Historical Association, 1995.

Wooster, Ralph A., and Robert Wooster. "A People at War: East Texas during the Civil War." *East Texas Historical Journal* 28 (1990): 3–16.

Wriggins, Jennifer. "Rape, Racism, and the Law." *Harvard Women's Law Journal* 6 (1983): 103–41.

Wright, J. Leitch, Jr. *Creeks and Seminoles: The Destruction and Regeneration of the Muscogulge People*. Lincoln: University of Nebraska Press, 1986.

Zuber, Macklyn. "Fire at Union Wells." *Frontier Times* (October–November 1963): 28.

Contributors

Victoria E. Bynum is Distinguished Professor Emeritus of History at Texas State University. She earned her Ph.D. in history at the University of California, San Diego, and taught antebellum, Civil War, and women's history in San Marcos from 1986 to 2010. She is the author of three books and numerous articles in various anthologies and journals, including *The Long Shadow of the Civil War: Southern Dissent and Its Legacies* (University of North Carolina Press, 2010), *The Free State of Jones: Mississippi's Longest Civil War* (University of North Carolina Press, 2001), and *Unruly Women: The Politics of Social and Sexual Control in the Old South* (University of North Carolina Press, 1992). Along with awards for scholarship and teaching from Texas State University, Bynum is the recipient of a National Endowment for the Humanities fellowship; the Lawrence T. Jones III Research Fellowship, Texas State Historical Association; and the Lena Lake Forrest Fellowship, Business and Professional Women's Foundation, Washington, D.C. In 2014, STX Entertainment obtained the movie rights to her book *The Free State of Jones*.

Rebecca A. Czuchry received her Ph.D. in history from Texas A&M University. She is Associate Professor and Chair of the Department of History and Director of African American Studies at Texas Lutheran University, where she teaches nineteenth and twentieth-century U.S. history, race and gender in the United States, the Atlantic world, the African diaspora, and borderlands studies. She is the author of "'Wantonly Maltreated and Slain Simply Because They Are Free': Racial Violence during Reconstruction in South Texas," in *African Americans in South Texas History*, ed. Bruce Glasrud (College Station: Texas A&M University, 2011); and "'To Punish and Humiliate the Entire Community': Violence Perpetrated against Black Women in Texas," in *Unrepentant*

Rebels: Violence and Turmoil in Reconstruction Texas, 1865–1874, ed. Kenneth Wayne Howell (University of North Texas Press, March, 2012). Her recent research has focused on racialized sexual violence during the Reconstruction period.

Jesús F. de la Teja is Jerome H. and Catherine E. Supple Professor of Southwest Studies and Director of the Center for the Study of the Southwest at Texas State University, where he is also a Regents' Professor of History. Between 1985 and 1991 he worked in the Archives and Records Division of the Texas General Land Office. He has published extensively on Spanish, Mexican, and Republic-era Texas, including the award-winning *San Antonio de Béxar: A Community on New Spain's Northern Frontier* (University of New Mexico Press, 1996), and most recently co-edited *Recollections of a Tejano Life: Antonio Menchaca in Texas History* (University of Texas Press, 2013) and edited *Tejano Leadership in Mexican and Revolutionary Texas* (Texas A&M University Press, 2010). He served as book review editor for the *Southwestern Historical Quarterly* from 1997 to 2014. He has served on the board of directors and as president of the Texas State Historical Association and currently serves on the board of directors of Humanities Texas and the San Jacinto Museum of History. He was the inaugural State Historian of Texas (2007–2009). He is a Fellow of the Texas State Historical Association and the Texas Catholic Historical Society and a member of the Texas Institute of Letters and the Philosophical Society of Texas.

Walter D. Kamphoefner earned his Ph.D. at the University of Missouri–Columbia in 1978 and came to Texas A&M University in 1988, where he is now Professor of History. He teaches in the fields of immigration, urbanization, and quantitative methods. He is the author and editor of numerous books and articles related to the German experience in the United States and Texas, including *Germans in the Civil War: The Letters They Wrote Home*, edited with Wolfgang Helbich (University of North Carolina Press, 2006); and "New Perspectives on Texas Germans and the Confederacy," *Southwestern Historical Quarterly* (1999). He is currently at work on an overview volume on German immigration and ethnicity and is serving (2015–17) as President of the Society for German American Studies.

Richard B. McCaslin received his Ph.D. from the University of Texas at Austin and is Professor of History at the University of North Texas. He has written or edited sixteen books, including *Tainted Breeze: The Great Hanging at Gainesville, Texas, October 1862* (Louisiana State University Press, 1994, winner of the Texas State Historical Association's Tullis Award), *Lee in the Shadow of Washington* (Louisiana State University Press, 2001, winner of the Slatten Award of the Virginia Historical Society and a nominee for the Pulitzer in Biography), and *Fighting Stock: John S. Rip Ford of Texas* (TCU Press, 2011, winner of the Texas State Historical Association's Bates Award), along with three volumes in the award-winning Portraits of Conflict series. A Fellow of the Texas State Historical Association, he is also a contributor to many other publications such as the *New Handbook of Texas* and a two-volume history of the Texas senate.

W. Caleb McDaniel is Associate Professor of History at Rice University and the author of *The Problem of Democracy in the Age of Slavery: Garrisonian Abolitionists and Transatlantic Reform* (Louisiana State University Press, 2013), which won the Merle Curti Award from the Organization of American Historians and the James Broussard First Book Prize from the Society for Historians of the Early American Republic. His articles on the Civil War era have appeared in the *Journal of the Early Republic*, *American Quarterly*, *Slavery and Abolition*, *Atlantic Studies*, and *Journal of the Civil War Era*.

Laura Lyons McLemore is William B. Wiener, Jr., Professor of Archives and Historic Preservation and head of LSU–Shreveport Archives and Special Collections, and Adjunct Professor of History at LSU–Shreveport. Before coming to Shreveport in 2004 she was College Archivist at Austin College in Sherman, Texas. She received her Ph.D. in history at the University North Texas. Her recent publications include "Women and the Texas Revolution in History and Memory," in *Women and the Texas Revolution* (University of North Texas Press, 2012); "Early Historians and the Shaping of Texas Memory," in *Lone Star Pasts: Memory and History in Texas* (Texas A&M University Press, 2007); *Inventing Texas: Early Historians of the Lone Star State* (Texas A&M University Press, 2004); "Adele Briscoe Looscan: Daughter of the Republic," in

Texas Women: Their Histories, Their Lives (University of Georgia Press, 2015); and *Adele Briscoe Looscan: Daughter of the Republic* (TCU Press, forthcoming).

Carl H. Moneyhon received his Ph.D. from the University of Chicago and has taught in the Department of History at the University of Arkansas at Little Rock since 1974. He is the author of five major works, including *Edmund J. Davis: Civil War General, Republican Leader, Reconstruction Governor* (TCU Press, 2010), *Texas after the Civil War: The Struggle of Reconstruction* (Texas A&M University Press, 2004), and *Republicanism in Reconstruction Texas* (University of Texas Press, 1980, reprinted by Texas A&M University Press in 2001). Along with scholarship awards from the University of Arkansas at Little Rock, Moneyhon has been honored as a Fellow of the Texas State Historical Association and received a Research Fellowship from the National Endowment for the Humanities.

Andrew J. Torget is a historian of nineteenth-century North America at the University of North Texas, where he directs a digital humanities lab. The founder and director of numerous digital humanities projects—including Mapping Texts and the Texas Slavery Project—he has been a featured speaker on the digital humanities at Harvard, Stanford, Duke, Johns Hopkins, as well as the National Archives. Torget was named the inaugural David J. Weber Research Fellow at the Clements Center for Southwest Studies at Southern Methodist University, and he is the coeditor of several books on the American Civil War, including *This Corner of Canaan: Essays on Texas in Honor of Randolph B. Campbell* (University of North Texas Press, 2013). His most recent book is *Seeds of Empire: Cotton, Slavery, and the Transformation of the Texas Borderlands, 1800–1850* (University of North Carolina Press, 2015).

Elizabeth Hayes Turner received her Ph.D. in American history from Rice University and is University Distinguished Teaching Professor and Professor Emeritus of History at the University of North Texas. She is the author of *Women and Gender in the New South, 1865–1945* (Wiley-Blackwell, 2009), and *Women, Culture, and Community: Religion and Reform in Galveston, 1880–1920* (Oxford University Press, 1997), which won three awards, including the Coral Horton Tullis Memorial Prize awarded by the Texas State Historical Association. She is coauthor of *Galveston and the 1900 Storm: Catastrophe and Catalyst* (University of Texas Press, 2000). Turner has authored several articles and coedited six volumes, including *Lone Star Pasts: Memory and History in Texas* (Texas A&M University Press, 2007), which won the T. R. Fehrenbach Award in Texas History from the Texas Historical Commission. In 2003 she was a Fulbright Lecturer to the University of Genoa, Italy. In 2011 she was awarded the William P. and Rita Clements Center Fellowship for the Study of Southwestern America, Southern Methodist University, and elected Fellow of the Texas State Historical Association. Her current book project explores the Juneteenth emancipation celebration.

Omar S. Valerio-Jiménez is Associate Professor of History at the University of Texas at San Antonio, where he teaches courses on Latinos, borderlands, and the U.S. West. His first book, *River of Hope: Forging Identity and Nation in the Rio Grande Borderlands* (Duke University Press, 2013), explores state formation and cultural change along the Mexico–United States border and traces changes in ethnicity, citizenship, and gender relations among borderland residents as jurisdiction over the area passed from native peoples to Spain, Mexico, and finally the United States. He is coeditor of the anthology *Major Problems in Latina/o History* (Wadsworth/Cengage Learning, 2014) and author of articles on divorce, regional identity, and immigration that have appeared in the *Journal of Women's History*, *Estudios Mexicanos/Mexican Studies*, and *Journal of American Ethnic History*. He is coediting *The Latina/o Midwest Reader* (University of Illinois Press, 2016), a collection of essays on the arts, politics, history, and labor of Latinos in the Midwest. His longer-term project is a transnational study of the U.S.-Mexican War that examines memory, identity, and civil rights.

Index

References to illustrations appear in italic type.